The Dog Dictionary:
Canine Lingo from A to Z

The Dog Dictionary:
Canine Lingo from A to Z

By Diane Morgan and John Warner

Irvine, California
A Division of BowTie, Inc.

Karla Austin, *Business Operations Manager*
Nick Clemente, *Special Consultant*
Jarelle S. Stein, *Editor*
Kendra Strey *Assistant Editor*
Jill Dupont, *Production*
Allyn A. Salmond, *Book Design, Layout*
Denice McAskin, *Cover Design*

Library of Congress Cataloging-in-Publication Data

Morgan, Diane, 1947-
  The dog dictionary : Canine lingo from A to Z by Diane Morgan.
     p. cm.
  ISBN 1-931993-61-0
  1. Dogs–Dictionaries. I. Title.

  SF422.M65 2005
  636.7'003–dc22

                                             2004025522

BowTie Press®
A Division of BowTie, Inc.
3 Burroughs
Irvine, California 92618

Printed and bound in the United States
10 9 8 7 6 5 4 3 2 1

For George Statler, my hero, patron saint of Mountainside Pet Rescue, whose love and compassion is without bounds.

—Diane Morgan

A

AAA: Animal Acupuncture Academy.

AAAA: Association for Applied Animal Andrology.

AAABEM: American Association of Acupuncture and Bio-Energetic Medicine.

AAD: Advanced Agility Dog (USDAA title).

AADC: Advanced Agility Dog of Canada (AAC title).

AAFCO: American Association of Feed Control Officials, an agency that develops guidelines and model regulations for commercial animal foods.

AAFHV: American Association of Food Hygiene Veterinarians.

AAHA: American Animal Hospital Association.

AAHV: American Association of Housecall Veterinarians.

AAPHV: American Association of Public Health Veterinarians.

AAVA: American Association of Veterinary Anatomists, also American Academy of Veterinary Acupuncture.

AAVC: American Association of Veterinary Clinics.

AAVDM: American Association of Veterinary Disaster Medicine.

AAVI: **(1)** American Association of Veterinary Immunologists. **(2)** American Association of Veterinary Informatics.

AAVLD: American Association of Veterinary Laboratory Diagnosticians.

AB: **(1)** Antibiotic. **(2)** Antibody.

Abady Dog Food Company: Telephone: (914) 473-1900.

Abandoned animal: In law, an animal whose owner has voluntarily relinquished it, but who has not assigned it to another person. Also an animal whose owner cannot be found.

Abasia: Inability to walk.

Abdominal: Pertaining to the belly cavity.

Abdominocentesis: Placing a needle into the abdominal cavity to check for abnormal fluids.

Abduction: In a veterinary exam, extending a limb away from the body.

Aberdeen terrier: Scottish terrier.

ABKA: American Boarding Kennels Association.

Abortifacient: Substance that can cause abortion.

Abortion: Premature delivery of a dead fetus.

Abrasion: **(1)** Excessive wear of the teeth due to contact with an external source. **(2)** Superficial scraping of the skin.

ABS: Animal Behavior Society.

Abscess: A localized, painful collection of pus in a fibrous cavity formed by the death of tissue due to a bacterial infection. Usually surrounded by inflamed skin. Treatment with antibiotics is effective if the abscess can be drained.

Absolute winner: Winner of a stake consisting of the winners of all other stakes at a field trial.

ABVA: Association of British Veterinary Acupuncturists.

ABVP: American Board of Veterinary Practitioners (veterinarians with expertise in clinical practice).

ABVT: American Board of Veterinary Toxicology.

Academy of Veterinary Homeopathy: 1283 Lincoln Street, Eugene, OR 97401. Telephone: (503) 342-7665.

Acanthosis nigrans: Literally, "thick black skin." Diffuse hyperplasia (thickening) of the spinous layer of the skin with gray, brown, or black pigmentation, usually beginning in the "armpit." A rare condition affecting dachshunds. There is no specific treatment.

Acariasis: Infestation with mites.

Acaricide: An agent that kills ticks and mites.

Accreditation: In the AKC, approval by the New Clubs Committee to conduct AKC-sanctioned events.

Accumulation points: In acupuncture, points on the meridian where the energy is greatest.

Accumulator: In dog racing, a multiple bet.

ACD: Australian cattle dog.

Ace: (1) Acepromazine. **(2)** Angiotensin-converting enzyme.

ACE inhibitor: Drug that decreases the function of the angiotensin-converting-enzyme (ACE). The ACE changes a compound called angiotensin I to angiotensin II. Angiotensin II is a potent blood vessel constrictor. ACE inhibitors have the effect of dilating blood vessels, since less angiotensin II is produced.

Acepromazine: Generic name for the tranquilizer acepromazine maleate, prescribed for sedation, scratching, and motion sickness. Sold under the name Promace.

Acetabulum: Socket of the hip bone that holds the femur.

Acetylcholine: A neutrotransmitter.

Acetylcysteine (N-acetylcysteine): Generic name for a medication used for dry eye, corneal ulcers, bronchitis, and poisoning from acetominophen (Tylenol).

Achalasia: Cricopharyngeal dysphagia.

Achilles tendon: Longest and strongest tendon, which functions as an anchor and extension for the calf muscle onto the fibular tarsal bone.

Achlorhydria: Inadequate production of stomach acid.

Achondroplasia: A kind of dwarfism characteristic of some breeds, such as basset hounds.

Acidophilus: Beneficial bacteria available as a dietary supplement.

Acidosis: A physiological state in which the body's pH becomes too low.

Acknowledgment of the pointing dog: Recognition of the presence of a pointing dog by a dog coming to honor.

ACL: Anterior cruciate ligament.

Aconitum Napellus: A homeopathic remedy, often used in the treatment of metritis.

Acquired aurotrichia: A condition in which silver or black hairs change to gold, especially on the abdomen.

Acquired defect or disease: A defect or disease that develops after birth; not congenital.

Acquired epilepsy: Epilepsy that is not inherited, but occurring as a result of trauma or disease.

Acral lick granuloma: A raised, bald sore found typically on the wrist, paw, or hock of the limbs and caused by incessant licking. Fairly common, and often linked to boredom. See Acral pruritic dermatitis.

Acral pruritic dermatitis: A condition caused by incessant licking at the same site, usually on the paw, producing a sore spot. See acral lick granuloma.

Acrodermatitis: Severe skin lesions, especially of the feet or paws.

Acromegaly: A condition accompanied by giantism, with large feet, bony growth or ridges above the eyes, and loose, thick skin, as in the Saint Bernard.

ACSMA: American Canine Sports Medicine Association.

ACT: (1) Activated clotting time. **(2)** American College of Theriogenologists, veterinarians with expertise in reproductive medicine.

ACTH: Adrenocorticotropic hormone.

ACTH stimulation test: Test to

indicate the presence of hyperadrenocorticism.

Actinic dermatitis: A condition in which pigmentation is lost, usually in the nose. The condition is aggravated by the sun and is also known as nasal solar dermatitis.

Actinic keratosis: Lesions associated with chronic sun exposure, generally seen in pale-skinned dogs with outside access. Lesions may progress to squamous cell carcinoma.

Action: A dog's movement.

Activated charcoal: An adsorbent, detoxifying medication used for poisonings and drug overdoses.

Active immunity: Immunity produced when an animal's own immune system reacts to a stimulus like a virus or bacteria, and produces antibodies and cells that protect it from the disease caused by the organism.

Active Life Pet Products: Telephone: (303) 415-1707. Web site: www.activelifepp.com.

Actors and Others for Animals: P.O. Box 33473, Granada Hills, CA 91394. Telephone: (818) 386-5870.

Acupoint: Location at which treatment of acupuncture is delivered.

Acupuncture: Ancient Chinese healing system of placing fine needles at selected points in the body along specific channels called meridians. The purpose is to stimulate, reduce, or balance the energy flow (*qi*). Acupuncture has been shown not only to relieve pain, but also to be a valuable treatment for problems of the musculoskeletal and nervous systems.

Acute: Sudden, rapid, and serious onset. It is often of short duration.

Acute hemorrhagic enteropathy (HE): Also called hemorrhagic enteritis or hemorrhagic gastroenteritis; clinical signs include bloody diarrhea, dehydration, and hemoconcentration.

Acute moist dermatitis (pyotraumatic dermatitis): Hot spot. A patch of extremely inflamed, itchy skin, often made worse by the dog's licking it.

Acute turn: In tracking, a turn of less than 90 degrees.

ACVA: American College of Veterinary Anesthesiologists.

ACVB: American College of Veterinary Behaviorists.

ACVCP: American College of Veterinary Clinical Pharmacology.

ACVD: American College of Veterinary Dermatology.

ACVECC: American College of Veterinary Emergency and Critical Care.

ACVIM: American College of Veterinary Internal Medicine (including specialties in cardiology, neurology, and oncology).

ACVN: American College of Veterinary Nutrition.

ACVO: American College of Veterinary Ophthalmologists.

ACVP: American College of Veterinary Pathologists.

ACVPM: American College of Veterinary Preventive Medicine.

AD: (1) Agility Dog (USDAA). **(2)** Right ear. **(3)** Aleutian disease. **(4)** In schutzhunds, a 12 $\frac{1}{2}$-mile endurance run.

Ad lib: Ad libitum.

Ad libitum: Free access to food and water.

Adaptive thermogenesis: Energy needed to maintain internal body temperature.

Adaptogen: A nontoxic agent that increases the organism's ability to adapt.

ADC: Agility Dog of Canada (AAC title).

ADCH: Agility Dog Champion (USDAA title).

Addison's disease (hypoadrenocorticism): A disease of the endocrine system, first described in humans in 1855. In Addison's disease, the adrenal cortex fails to supply adequate secretions of two types of cortisone critical to the dog's ability to use energy-containing glucose and to balance levels of critical minerals such as sodium and potassium. Signs include recurrent periods of appetite loss, vomiting, diarrhea, and weakness. It is more common in young and middle-aged female dogs, and although it can occur in any breed, there is a familial predisposition. The cause is unknown. The disease is treatable but not curable.

Additive: Anything added to a dog food; additives may be nutritive (including vitamins and minerals), preservative, or flavor-enhancing.

Adduction: In a veterinary exam, moving the body part toward median (inside) plane, as in tucking a limb under the body.

Adenocarcinoma: Malignant, rapidly metastasizing tumor that originates in the glandular tissue. Compare with adenoma.

Adenohypophysis: Anterior lobe of the pituitary gland.

Adenoma: A benign tumor originating in glandular tissue. Compare with adenocarcinoma.

Adenomatous polygeniceps: Benign neoplasm of the rectum or colon.

Adequan: Injectable substance (glucosamine and chondroitin sulfate) derived from the tracheas and lungs of cattle; it is a purified glycosaminoglycan (GAG) sulfate, used for the treatment of arthritis in dogs and horses.

ADF: Acid detergent fiber, the percentage of highly indigestible or slowly digestible fiber in a feed or forage.

ADH: Antidiuretic hormone (vasopressin).

Adhesions: The binding together of tissues that are not normally bound together.

ADI: Assistance Dogs International.

Adipocyte hyperplasia: An increase in the number of fat cells.

Adipocyte: Specialized cells that store fat (triglycerides).

Adipose: Fatty body tissue.

Adipsia: Absence of thirst or avoidance of drinking.

Adjutant: A black Labrador gundog that was whelped on August 14, 1936, and died on November 20, 1963, aged twenty-seven years, three months. The world's longest-lived dog, according to *Guinness World Records.*

Adjuvant: Substance added to a killed vaccine to enhance local reaction and create better immunity. Common adjuvants contain aluminum compounds.

Adnexa: Accessory organs in the eye or uterus, or of the skin such as hair, sweat glands, and claws.

Adnexal tumor: Tumor of the adnexa.

Adonis: The first registered dog in the *American Kennel Club Stud Book* (1878). An English setter.

ADP: Adenosine diphosphate.

ADR: "Ain't doin' right" (veterinary notation).

Adrenal: (1) Referring to the adrenal glands. **(2)** Homeopathic remedy for inappropriate urination and hypothyroidism.

Adrenal gland hyperfunction: Production of excess cortisol.

Adrenal glands: Two small endocrine glands near the kidneys that produce adrenaline and corticosteroids.

Adrenal sex-hormone dermatosis: A syndrome similar

to growth hormone-responsive dermatitis. It appears to be due to abnormal sex hormone production by the adrenal glands, causing secondary changes in growth hormone levels.

Adrenal tumor (AT): Form of hyperadrenocorticism stemming from adrenal gland dysfunction.

Adrenalectomy: Surgery to remove the adrenal gland.

Adrenaline (epinephrine): A hormone produced by the adrenal glands that stimulates the heart and increases blood pressure.

Adrenergic stimulation: Communication between the nerves and muscles that uses epinephrine as the "messenger." Adrenergic stimulation is involved in the fight-or-flight response. Adrenergic stimulation results in an increased heart rate, sweating, and increased blood pressure.

Adreno-: Pertaining to the adrenal gland.

Adrenocorticotropic hormone (ACTH): Hormone produced by the pituitary gland that stimulates production of corticosteroids by the adrenal cortex.

Adv: "Advice" (veterinary notation).

Adverse drug reaction: Undesirable response to a drug.

Aerobic bacteria: Bacteria that grow only in the presence of air, as opposed to anaerobic bacteria.

Aesculus Hippocastanum: A homeopathic remedy often used in the treatment of constipation.

AFC: Amateur field trial champion. This title indicates great field ability. In four breeds (German shorthaired pointer, German wirehaired pointer, Weimaraner, vizsla), it indicates retrieving ability. In two breeds (German wirehaired pointer, Weimaraner), it indicates water-retrieving ability.

Affenpinscher: The name means "monkey-terrier" and accurately describes the animal. Size: about 10 inches, 7 to 8 pounds. The coat is harsh, wiry, and medium-long. The preferred color is black, but also comes in black and tan, red, and dark gray. Origin: Germany, 1600s.

Affix: The registered kennel name of the breeder or owner.

Afghan hound: Dignified and aloof sight hound with long, silky hair of any color. Size: 25 to 27 inches, 50 to 70 pounds. Origin: Afghanistan, antiquity.

Afghan myelomalacia: Softening of the spinal cord tissues, eventually leading to paralysis; seen primarily in Afghans.

A-frame: In agility, two nine-foot ramps leaning against each other to form a "go-up" at least six feet high. Also called an A-ramp, or scale.

African Lion Hound: Rhodesian ridgeback.

African wild hunting dog (*Lycaon pictus*): Wild canid dwelling on African plains.

Afterbirth: Placenta and fetal membranes expelled from the womb after a puppy is born.

AG: (1) Anal glands (veterinary notation). **(2)** Antigen.

Agalactia: Failure to produce milk.

AGC: American Greyhound Council, Inc.

Agenesis: Absence of an organ at birth.

Agglutination: Abnormal clumping of red blood cells or other cells such as bacteria.

Aggravation: In homeopathy, the "healing crisis." Sometimes follows administration of homeopathic remedy, wherein the patient experiences a brief intensification of symptoms. Also used in homeopathy to describe the correct medication at incorrect dosages.

Aggression: Dominant or attack behavior. While some aggression is normal toward other dogs or against humans if the dog is a trained attack dog, most aggression against humans is inappropriate and dangerous. Causes include poor socialization, hormonal changes, fear, and pain. However, a great deal of aggression is hereditary, which cannot be cured, only controlled. Holistic treatments include belladonna, hydrophobinum, nux vomica, Rescue Remedy, detoxification, PC6, and exercise.

AGID: Agar gel immunodiffusion.

Agility Excellent: Title awarded to a dog earning three qualifying scores in Excellent agility classes under at least two different judges.

Agility trial: A performance event in which the handler directs his or her dog over a timed obstacle course. The scoring revolves around faults, similar to equestrian Grand Prix jumping.

Aging: In tracking, the time elapsed between the laydown of the scent and start of the event.

Agonistic: Any behavior displayed during conflict, aggression, or fear.

Agoraphobia: Fear of going outside or fear of new places.

Agouti: The so-called "wild" color used for Siberian huskies and other breeds. In this color, guard hairs are banded, with black at tips and roots and yellow in the middle.

AGTOA: American Greyhound Track Operators Association.

Aguirre syndrome: Unilateral depigmentation around the eyes. It may be associated with Horner's syndrome.

AHBA: American Herding Breeds Association.

AHVMA: American Holistic Veterinary Medical Association.

AI: Artificial insemination.

AIHA: Autoimmune hemolytic anemia.

Airedale terrier: The largest of the terrier breeds. Hardy, loyal, alert, and active. Colors include black or grizzle and tan. Size: 22 to 24 inches, 45 to 50 pounds. Origin: England.

Air-scenting dog: A search and rescue dog that sniffs across the prevailing wind for airborne human scent and follows it to its source. Usually does not discriminate between different human scents.

Aitches: The pelvic tubers.

Akbash: A white-coated, flock-guarding breed. Size: 28 to 34 inches, 85 to 140 pounds. May be short- or long-coated. Origin: Turkey.

AKC: American Kennel Club.

Akebia: A Chinese herbal formulation used to prevent bladder stones and cystitis.

Akela: Wolf pack leader in Rudyard Kipling's *The Jungle Book*.

Akita: A large, alert breed of Japanese spitz-type dog originally bred to hunt bears. Dominant toward other dogs and very protective. Any color acceptable. Size: 24 to 28 inches, 75 to 110 pounds.

Akita inu: Akita.

Alani: "Hunting dogs;" a Greek name for the Scythian tribes who worshiped Artemis as the Sacred Huntress. The word is still echoed in the names "Alan" and "Alaunt" (see Alaunt).

Alariasis: Intestinal infection caused by ingestion of flukes.

Alarm points: In acupuncture, points located on the ventral part of the abdomen. Also called Mu points.

Alaskan malamute: Powerful, heavy, ancient Arctic breed used for freighting. Friendly but stubborn. Colors from light gray to black, gold to red, or liver with white markings. Solid white acceptable. Size: 23 to 28 inches, 84 to 123 pounds. Origin: Alaska.

Alaunt: A large, mastiff-like hound using as a hunting companion during the Middle Ages and Renaissance in Europe.

Albinism: Recessive trait resulting in deficiency of pigmentation, which can cause white hair, pink skin, and pink or blue eyes.

Albino: An animal that is white because it lacks melanin pigmentation.

Albumin: A small protein in blood (produced by the liver) that acts to keep fluid within the blood vessels. Low albumin on a lab test indicates dehydration.

Albuterol: Generic name for a bronchodilator prescribed for asthma, cough, and bronchitis.

Aldosterone: The main mineralocorticoid secreted by the adrenal gland.

Alert: In search and rescue dogs, an indication that an air-scenting dog has detected scent.

Alfalfa (*Medicago sativa*): Used in herbal medicine as a blood purifier and to treat arthritis.

Alfalfa meal: In dog food, the aboveground part of the alfalfa plant, sun-cured and finely ground.

Alimentary: Referring to the digestive system.

Alkaline phosphatase: An enzyme normally present in the serum that can become elevated in the presence of certain cancers or certain bone, muscle, or liver diseases.

Alkaloids: Nitrogen-containing compounds, including caffeine and codeine, found naturally in plants or derived from these natural products. Many are medicines or poisons.

Alkalosis: A physiological state in which the body's pH becomes too high.

All-Age Stakes: In pointing breeds, all-age field trial stake, the highest level of competition, including all ages of dogs. In addition, the dogs are run wider than regular *Field Dog Stud Book* shooting trials. In the AKC, the dogs are run wider than in the gundog stakes.

All-America Team: The top eight racing greyhounds selected each year by AGTOA.

All-Breed Club: An organized group of dog fanciers, recognized by the Canadian Kennel Club (CKC) and/or American Kennel Club (AKC) to hold all-breed dog shows and performance events within their geographic boundaries.

All-Breed Dog Show: Offers conformation competitions for more than 150 breeds and varieties of dogs recognized by the AKC.

Allele: The specific form of a particular gene. One allele is inherited from each parent.

Allelomimetic behavior: Behavior that copies another animal, as when one dog barks because another does.

Allergen: Substance (usually a protein) causing an allergic reaction. Common allergens include flea saliva, pollen, mold, ragweed, and dust mites. Certain foods also can cause allergies.

Allergic hot spot: Self-induced skin condition brought about by biting or licking an itchy spot, such as that produced by a fleabite.

Allergic pneumonitis: Pneumonia produced by an allergic response.

Allergy Formula: A dog food excluding common foods that

often cause allergies, such as wheat, corn, soy, dairy, chicken, and beef.

Allergy: Immunological hypersensitivity to certain foreign antigens. Genetically predisposed condition, but also can be brought about by chronic exposure. Common in Labradors, golden retrievers, and the smaller terriers.

Allogrooming: Licking or grooming of others in the same social group.

Allopathy: Homeopathic term to describe conventional medicine; generally refers to the use of drugs to treat a disease.

Allopurinol: Generic name for an enzyme inhibitor, prescribed for the prevention of certain urinary stones.

Allorhythmia: Irregularity of the pulse.

Allotriophagia: See Pica.

All Stages: In dog food manufacturing, a reference to all life stages of a dog, including puppies, pregnant or nursing bitches, and regular adults.

Almond eye: An elongated eye; its appearance is due to folds or shrinkage surrounding tissue.

Aloe Socotrina: A homeopathic remedy often prescribed for constipation.

Aloe Vera: A soothing gel derived from the leaves of the plant of the same name. Used topically to treat minor burns, skin lesions, itching, and cracked pads on paws.

Aloof: Standoffish.

Alopecia: Hair loss from skin where it is normally present.

ALP: Alkaline phosphatase.

Alpha: The "top dog" or dominant animal in a pack.

Alpha-1–antitrypsin related hepatitis: A form of chronic progressive hepatitis.

Alpha-linolenic acid (ALA): An essential omega-3 polyunsaturated fatty acid.

Alpine mastiff: Saint Bernard.

Alpo (Friskies) Dog Food Company: Telephone: (800) 745-3402.

Alsatian: German shepherd (Deutscher schaferhund).

ALT: Alanine aminotransferase (a liver enzyme), also called SGPT.

Alter: To surgically remove the reproductive ability of animals either through spaying (females) or through neutering (males).

Altricial: Requiring parental care and feeding for survival at birth.

Aluminum hydroxide: (1) A common adjuvant of killed vaccines. **(2)** Medication used to reduce stomach acidity in the treatment of ulcers.

Alveolar bone: The bone around the roots of a tooth.

Alveoli: Microscopic sac-like structures within the lung that facilitate oxygen uptake.

Am/Can: American/Canadian.

AMA: Against medical advice (veterinary notation).

Amateur: In AKC field trials, one who does not make all or part of his living training and handling dogs.

Amateur All-Age Stake: A field trial stake for dogs over six months old, in which only amateurs are permitted to handle a dog. Otherwise identical to the Open All-Age stake except that the dogs may be handled only by non-professional trainers.

Amateur Field Champion: For pointing breeds, a dog that has won ten points at three trials, with at least one win of three points or more in Amateur All-Age, Amateur Gun Dog, Amateur Limited All-Age, or Amateur Limited Gun Dog. No more than two points in Amateur Walking Puppy and no more than two points in Amateur Walking Derby are allowed. For retrievers, a dog that has won a National Championship Stake, Handled by an Amateur or that has won fifteen points with at least one win of five points or better in: Open All-Age, Limited All-Age, Special All-Age, Amateur All-Age, Owner Handler All-Age, or Restricted All-Age stakes. Not more than five points can be awarded in trials not open to all breeds of retrievers. For English springer spaniel, cocker spaniel, or English cocker spaniel, the dog must win one of the following: one National Championship stake or two Amateur All-Age stakes at different trials with at least ten starters in each stake, or one Amateur All-Age stake and ten Amateur Championship points with ten starters in each stake. The handler must be an amateur.

Amateur stakes: Includes amateur derby, amateur all-age and also competition held only for handlers deemed amateurs by the sponsoring organization.

Amaurosis: A disease condition of German shorthaired pointers marked by nervousness and low trainability. Also known as familial amaurotic idiocy.

Amble: A relaxed, easy trot between the walk and the show ring gait.

AMBOR: American Mixed Breed Obedience Registration.

Ambulate: Walk or run.

Ambylopia and quadriplegia: Lethal inherited condition of Irish setter. Puppies are unable to walk, eventually blindness and seizures occur.

Ameba: Class of single-celled protozoa. Also amoeba.

Amebiasis: Infected with amebas.

Amebicide: Substance that destroys amebas.

American Academy of Veterinary Acupuncture (AAVA): P.O. Box 419, Hygiene, CO 80533-0419.

American Animal Hospital Association (AAHA): An international association of more than 17,000 veterinary care providers who treat companion animals. The association was established in 1933. P.O. Box 150899, Denver, CO 80215. Telephone: (800) 252-2242. Web site: www.healthypet.com.

American black and tan coonhound: Black and tan coonhound.

American Boarding Kennels Association: This is the trade association for kennels. 4575 Galley Road, Suite 400A, Colorado Springs, CO 80915.

American-bred: In a conformation dog show, a not-finished dog whose parents were mated in America and who was born in America.

American Canine Sport Medicine Association: A group of veterinarians, trainers, physical therapists, and other professionals who are experts in the diagnosis and management of injuries, diseases, nutritional problems, rehabilitation procedures, and physiologic functions of dogs involved in field sports and working endeavors.

American cocker spaniel: Cocker spaniel.

American College of Veterinary Behaviorists: College of Veterinary Medicine, Cornell University, Ithaca, NY 14853-6401.

American Dog Breeders Association: P.O. Box 1771, Salt Lake City, UT 84110. Telephone: (801) 298-7513.

American Dog Owners' Association: 1654 Columbia Turnpike, Castleton, NY 12033.

American Dog Trainers Network: (212) 727-7257

American Eskimo dog: A white spitz-type dog developed in America from the German spitz. Comes in three sizes, including toy (9 to 12 inches), miniature (12 to 15 inches), and standard (over 15 inches).

American Field: The organization that publishes the Field Dog Stud Book and maintains a registry for hunting dogs.

American foxhound: Descended from English foxhounds, the American foxhound is taller and rangier than its ancestor. Any color. Size: 21 to 25 inches. Origin: colonial America.

American Holistic Veterinary Medicine Association. 2214 Old Emmorton Road, Bel Air, MD 21015. Telephone: (410) 569-0795.

American Humane Association: P. O. Box 3597, Englewood, Colorado 80155. Telephone: (303) 792-9900. Works to prevent cruelty to children and animals, especially in the film industry. Founded in 1877.

American Kennel Club (AKC): Founded in 1884 to oversee the registration and showing of dogs. It is composed of more than 530 independent purebred dog clubs. Has breeder referral representative service. 5580 Centerview Drive, Raleigh, NC 27606 and 51 Madison Avenue, New York, NY 10010. Telephone: (212) 696-8245. Web site: www.akc.org.

American Massage Therapy Association: 820 Davis Street, Suite 100, Evanston, IL 60201.

American Mixed Breed Registry (AMBOR): An organization that enables dogs of mixed heritage to earn title by receiving verification from a licensed judge in that event.

179 Niblick Road, Suite 113, Paso Robles, CA 93446. Telephone: (805) 226-9275. Web site: www.amborusa.org.

American Rare Breed Association: P. O. Box 76426, Washington, DC 20013.

American Shih Tzu Club: 5252 Shafter Avenue, Oakland, CA 94618. E-mail: hanashihtzu@compuserve.com.

American Society for the Prevention of Cruelty to Animals (ASPCA): 441 East 92nd Street, New York, NY 10128. Telephone: (212) 876-7700, (212) 348-3031. Web site: www.aspca.org. Founded in 1866 by Henry Berg. It was originally a New York-based institution, but many American cities copied the idea. Today humane societies operate largely on a local level.

American Staffordshire terrier: Developed from Staffordshire bull terriers, but larger and more pugnacious. A small but strong dog with a short coat of any color. Size: 17 to 19 inches.

American Veterinary Chiropractic Association (AVCA): 442154 East 140th Road; Bluejacket, OK 74333. Telephone: (918) 784-2231. E-mail: AmVetChiro@aol.com.

American Veterinary Medical Association (AVMA): 1931 North Meacham Road, Suite 100, Schaumburg, IL 60173-4360. Telephone: (847) 925-8070, (800) 248-AVMA. Web site: www.avma.org.

American Veterinary Society of Animal Behavior: Veterinary Behavior Consultations. 253 South Graeser Road, St. Louis, MO 63141.

American veterinary specialty boards: The American veterinary boards and American veterinary colleges that hold examinations and award diplomas in veterinary specialties to graduate veterinarians.

American water spaniel: Related to the Irish water spaniel. Excellent retriever and all-around hunting dog. Size: 15 to 18 inches, 25 to 45 pounds, colored solid liver, brown, or chocolate.

AMHB: Association of Masters of Harriers and Beagles. Web site: www.amhb.org.uk/

Amine: An organic compound containing nitrogen; specifically, one that contains an amino (NH2) group.

Amino acids: The building blocks of protein; they have both an acid and an amino group.

Aminoglycoside antibiotics: Generic name for a class of medications primarily designed to kill gram-negative bacteria such as *E. coli* and *Salmonella*. Antibiotics in this class include gentamicin (Gentocin), kanamycin, neomycin, streptomycin, tobramycin, and amikacin. Many of these antibiotics are not well-absorbed from the animal's digestive system, so they are often administered as injections or used topically. Not effective against most gram-positive bacteria, such as *streptococcus* and *staphylococcus*, or against anaerobic bacteria.

Aminopentamide: Generic name for certain antispasmodic drugs given to prevent vomiting, diarrhea, nausea, and other gastrointestinal spasms.

Amitraz: Generic name for a number of pesticidal drugs used for **(1)** treatment of demodectic mange and **(2)** killing ticks (in a tick collar).

Amitriptyline: Generic name for a class of tricyclic antidepressants prescribed for compulsive behaviors, anxiety, and fear.

Ammonium chloride: Urine acidifier prescribed for cystitis, urinary stones, and urinary tract infections.

Amnion: Inner layer of the membrane surrounding an embryo in the uterus; contains the amniotic fluid.

Amniotic fluid: Fluid surrounding a fetus.

Amoeba: Alternate spelling for ameba.

Amoxicillin: Synthetic improvement on the original penicillin molecule. Amoxicillin is better able to resist damage from stomach acid, so less of an oral dose is wasted. While it is still susceptible to destruction by staphylococcal enzymes, it has a broader spectrum against the gram-negative cell wall and lasts a bit longer.

Amphotericin B: Generic name for a number of antifungal drugs, prescribed for deep (systemic) fungal infections.

Amplification: Copying a section of DNA chemically billions of times, using polymerase chain reaction (PCR).

Amputation: The removal of a limb or other body part.

Amylase: An enzyme produced by the pancreas that contributes to the digestion of food, especially carbohydrates.

Amyloid glomerulonephritis: Amyloidosis.

Amyloidosis: Abnormal deposits of amyloid protein into various tissues or organs, resulting in progressive organ dysfunction.

Anabolic steroid: A type of steroid (not a corticosteroid like prednisone, cortisone, or dexamethasone) that promotes the building of tissues, including muscle.

Anabolism: The constructive phase of metabolism in which body cells repair and replace tissue.

Anaeorbic bacteria: Bacteria that grow only in the absence of oxygen.

Anagen: The phase of the hair-growing cycle when the hair is being synthesized.

Anal adenomata: Subcutaneous tumor located around the anus.

Anal sacs: Located on either side of the anal opening. Often filled with foul-smelling liquid. Domestic animals have largely lost their ability to empty these sacs voluntarily, but normally the anal sacs empty with each bowel movement. If anal sacs become impacted (the dog may start scooting), they can be "expressed" by applying gentle pressure at four o'clock and eight o'clock positions.

Analgesia: Loss of pain sensation. Other sensations are still felt.

Analgesic: Pain-relieving substance.

Anamnestic response: The faster and greater immune response produced by an animal that has previously encountered that specific antigen. Memory cells are responsible for this more efficient response. Also called secondary response.

Anaphylactic: Relating to anaphylaxis or shock.

Anaphylaxis: Severe hypersensitivity reaction. It can result in hives, edema in the respiratory tract, shock, and death. Also called anaphylactic shock.

Anaplastic sarcoma: A poorly differentiated malignant soft-tissue tumor derived from the mesenchymal connective tissues.

Anasarca: Swelling of legs and body due to fluid retention in the limbs or under the skin; edema.

Anatolian sheepdog: Large breed originating in ancient Turkey. Used for guarding, military work, and shepherding. Colors are cream to fawn with black mask and ears. Size: 28 to 32 inches, 88 to 140 pounds.

Anatomy: Physical structure of the body.

Anconeal process: A part of the bone of the elbow.

Ancylostomiasis: Hookworm infestation.

Androgen: Male sex hormone, primarily androstenedione and testosterone.

Anemia: Insufficient number of red blood cells (or enough hemoglobin) to carry oxygen through the body. Most commonly caused by internal or external bleeding, rat poisons, or even a heavy flea infestation. It can also result from disease to the bone marrow. Dogs with anemia often have pale gums (in the case of dark-pigmented gums, check the inside of the lower eyelid). Anemic dogs are often lethargic.

Anesthesia: Temporary unconsciousness.

Anesthetic sensitivity: Condition characteristic of many sight hounds. Such animals also are often sensitive to certain flea-control products.

Anesthetic: Substance that produces temporary unconsciousness.

Anestrus: The period during which there is no reproductive activity in the female dog. Typically lasts four or five months.

Angulation: Angles created by bones meeting at their joints, usually applied to the fore- and hindquarters.

Animal: In dog-food manufacturing, an ingredient derived from cattle, swine, sheep, goats, horses, poultry, or fish.

Animal Behavior Society: The purpose of this society is to promote and encourage the biological study of animal behavior in the broadest sense, including studies at all levels of organization using both descriptive and experimental methods under natural and controlled conditions. Animal Behavior Society, Indiana University, 2611 East 10th Street #170 Bloomington, IN 47408-2603.

Animal by-product meal: In dog-food labeling, the rendered product from animal tissues, exclusive of any added hair, horn, hoof, hide trimmings, manure, and stomach and rumen products, except in such amounts as may unavoidably occur in good processing practices.

Animal communicator: One who attempts to communicate with animals via mental means.

Animal fat: In dog-food manufacturing, fatty acids obtained from the process of rendering tissue from mammals or poultry, with no addition of free fatty acids.

Animal Legal Defense Fund: A group of private attorneys working to promote the welfare and rights of animals.

Animal Protection Institute: P.O. Box 22505, Sacramento, CA 95822. Telephone: (916) 731-5521, (800) 348-7387. Web site: www.api4animals.org.

Animal reservoir: An apparently unaffected animal harboring a disease and capable of passing it on.

Animal shelter: Facility, often run by the county pound, a humane society, or animal welfare authority, that provides for the care of discarded pets.

Animal therapy: A kind of medical therapy employed by long-term-care facilities and their volunteers that uses pets to entertain, comfort, or aid the well-being of patients.

Animal Welfare Act: A federal statute (U.S. Public Law 91-579) that mandates standards of minimum care for animals in the areas of sales, breeding, and transportation.

Animal Welfare Information Center: A federally funded group originally set up with the Health Research Information Act (1985), with the mandate to look for alternatives to the use of animals in research.

Animal Welfare Institute (AWI): A nonprofit charitable organization founded in 1951 to reduce the sum total of pain and fear inflicted on animals by humans.

Anipryl (Selegiline): An MAOI used in humans for Parkinson's disease and in dogs to control signs of canine cognitive dysfunction (senility). It works by increasing levels of dopamine, a neurotransmitter in the brain.

Anise: Used in herbal medicine as an expectorant and to reduce coughing.

Anisocoria: Pupils of unequal size. Problem may be in the eye itself or in the nerves that lead to it.

Anisocytosis: Blood cells of unequal size.

ANKC: Australian National Kennel Council.

Ankylosis: Bones abnormally fused.

Annulus fibrosi: The tough, outer fibrous area that encircles the pulpy center of the vertebra.

Anoplasty: Surgical repair of the anus.

Anorexia: A lack of appetite.

Ant: Anterior (veterinary notation).

Antacids (phosphate binders): Drugs prescribed for the treatment of stomach ulcers and gastrointestinal reflux. Active ingredients include aluminum hydroxide, magnesium hydroxide, and sodium bicarbonate.

Anterior: Directed toward the front. In the eye, closer to the cornea or front part of the head. In gaiting, the portion carried foremost in normal locomotion.

Anterior chamber: Portion of the eye between the cornea and iris and filled with aqueous fluid.

Anterior cruciate ligament rupture: The most common cause of rear leg lameness in dogs. This injury allows degenerative changes to occur in the knee joint, which must be repaired before permanent damage is done. The injury usually occurs when the dog is making a sudden turn.

Anterior uveitis: Inflammation of the iris and ciliary body of the eye.

Anthelmintic: Medication given to remove or kill worms.

Anthropomorphic: Attributing human qualities to animals.

Antibiotic sensitivity: A laboratory test to determine which antibiotics are effective against bacteria cultured from an infected patient.

Antibiotics: Medications that kill bacteria but not viruses. Common antibiotics include penicillin, ampicillin, cephalosporins, amilgycosides, neomycin, kanamycin, streptomycin, gentamicin, tetracyclines, chloromycetin, panalog, erythromycin, lincomycin, tylosin, sulfa drugs, furacin, and others.

Antibody: A protein formed by the white blood cells when confronted with an allergen.

Antibody titer: A measurement of the amount of antibodies in the blood.

Anticholinergic: Stopping the communication between certain nerves and muscles, including those of the gastrointestinal tract and heart. These parasympathetic nerves do such things as constrict the pupils of the eye, stimulate contractions of the muscles in the intestine, and slow the heart rate. Anticholinergic drugs would have the effect, then, of dilating the pupil, slowing contractions of the intestines, and increasing the heart rate.

Anticholinesterase: A drug that blocks the enzyme acetylcholinesterase; this results in stimulation of the parasympathetic nervous system.

Anticipation: In genetics, when an inherited disease occurs with earlier onset in successive afflicted generations.

Anticoagulant: Blood-thinning drug.

Anticonvulsant: A drug used to prevent or decrease the severity of convulsions.

Antiemetic: Medication to halt vomiting.

Antifreeze (ethylene glycol): Fluid is used to maintain automobile engines. Its sweet taste makes it attractive to dogs, but if ingested causes lethal damage to the kidneys.

Antifungal: Medication designed to treat a disease caused by a fungus.

Antigen: A substance, often a protein, that causes the body to produce immune antibodies (to elicit an immune response).

Antigenicity: The capacity to stimulate the production of antibodies.

Antihistamine: A medication to relive symptoms of allergic reactions or skin conditions.

Antilithic: A substance that helps prevent the formation of stones in the urinary system.

Antimicrobial: An agent that kills or suppresses the growth of microorganisms.

Antiopathy: In homeopathy, a system of medicine using agents whose action is opposite to the symptoms.

Antioxidant: (1) Substance that eliminates free radicals or reduces cellular oxidation in the body. **(2)** A synthetic or natural substance added to food to prevent its deterioration.

Antiparasitic: A substance that destroys or repels parasites.

Antiprotozoal: An agent that kills protozoa, which are one-celled organisms such as Giardia.

Antipruritic: A substance that relieves itching.

Antipyretics: Drugs to suppress fever.

Antiseborrheic: A substance active against seborrhea, usually by removing excess oil from the skin.

Antiseptic: A substance that inhibits the growth of bacteria but does not kill them.

Antispasmodic: An agent that relieves or decreases spasms in muscle.

Antitussive: Effective against coughs by inhibiting or suppressing them.

Antivenin: An antitoxin to venom.

Anubis: Egyptian jackal god.

Anuria: Not producing urine.

Anus: Muscular tissue at the end of the rectum.

Anxiety: Uneasiness or apprehension. Holistic treatment includes aconite, ignacia, nux vomica, Rescue Remedy, Kidney Diet, and Willard Water.

AOM: Award of Merit.

AON: "All others normal" (veterinary notation).

Aortic stenosis: A condition in which there is a partial obstruction to the flow of blood as it leaves the left side of the heart (the left ventricle) through the main blood vessel (the aorta) that carries blood to the rest of the body. The obstruction causes the heart to work harder. The condition appears to be inherited.

AP: (1) Anterior-posterior. **(2)** Alkaline phosphatase.

Apex: The pointed end of a cone-shaped structure.

Apical abscess: Abscess in the root of the tooth.

Apical: Toward the apex.

Apis mellificia: Homeopathic remedy commonly given for insect bites.

Aplastic anemia: A serious condition in which red blood cells, white blood cells, and platelets are not produced in sufficient quantity.

Apnea: Absence of breathing.

Apocrine sweat glands: Sweat glands present in the skin, opening into hair follicles.

Apomorphine: Emetic drug prescribed to induce vomiting.

Appendicular achondroplasia: Scant growth of cartilage at the ends of the long bones.

Appenzell mountain dog: Also called the Appenzeller, the Appenzell Cattle Dog, or the Appenzeller Sennenhund. A muscular, hardworking dog with a wide, flat head, pendant ears, and a muzzle that narrows toward a black nose. Its tail is carried rolled up on its back. Its short double coat comes in black or brown with symmetrical white and rust markings. European breed, a sheep herder and cart puller.

Appetite loss: A depressed appetite can be caused by tooth or gum problems, sickness, change in diet, a new routine, or distraction.

Apple head: A very round skull top, as in the Chihuahua.

Apricot: Reddish-yellow, referring to color in some poodles.

Apron: (1) Frill or long chest hair below the neck. **(2)** An area located next to the racetrack, where patrons may watch greyhound racing up close, like the paddock in thoroughbred racing.

APTT: Activated partial thromboplastin time.

Aqueous humor: The clear liquid filling the anterior and posterior chambers of the eye.

Aqueous: Watery, or prepared with water.

Aquiline: Curving down like an eagle's beak.

Arabian hound: Saluki.

Arachidonic acid: An essential twenty-carbon fatty acid.

ARBA: American Rare Breed Association.

Arched loin: Well-muscled over the loin; not to be confused with a roach.

Arched skull: A skull that arches from side to side or sometimes lengthwise.

Arched toes: Strong, well-knuckled feet; cat feet.

Arctic husky: Siberian husky.

ARF: Acute renal failure (veterinary notation).

Argos: Favorite dog of the Greek hero Odysseus.

Arm: Region between the shoulder and elbow.

Armadillo Westie syndrome: A yeast infection of West Highland white terrier in which the skin becomes inflamed, greasy, and itchy.

Armat: An Egyptian sheepdog.

Armband: In a dog show, a number printed on paper that an exhibitor wears to indicate the entered dog's (or Junior's) reference number in the judge's book and catalog. This number is the only identification that the judge is allowed access to before and during the competition.

Arnica: Homeopathic remedy commonly prescribed for cuts, bruising, shock, arthritis inflammation and pain, dog bites, fracture pain, and inflammation. It is frequently used in after-injury care.

Aromatherapy: A therapy using the essential oils derived from plants. These oils are obtained through distillation. Practitioners claim that aromatherapy is useful in the treatment of eczema (lavender and rosemary); heart and circulatory problems (mint); and cystitis (juniper and sandalwood). Oils can be administered by mouth (for experienced practitioners only), massage, or diffusion.

Aromatic: Having a strong, usually pleasant odor that can stimulate the digestive system.

Arrhythmia: A variation from normal heart rhythm. Also called dysrhythmia.

Arsenic: Combined with metaldehyde, a poison used in slug and snail bait, ant poisons, and weed killers.

Arsenicum Album: Homeopathic remedy used for treatment of dry, scaly skin and harsh coats.

Artery: Blood vessel that carries blood away from the heart.

Arthritis: Joint inflammation, of which there are more than one hundred different varieties. Can be due to infectious disease, metabolic disorder, trauma, or age-related wear-and-tear. The most common form is called osteoarthritis. Although it can develop in any joint, it usually affects the hip and leg joints. Signs include stiff movement, obvious pain, snappish behavior, incontinence, depression, loss of appetite, and long hours of sleep. It can be definitively diagnosed by X-ray and other medical tools. Treatment may include NSAIDS.

Arthro-: Pertaining to joints.

Arthroscopy: Visual examination of the joint cavity using a fiber-optic needle.

Article: The object to be found in a tracking event, usually a leather glove.

Articular: Referring to joints.

Articular surface: Articulation, location where bones meet to form joints.

Articulation: A joint; the place where one bone connects with another.

Artificial insemination: Reproduction without contact between the male and female dogs. Semen is placed within the female. The frozen semen is thawed and injected into the lumen of the bitch's uterus.

Artificial respiration: Emergency procedure used to assist breathing in an unconscious dog.

As fed basis: An expression of nutrient content with moisture included.

ASCA: Australian Shepherd Club of America

Ascarid: Common form of roundworm, a parasitic nematode.

Ascending paralysis: Loss of sensation or ability to move, starting in the hindquarters and progressively moving forward.

Ascites: Accumulation of fluid in the abdominal cavity, causing swelling. Usually associated with heart or liver disease.

ASCOB: Any solid color other than black. Used for cocker spaniels.

Ascorbic acid: Vitamin C.

ASD: Atrial septal defect.

Aseptic: Free of disease organisms.

Ash: **(1)** The inorganic mineral content of plants and animals. **(2)** In dog-food manufacturing, the total mineral content as measured by burning a food sample at 600 degrees C for two hours.

ASPCA National Animal Poison Control Center. Telephone: (800) 548-2423. Consultation fee, payable by credit card. Open twenty-four hours, every day.

ASPCA: American Society for the Prevention of Cruelty to Animals.

Aspergillosis: An opportunist fungal infection, generally appearing as a nasal and frontal sinus infection. Long nosed breeds mostly affected.

Aspic: In dog-food manufacturing, a solid or semisolid flavor enhancer, made by mixing a gelling agent with seasoning and flavors, often an extract of meat or poultry.

Aspirate: Withdraw cells or fluid by means of suction.

Aspiration biopsy: See aspiration.

Aspiration pneumonia: Lung disease resulting from food, saliva, or regurgitated stomach contents entering the respiratory tract.

Aspiration: (1) Removal of fluid from any part of the body (usually a cyst or tumor) using a fine sterile needle and syringe. **(2)** Inhaling of food or other materials into the airways.

Aspirin: Acetylsalicylic acid sometimes prescribed as an anti-inflammatory drug for dogs despite newer NSAIDS. Usually taken twice a day. Measured in grains, the prescription is usually one 5-grain tablet for every 60 pounds of weight every 12 hours. A 5-grain tablet equals 325 milligrams. Aspirin taken over an extended period can cause stomach distress in some dogs.

Assimilation: Process of transforming food into a state in which it can be absorbed.

Assistance Dog Institute: P.O. Box 2334, Rohnert Park, CA

94927. Telephone: (707) 585-0300 (voice/TTY).

Association of American Feed Control Officials (AAFCO): An agency that develops model regulations for the production and labeling of animal feeds.

Association of Masters of Harriers and Beagles: Association of hunting dog owners formed in England in 1873.

Association of Pet Dog Trainers: This organization promotes non-force methods of training. 17000 Commerce Parkway, Suite C, Mt. Laurel, NJ 08054. Telephone: (800) 738-3647. Website: www.apdt.com.

Association of Veterinarians for Animal Rights: P.O. Box 6269, Vacaville, CA 45656-6269. Telephone: (707) 451-1391.

Association points: In acupuncture, points located along the bladder meridian along the back.

AST: Aspartate aminotransferase (SGOT), a liver enzyme.

Asthma: Condition marked by labored breathing, wheezing, and gasping.

Astringent: A drying agent. In herbal medicine, an agent with a constricting or binding effect. Astringents may be used to stop hemorrhages, discharges, and secretions.

Asymptomatic: Without symptoms or signs.

Ataxia: Incoordination.

Ataxic: Uncoordinated.

ATD: Advanced Trial Dog, title for herding dogs awarded by the Australian Shepherd Club of America.

Atelectasis: Rupture of the small sacs in the lung; produces chronic coughing.

Atenolol: Beta blocker prescribed for dilated cardiomyopathy, high blood pressure, and abnormal heart rhythms.

Atlantoaxial luxation: Instability or dislocation of the cervical vertebrae.

Atlas: First cervical vertebra.

Atony: Lack of normal tone or strength.

Atopic allergy: Inherited sensitivity to environmental allergens such as pollens.

Atopy: (1) A genetically determined predisposition to produce IgE antibodies in response to an allergen (usually ragweed, pollen, house dust, house dust mites, mold, animal dander, feathers, grasses, trees, or shrubs). These allergens can be inhaled, can pass through the foot pads, or can even be ingested. (2) Skin allergy. Also called atopic dermatitis. This condition is often caused by pollen. Dogs with such allergies scratch, but their skin often appears normal. More rarely a dog may vomit, sneeze, wheeze, or have a runny nose. Very severe itching may indicate an active case of fleas, mange, or food allergy. Dogs that begin scratching at the same time every year are probably allergic to some type of vegetation.

ATP: Adenosine triphosphate; a compound used for energy by cells.

Atresia: Congenital absence or closure of a normal body opening or tubular structure.

Atrial anomalies: Defects of the upper chambers of the heart.

Atrial fibrillation: A heart condition in which the atria (chambers of the heart that receive the blood) contract rapidly, irregularly, and independently of the ventricles (the chambers of the heart that pump the blood). Also called atrial flutter.

Atrial septal defect (ASD): A hole in the heart wall that separates the right and left atria.

This problem is rather uncommon, but boxers, Doberman pinschers, Samoyeds, and Old English sheepdogs are considered to have an increased risk for ASD. The mode of inheritance is not known.

Atrium: One of the two chambers that make up the top of the heart.

Atrium: One of the two smaller upper chambers of the heart that receive blood. The right atrium receives venous blood from the body. The left atrium receives oxygenated blood from the lungs. (Plural: atria).

Atrophy: Decreased size of an organ, due to withering away.

Attempt: In herding, when the livestock crosses the plane of the obstacle.

Attenuation: Reduction in virulence of an infective agent.

AU: Each ear (veterinary notation).

Auditory ossicles: The smallest bones of the body, located within the ear. They are the hammer, anvil, and stirrup bones.

Aura: In epilepsy, the start of the seizure. Signs include restlessness, nervousness, whining, trembling, salivation, affection-seeking, wandering, hiding, and hysterical running.

Aural: Pertaining to the ear.

Aural hematoma: Accumulation of blood in the space between the skin and the cartilage in the ear flap.

Auricle: Pinna, the part of the ear outside the skull.

Auscultate: To listen for sounds produced within the body, usually with the aid of a stethoscope.

Australian cattle dog: Also known as the blue heeler or Queensland cattle dog, the breed originated in Australia in the 1840s. Used for driving cattle, but can handle any kind of stock, including ducks. Size: 17 to 20 inches, 35 to 45 pounds. Colors include blue, blue-mottled, blue-speckled, and red-speckled.

Australian heeler: Short coated breed with tipped ears and a long tail. Usually black and tan. Size: about 45 pounds.

Australian kelpie: Strong, medium-sized sheepdog. It was developed from English North Country collies.

Australian National Kennel Council (ANKC): The principal dog registry for purebred dogs in Australia. It recognizes the same breeds as the Kennel Club of Great Britain and adopts the same standards, except for the Australian national breeds such as the Australian kelpie. Established in 1958.

Australian Shepherd Club of America: P. O. Box 3790, Bryan, TX 77805. Telephone: (800) 892-2722. Web site: www.asca.org.

Australian shepherd: Despite its name, this breed was developed in the United States. Originally used to herd sheep, it now excels in agility trials. Size: 18 to 23 inches, 50 to 70 pounds with a straight-to-wavy medium-length coat, which is often merled.

Australian silky terrier: Silky terrier.

Australian terrier: Along with the silky terrier, the only well-known terrier breed not developed in Great Britain. The Australian terrier was created from a blend of terriers imported from northern England and Scotland. A typical terrier, and a good family dog. Colors include blue, steel blue, dark gray, blue with tan, sandy, and red. Size: 10 to 11 inches at the withers, about 14 pounds.

Autoimmune disease: A disease in which the body rejects or destroys its own tissues; the T cells begin attacking other cells. Also called immune-mediated condition.

Autoimmune hemolytic anemia (AIHA): A disease in which red blood cells are destroyed faster than new ones can be produced, resulting in a decrease in the oxygen-carrying capacity of the blood. The disease may develop in response to an infection, and the signs include pale gums and other signs of anemia.

Autolesion: Self-inflicted injury.

Autologous chondrocyte implantation (ACI): Surgery used in humans and experimentally in dogs in which healthy cartilage is grafted into an arthritic joint.

Automatic strike dog: Hound that barks as soon as turned loose in a competitive event.

Autonomic: Not subject to voluntary control.

Autosomal dominant disease: When inheritance of only one mutant allele on any non-X or non-Y chromosome results in a disease.

Autosomal: Chromosomes other than the sex pair, the X and Y chromosomes.

AV: Atrioventricular.

Available protein: The portion of crude protein that actually can be used by an animal.

Avalanche dog: A dog trained to find human beings trapped under snow. These dogs are able to discriminate between living and dead persons.

Avascular necrosis: Cellular death due to lack of blood supply.

Avascular: Lacking a blood supply.

AVCA: American Veterinary Chiropractic Society.

AVDC: American Veterinary Dental College.

Aversion therapy: Treatment of a behavior problem involving mild physical or mental discomfort.

Avidin: Enzyme in raw egg white that interferes with absorption of biotin.

AVMA: American Veterinary Medical Association.

AVSAB: American Veterinary Society for Animal Behavior.

AWE: Acute wet eczema.

AWTA: American Working Terrier Association.

AX: Agility Excellent (AKC title). Title is added after the dog's name.

Axilla: Armpit.

Axis: Second vertebra of the neck.

AXJ: Excellent Agility Jumper (AKC title). Title is added after the dog's name.

Azathioprine: Immunosuppressant prescribed for autoimmune diseases, especially of the skin, gastrointestinal tract, and eyes.

Azotemia: The increase of nitrogen-containing waste products (such as urea) in the bloodstream due to kidney failure.

AZT: Azidothymidine.

B

B cell: Also called B lymphocyte. The type of lymphocyte that produces antibodies.

B/W: Black and white.

B: (1) Booster (veterinary notation). (2) In schutzhund, the German equivalent of a CD and CGC test in one.

Babbler: A hound that vocalizes even though it is not on the scent.

Babesiosis: (Nantucket disease): Tick-borne disease caused by a protozoan that destroys red blood cells and leads to hemolytic anemia.

Bach flower essences: Named after Dr. Edward Bach, a homeopath who became interested in the healing properties of flowers. Eventually Bach produced thirty-eight different essences, each designed to treat a separate problem. In addition, and most popular of all, is Rescue Remedy, a combination of star-of-Bethlehem, impatiens, cherry plum, and clematis, designed to alleviate shock, anxiety, and trauma. The essences can be administered by mouth or added to food or water. Normally several weeks are required for full effect.

Back: In brace work during pointing breed field trials, the sight point of another dog on point. Another term for Honor.

Back crossing: A type of inbreeding where a dog is mated to its parent.

Back dropping through withers: A topline in which the front section of the back right behind the withers is hollowed out.

Backcast: Referring to a dog moving behind the handler, below nine o'clock or three o'clock relative to that handler's direction of travel.

Backtrack: (1) In tracking, retracing steps over a portion of the track that has already been completed. Also known as "double-" or "triple laying" a track. (2) In hound trials, backtrack refers to a dog's running the track in the wrong direction from the one in which the game has traveled.

Backyard breeder: Term used to describe a person who breeds purebred dogs in a casual way, disregarding the breed standard, genetically linked defects, or temperament.

Bacteremia: Presence of bacteria in the blood.

Bacterial folliculitis: Infection of the hair follicle.

Bacterin: A killed bacterial vaccine.

Bacterium: A single-celled organism lacking a true nucleus. Its genetic material consists of a single double-stranded DNA or RNA molecule.

Bad breath: Causes include tooth and gum problems, poor digestion, and kidney problems.

Bad doer: A dog that fails to thrive despite normal care.

Badger: Coat color blending brown, gray, black, and white.

Badger-pied: Unequally portioned patches of black and white or tan and white, mixed together.

BAER test: Brainstem Auditory Evoked Responses. A hearing test.

Baiting: Using a treat to spark a dog's interest during a show.

Baking soda: Sodium bicarbonate. Use to relieve itching and sunburn.

BAL: Dimercaprol.

Balaeric dog: Ibizan hound.

Balance: (1) In herding, the point, usually opposite the handler, where the dog has the most influence on the stock, in order to control their behavior and move them in the desired direction. (2) In conformation, a term used to describe the similar characteristics of the dog's parts; proportions.

Balanced food: A food that supplies the proper amount and proportion of nutrients needed.

Balanced head: A head in which the skull and foreface are equal in length, as in the Gordon setter.

Balanic: Pertaining to the glans penis or glans clitoridis.

Balanitis: Infection or inflammation of the glans penis.

Balk: In field trials, when a dog refuses to leave line when ordered to do so. Also called a "no go."

Balto: Siberian Husky who led the famous 650-mile run from Nenana to Nome, Alaska, to deliver diphtheria serum in 1925. The run is commemorated in the annual Iditarod sled race held each year in March.

Baluchi hound: Afghan hound.

Band cells: Immature neutrophils.

Bandog: A dog tied by day, released at night.

Bandy-legged: Wide, bow-legged rear legs. The opposite of cow-hocked.

Banker: In dog racing, an animal generally expected to win.

Bar and goggles: The face markings found on some malamutes, particularly black-and-white ones.

Bar: (1) Arm or humerus. (2) A stripe of dark color running from the forehead down to the nose, particularly in malamutes.

BAR: "Bright and responsive" or "bright, alert, responsive" (veterinary notation).

Barbichon: Old name for a Bichon frise.

Barbon: Standard or miniature poodle.

Barghest: Legendary dog from Wales and parts of Great Britain. Also known as Gwyllgi, the Dog of Darkness, or Mauthe Doog.

BARH: "Bright, responsive, alert, hydrated" (veterinary notation).

Barium series: GI diagnostic tests in which a dog is fasted for fourteen hours, given barium (a white, chalklike fluid) and then radiographed. The barium will highlight abnormalities or stoppages in the intestinal tract.

Barking: Characteristic short, loud cry of a dog. While some barking is normal, excessive barking can be triggered by overactive territorial instincts, boredom, fear, or separation anxiety.

Barkless dog: See basenji.

Barks per minute: In treeing competitions, the number of barks during each minute of treeing.

Barrel chest: Round, sometimes oversprung rib cage.

Barrel hocks: Turned-out hocks, also called spread hocks or divergent hocks.

Barring: Stripes.

Barry: Famous alpine Saint Bernard (1800–1814), credited with saving more than forty human lives.

Basal cells: Bottom cell layer of the epidermis.

Basal cell tumor: Common benign skin tumor.

Basal energy requirement (BER): The energy requirement for a normal resting animal in a comfortable environment.

Baseball: In retriever training, a beginning drill used to teach the dog to take hand signals. A precursor for blinds.

Base coat: Primary coat color.

Basenji: Small- to medium-sized dog of primitive African ancestry. It does not bark but has a variety of other vocalizations, including yodeling. Independent and aloof. Also called the barkless dog. Very clean and easy to house train. Colors include black, black and tan, white, black and white, and red and white. Size: 16 to 17 inches, 21 to 24 pounds.

Basenji enteropathy: Progressive intestinal malabsorption of Basenjis, resulting in protein loss, diarrhea, and loss of weight. Also called lymphocytic-plasmacytic enteritis.

Basewide: Wide footfall in gaiting.

Basket: In dog sledding, the bed of the sled.

Basset fauve de Bretagne: French breed notable for its dense, wiry coat. Traditionally used for hunting game, but also a fine family pet. Colors include wheaten, fawn, and red. Size: 12 to 15 inches, 35 to 40 pounds.

Basset hound: Willful, sweet-natured scent hound characterized by very long ears, large feet, and short stature. Colors include red and white, lemon, and tricolor. Size: 13 to 15 inches, 40 to 60 pounds.

Basset hound thrombopathia: See thrombopathia.

Bat ear: A rounded, broad-based erect ear, as in the French bulldog.

Bawl mouth: Long, drawn-out bark. A hound trait.

Bay: The prolonged cry of a hunting hound; a howl.

Baytril: See enrofloxacin

BBE: Bred by exhibitor.

BC: Border collie.

Beady: In reference to the eye, small and unpleasantly glittering.

Beagle: Small, friendly scent hound, with dense fur, usually tricolor or brown and white. It is known for retaining a "puppy face" throughout its life. Size: 13 to 16 inches, 20 to 30 pounds.

Beard: Thick, long hair underneath the chin.

Bearded collie: Medium to large-sized dog used as a family pet or guard dog. Has a harsh, flat, shaggy outer coat in a variety of browns and blues. Puppies change color as they age. Also called the Highland Collie, the Mountain collie, or the Hairy Mouthed Collie. Size: 20 to 22 inches.

Bear ear: Ears with very rounded tips.

Beauceron: A French sheep and guard dog whose ancestry goes back more than 500 years. This breed is not recommended for a novice owner. Noted for its double dewclaws. Colors include black and tan or harlequin. Size: 26 to 28 inches, 80 to 110 pounds.

Also called Berger de Beauce, Beauce, and bas rouge.

Beaver: In fur, a mixture of gray, white, brown, and black hairs.

Bedlington terrier copper-associated hepatopathy: An inherited copper storage disease, in which the animal accumulates copper in the liver. The disease is incurable but can be managed with decoppering agents such as D-penicillamine.

Bedlington terrier: Soft-coated, curly-haired, roman-nosed terrier from northeast England used by miners and ironworkers to hunt rats. Said to look like a lamb with the heart of a lion. Origin: Bedlington, England. Colors include blue, liver, or sandy with or without tan. The breed is subject to retinal dysplasia and copper-associated hepatopathy. Size: 16 inches, 17 to 23 pounds.

Bee sting tail: A strong, straight tail that tapers to a point.

Beef: In dog-food labeling, the clean, striated muscle flesh from slaughtered cattle.

Beefy: A dog with overdeveloped hindquarters.

Beet pulp: Dried residue from sugar beets. Sometimes found in dog food.

Beethoven: Screen name of the Saint Bernard in the film of the same name. Real name: Kris.

Beezer: Colloquial, affectionate name for the Ibizan hound.

Behavior: Anything a dog does.

Belge: Coat of black and reddish brown, characteristic of the Brussels griffon.

Belgian cattle dog: Bouvier des Flandres.

Belgian griffon: Brussels griffon.

Belgian Malinois: One of the Belgian shepherd dogs. Short-haired, fawn-colored dog, with a black mask. Size: 22 to 26 inches, 55 to 60 pounds.

Belgian sheepdog: One of the Belgian shepherd dogs. Black, long-haired herding dog with upright ears; used as a herd dog and guard dog. The modern breed was developed in the late-nineteenth century. Also called the Groenendael. Size: 22 to 26 inches, 55 to 60 pounds.

Belgian Tervuren: One of the Belgian shepherd dogs, the Tervuren is similar to the Belgian sheepdog, although its coat is predominantly fawn.

Belladonna: A homeopathic remedy frequently used for aggressive behavior, ear problems, and acne.

Bell ear: Big, wide ear that sticks out, like Dumbo's.

Bell hound: In a group of dogs, the one that initiates the baying.

Belly: The under-part of the abdomen.

Belton: Intermingled white and colored hairs. Also called a ticking or roan pattern. Used for English setters. The word comes from a village in Northumberland, England.

Benadryl (diphenhydramine): Antihistamine safe for use in allergic, itchy dogs.

Benched show: A dog show in which the exhibitors are required to display their dogs on platforms during the show. In the United States, only a few benched shows remain; among them the prestigious Westminster Kennel Club Show of New York. The others are in Detroit, San Francisco, Philadelphia, and Chicago.

Benign: Not harmful, invasive, or malignant; or not progressive. Term is usually used in reference to tumors.

Benzoyl peroxide: Topical antibacterial, anti-itch, anti-scale, degreasing gel or shampoo prescribed for skin problems.

BER: Basal energy requirement.

Berberis Vulgaris: Homeopathic remedy commonly administered for kidney disease.

Berger de Brie: Briard.

Berger de la Camargue: One of the five varieties of Languedoc sheepdogs.

Berger de la Garu: One of the five varieties of Languedoc sheepdogs.

Berger des Carrigues: One of the five varieties of Languedoc sheepdogs.

Berger du Larzac: One of the five varieties of Languedoc sheepdogs.

Bergomasco sheepdog: Coarse-coated, knotty-haired breed originating in Bergamo (northern Italy), best suited for guarding sheep in large fields. A vigilant watchdog. Renowned for the "flocks" to the coat, which need to be split by hand. Colors include solid gray, dull black, Isabella, or light fawn. Size: 21 to 25 inches, 57 to 84 pounds.

Berner sennenhund: Bernese mountain dog.

Bernese cattle dog: Bernese mountain dog.

Bernese mountain dog: One of the Swiss mountain breeds. Strongly built and with a long coat. Tricolor. Size: 23 to 28 inches, 88 to 97 pounds.

Bertillon card: A greyhound's identification card, listing fifty-six physical identifying points for every registered racing greyhound. The greyhound's Bertillon number is tattooed in its ear.

Bessie: Collie owned by Calvin Coolidge.

Best in Show: Award given to the one dog that defeated all other dogs of all breeds entered in an all-breed show.

Best Junior Handler: The award given to the one Junior Handler at an all-breed or specialty show who is judged to have exhibited the highest degree of skill in presenting his or her dog.

Best of Breed: In a conformation show, the dog judged as the best in its breed category.

Best of Opposite Sex: In a conformation show, the best dog that is the opposite sex of the Best of Breed winner.

Best of Winners (BOW): In a conformation show, the dog judged as the better of the Winners Dog (WD) and Winners Bitch (WB). The BOW receives the highest number of points given to that breed's WD or WB that day.

Beta blockers: Heart medications that block receptors in the heart called beta receptors. The beta receptors receive signals that generally increase the heart rate. If the heart rate is abnormally fast and uneven, beta blockers will help stabilize the rate and rhythm of contractions.

Beta-carotene: A plant pigment that can be converted to vitamin A by many animals.

Beta cells: Cells that produce insulin in the pancreas. Also called islet cells.

Betadine: Used to treat minor burns.

Bethanechol: Smooth-muscle stimulant prescribed to stimulate bladder contraction.

Bevy: A flock of birds.

Bewick, Thomas: Early writer of dog history. Most famous work is the General History of Quadrupeds (1790).

BHA: Butylated hydroxyanisole.

BHI Arthritis: A homeopathic remedy for arthritis.

BHI Trameel: A homeopathic remedy often administered for arthritic inflammation and pain.

BHS: Beta-hemolytic streptococci.

BHT: Butylated hydroxytoluene.

Biarticular: Affecting two joints.

Bichon a poil frise: Bichon frise.

Bichon frise: An ideal family dog. Curly coated with minimal shedding. Origin: Canary Islands. Color: White. Size: 9 to 11 inches, 7 to 12 pounds.

Bichon Havanese: Havanais.

Bichon Maltiase: Maltese.

Bichon Tenerife: Bichon frise.

Bicolor: Composed of two colors.

bid: Twice daily (veterinary notation).

Biddable: Responds readily to commands.

Bi-eye: One blue eye, one brown.

BIF: Best in Field winning.

BifN: Back if necessary (veterinary notation).

Big Ben: Fox Terrier owned by Herbert Hoover.

Big hunt: In retriever field trials, when a dog cannot find a mark and runs all over the field looking for it.

Bilateral: On both sides.

Bilberry: In herbal medicine, administered for diarrhea and blood disorders.

Bile: A salty yellow fluid produced by the liver and stored in the gall bladder that helps in the digestion of fat.

Bile acids: Substances produced by the liver and secreted in the bile that aid digestion.

Bilirubin: A bile pigment produced when old red blood cells are destroyed in the body. Abnormal amounts of bilirubin cause jaundice.

Bingley terrier: Airedale terrier.

Bioavailability: A measure of how well nutrients are used in the body.

Biochemical profile (SMA-20): A series of blood tests evaluating internal organs such as the liver and kidneys.

Biochemical tissue therapy: Treatment program similar to homeopathy, using twelve "biochemical tissue salts."

Biologically inactive hormone: A defective hormone that cannot produce its expected effects in the body.

Biological score: An index that compares the amino acid

composition of a given protein source with the amino acid pattern of very high quality protein (usually egg), which is given a score of 100.

Biological value: The percentage of absorbed protein retained by the body, or the amino acids actually converted into body tissue.

BIOP: "Been in owner's possession" (veterinary notation).

Biopsy: A minor operation that removes a portion of suspect tissue for microscopic examination.

Biotin: A member of the vitamin B complex, required by all life forms. It is essential to protein metabolism, growth, and healthy skin. Found in meat, fish, and liver.

Bird dog: Sporting breeds developed to hunt birds, primarily the pointing breeds other than spaniels or retrievers. Bird dogs track birds by air-scenting rather than trailing.

Bird of prey eyes: Light, yellowish eyes, usually accompanied by a hard expression.

Birdboy: See birdplanter.

Birdfield: A marked-off area at the back of the course, where at least two birds are planted per brace in a field trial or hunting test.

Bird-finding ability: A judging category of the AKC Pointing Breed Hunting Tests that evaluated the dog's scenting abilities and intelligence.

Birdless: In pointing tests and trials, a dog completing its brace without finding game.

Birdplanter: Person who plants blinds and liberates birds at field trials.

Birdy: Demonstrating the presence of game, a term used for pointing breeds.

BIS: Best in Show.

Bisacodyl: A laxative.

Biscuit: A blended and baked dry dog food, often used as a treat.

BISmap: Genetic map that is maximally informative for a particular breed.

BISmarkers: Breed informative set of genetic markers that constitute the most informative markers available for a given breed.

Bismuth subsalicylate: Antidiarrheal medication.

BISS: Best in Specialty Sweepstakes.

Bitch: Female dog.

Bitchy: A male dog showing female characteristics.

Bite: Occlusion; the way the upper and lower teeth meet.

Bitter: In herbal medicine, bitter herbs are used as stimulants to the digestive system through the taste buds.

Bitter tonic: Substance that stimulates digestive functions, first in the mouth and then in the stomach.

BIW: "Before, if worried" (veterinary notation). Instruction to bring dog back before scheduled reexamination date if owner is worried about its progress.

BJ: Broad jump or bar jump.

BJH: Best Junior Handler.

Black and tan: Color markings characteristic of Gordon setters, certain Doberman pinschers, and coonhounds.

Black and tan coonhound: Developed in America from ancient European hounds. Trails game slowly but relentlessly. A good, loyal companion. Size: 23 to 27 inches.

Black and tan terrier: Manchester terrier.

Black and tan toy terrier: Toy Manchester terrier.

Blackberry: Chow chow owned by Calvin Coolidge.

Black Jack: Terrier owned by Theodore Roosevelt.

Black-legged tick: Major transmitter of Lyme disease in the southern United States.

Black skin disease: Another name of alopecia X, or hair loss. The disease is cosmetic only.

Bladder: The sac-like structure that stores urine until it can be passed.

Bladder stones: Stones formed within the bladder, also called uroliths. Minerals that, instead of passing through the dog in solution, clump together to form a stone that irritates the bladder lining. Once a stone forms, more minerals cling to it.

Blade-bone: The shoulder blade.

Blaireau: Similar to badger color, a mixture of brown, black, gray, and white.

Blanco: Collie owned by Lyndon Johnson.

Blanket: (1) A solid coat color that extends from the neck to the tail and down part of the sides. **(2)** In lure coursing, a solid-colored cloth worn by each hound during competition.

Blanketback: A dog with a black or nearly black back, like a blanket.

Blaze: Wide central facial stripe between the eyes. Usually wider than the nasal bones.

Bleeding disorder: Any condition that interferes with blood clotting in a wound.

Blenheim: Chestnut red patches found on a white background. Used in reference to cavalier King Charles spaniels, as well as the Japanese chin.

Blepharitis: Inflamed eyelid. The lid becomes thick and red.

Blepharospasm: Spasm of the eyelids often resulting in complete closure of the lids due to eye pain, such as seen with a scratch on the cornea.

Blind: A bird or dummy planted where the handler knows the location but the dog does not.

Blind, quiet eye: Blind, quiet eye describes the condition in which loss of vision happens without any obvious external signs (such as reddened eyes) of eye damage. The loss of vision may stem from a problem with the eye itself, resulting from a change in how the eye focuses or transmits images to the brain. The loss of vision also may be caused by the brain's inability to receive or interpret these images.

Blind retrieve: A retrieve in which the dog is directed by the handler to a hidden bird or dummy.

Blind track: In tracking, a track laid by another person and totally unknown to the handler. No flags or turn markers are used.

Blinker: A dog that points a bird and then leaves it.

Blinking or blinking birds: (1) In pointing breeds, the refusal of a dog to acknowledge the presence of game or of another dog on point. **(2)** In retrievers, the refusal of a dog to pick up a bird or training dummy.

Bloat: Common name for gastric dilatation-volvulus. A recurring, often fatal condition in which the stomach swells with food, water, and gas and then twists, cutting off the blood supply. Occurs primarily in large, deep-chested breeds, such as Great Danes and German shepherds.

Blocky: Squarish or cube like; can refer to the body or the head, as in the Boston terrier.

Blondi: German shepherd owned by Adolf Hitler.

Blood gases: Gases, such as oxygen or carbon dioxide, that are in the blood.

Blood glucose (sugar) test: Test to diagnose diabetes (high blood sugar) and hypoglycemia (low blood sugar).

Blood test: A diagnostic tool that provides a complete blood count, platelet count, red blood cell count, white blood cell count, and so forth.

Blood transfusion: The introduction of whole blood or plasma directly into a dog's vein by means of a catheter.

Blood urea nitrogen test (BUN): A blood test to determine whether the kidneys are properly removing nitrogen wastes from the body. A high BUN count can indicate kidney disease, heart disease, or dehydration.

Blooded: Of good breeding.

Bloodhound: Heavily built scent hound. Needs kind, sympathetic training and lots of exercise. Colors include black and tan, liver and tan, and red. Size: 24 to 26 inches, 79 to 110 pounds.

Bloodline: The pedigree for a given dog, usually referred to in the sense of a specific kennel.

Bloody diarrhea: Sign of acute parvovirus infection.

Bloody stools: Can be caused by parasites (hookworm and whipworm), infections, sharp objects, diet change.

Bloody urine: Often caused by bladder or kidney infection, or prostate problems in older male dogs. Bright red blood usually indicates bladder infection. Dark, foul-smelling urine indicates kidney infection.

Bloom: (1) Top condition. **(2)** Glossy coat.

Blousy: Soft, woolly coat.

Blown: A coat that is shed out.

Blue: Diluted black coat color, caused by a recessive gene.

Blue black: Hair with blue base and black tip.

Blue cream: Coat color combining blue with cream.

Blue eye: Clouding of the eye, caused by inflammation of the cornea.

Blue heeler: Australian cattle dog.

Blue merle: Blue and gray mixed with black; marbled.

Blue ribbon: Awarded for first place in any regular class in a dog show.

Blue slip: Registration application, for a dog that has not been individually registered with the AKC. Owner chooses a name, pays a small fee, and fills out the slip. An official registration certificate will be returned by the AKC in about one month.

Bluetick coonhound: A hunting breed.

Bluies: Gray- or blue-colored portions of the coat, associated with light-colored eyes, eye rims, and nose and lip pigment.

Blunt muzzle: Square-cut nose, as in the mastiff.

Blunt triangle head: A V-shaped head with square or rounded ends.

Blunt-tipped ears: Erect ears that are rounded rather than pointed, as in a chow chow.

BMD: Bernese mountain dog.

BMR: Basal metabolic rate.

Boat feet: Slipper feet.

Boatswain: A Newfoundland made famous in an epitaph by Lord Byron.

Bob tail or bobtail: Short, stumpy tail, as in the Old English sheepdog. Also used for any dog with a very short tail.

Bodied up: Mature, well developed.

Body: (1) Anatomical section between the forequarters and hindquarters. **(2)** Good depth of chest.

Body scans: Examination of the interior of the body using radio waves or radioisotopes.

Body spots: Patches of color on the skin, but not the coat.

Boerbul: Mastiff-type dog native to South Africa.

BOH: Breeder/Owner/Handler.

Bolognese: White dog from antiquity. Minimal shedding and excellent family pet. Size: 10 to 12 inches, 6 to 9 pounds.

Bolo pads: White hairs under the feet of some Labrador retrievers, a characteristic traced back to a dog named Banchory Bolo.

Bolt: In field trials, when a dog leaves a test to go off hunting by itself, refusing commands to stop or return to the handler.

Bolter: A dog that habitually bolts.

Bone: (1) Major component of the skeleton. **(2)** Informally: clean, big, strong bones.

Bone cancer: Most common in large and giant breeds. See Osteosarcoma.

Bone marrow: The soft center of bones that produces blood cells.

Bone marrow aspiration: Removal of a bit of bone marrow for microscopic evaluation.

Bone meal: In dog-food labeling, the dried and ground sterilized product resulting from cooking fresh bones. Fat, gelatin, and meat may or may not be removed.

Booties: Foot coverings worn by sled dogs to protect their feet.

Borborygmus: A rumbling of the stomach or intestine.

Bordeaux mastiff: Developed in France, the breed's original purpose was to hunt boar and bear, as well as to fight bulls.

Border collie: Ancient, highly intelligent breed, considered the closest purebred representative of the old collies of Scotland. Most noted for its "strong-eye." This workaholic breed needs a real job, not just exercise. Comes in various colors. Size: 21 inches, 31 to 48 pounds.

Border terrier: Rough-coated dog, milder mannered than many other terriers. Not always good with cats. Colors include red, tan, wheaten, grizzle, and blue and tan. Size: 10 to 11 inches, 11 to 15 pounds.

Bordetella: Organism that causes kennel cough.

Bordetellosis: Bacterial infection that affects the respiratory system.

Boric acid: Topical antiseptic and antifungal prescribed for ear, eye, and skin infections.

Borrelia burgdorferi: Bacterial organism (spirochete) that causes Lyme disease.

Borreliosis: Commonly referred to as Lyme disease. An infectious arthritis caused by a spirochete bacterium.

Borzoi: Large, speedy, silky-coated sight hound in any color. Gentle and reserved. Size: 27 to 29 inches, up to 105 pounds.

BOS: Best of Opposite Sex to Best of Breed.

Bossy: Over-developed shoulder muscles.

Boston Beans: Bulldog owned by Calvin Coolidge.

Boston terrier: Intelligent, smooth-coated brindle-and-white terrier. An ideal family dog and excellent apartment pet. Size: 15 to 17 inches, up to 25 pounds.

BOSV: Best of Opposite Sex Variety.

Bouledogue Français: French bulldog.

Bounce: Movement characterized by great springiness and elasticity.

Bouvier des Flandres: Cattle-herding breed originating in the border region between France and Belgium. Used today as a guide, military, and police dog. Loyal and intelligent. Has a tousled, double coat. Colors include black, fawn, and brindle. Size: 23 to 27 inches, 59 to 88 pounds.

Bowed front: Forelegs that curve out between the elbows and pasterns.

Bowed legs: Barrel hocks in the rear or fiddle front in the fore.

Bow-hocked: Hind legs that curve outward away from each other. The opposite of cow-hocked.

Boxer: Medium-sized dog, with a short brown coat, white markings, docked tail, and often cropped ears (in the United

States). Originally a hunting breed, the boxer gained fame as a police and military dog. Origin: Germany. Colors include red, fawn, and brindle with or without white. Size: 21 to 25 inches, 55 to 70 pounds.

Boykin spaniel: An American breed of dog, originating in South Carolina as a turkey- and waterfowl-hunting dog. Size: 30 to 38 pounds, with a liver-colored, curly coat.

BP: Blood pressure.

Bracco Italiano: The "Italian Pointer." Medium to large Italian gundog. Colors include orange/white, chestnut/white, orange roan, and chestnut. Size: 22 to 26 inches, 55 to 88 pounds.

Brace: (1) In conformation, a pair of matched dogs (same breed and ownership) to be judged together in order to display the breeder's consistency in his or her breeding program. Brace competition is a nonregular competition and no points are awarded. **(2)** In field events, two dogs run at the same time. They are competitors.

Bracelets: In poodles with a Continental clip, the unshaven area of hair on the hind legs.

Brachury: An abnormally short tail.

Brachycephalic: Broad head with a flat face and short muzzle, like a bulldog or pug. Associated medical conditions can include difficult birth, chewing difficulties, breathing problems, and eye problems.

Brachygnathism: Protrusion of the lower jaw.

Bradycardia: A slower-than-normal heart rate.

Brand-name drug: Drug with a specific trade name rather than a generic name.

Break in ear: Line of crease of the fold in a semidrop ear.

Break: (1) To train. **(2)** The action of mistakenly chasing after a shot bird. **(3)** Term used to describe the change of coat color from puppy to adult stages.

Breakaway: In a pointing breed field trial, the point at which a course begins. A fast breakaway is desirable.

Breaking: In a field trial, leaving without having been sent or without having been released by the handler.

Breaking scent: Scent of unwanted game that is used to break dog from running that particular animal.

Breast bone: Sternum.

Bred by exhibitor: In dog shows, a class for non-finished dogs that were bred, owned, and handled by the same person.

Breech: Area designated by the inner thigh muscle groups around the buttocks.

Breech birth: A birth in which the hind end of the puppy comes out first, rather than the head.

Breeches: In long-coated dogs, the fringe of longer hair on the thighs or buttocks.

Breeching: The tan marking at the back of the thighs of a black-and-tan dog, such as a Gordon setter or Manchester terrier.

Breed: (1) A group of genetically related domesticated animals possessing a uniform appearance, distinguishable from other animals in the same species. Offspring will resemble the parents. **(2)** To mate dogs.

Breed club: Organization made up of dog fanciers devoted to the promotion and improvement of a particular breed of dog.

Breed council: A select group of dog-association members involved in exhibiting and breeding dogs of a specific breed. The council makes proposals to the main association about changes for the official breed and judging standards.

Breeder's Choice Pet Foods: Telephone: (800) 255-4286. Web site: www.breeders-choice.com

Breeding particulars: Sire, dam, date of birth, sex, color, and so on.

Breed rescue: An organization dedicated to finding good homes for unwanted, abused, or abandoned purebred dogs.

Breed ribbon: Award given to the Best of Breed in each ring.

Breed split: The situation in which two distinct breed types have emerged, one for "show" and one for use in hunting or other practical endeavors.

Breed standard: A written description listing the key characteristics of the perfect specimen of each breed.

Brewer's rice: A dried, extracted residue of rice resulting from the manufacture of malt or beer.

Briard: Known as the "dog of the grasslands," a highly intelligent sheepdog. The coat is long and dry. Colors include black, fawn, and slate gray. Size: 22 to 27 inches, 73 to 77 pounds.

Brick-shaped: Rectangular. Used in reference to head shape.

Brindle: Even, vertical bands of dark hair over a lighter coat color such as tan, brown, or gold.

Brisket: Breastbone or sternum, the lowest point of the thorax.

Bristle coat: a coat that is short, wirehaired, and stiff.

Britches: Longer hair found on the upper rear area of the legs.

Brittany: Size: 30 to 40 pounds, 17 to 21 inches. Color is usually orange and white or liver and white in parti- or piebald patterns. All-around hunting, pointing, and retrieving breed. Developed in northern France, as the name suggests, in the seventeenth century or earlier.

Brittany spaniel: The name by which the Brittany was officially known until 1982. The "spaniel" was dropped when it was agreed that the breed hunts more like a setter than a spaniel.

Broad jump: In obedience, an obstacle consisting of four separate hurdles spaced to cover a distance equal to but not less that two-and-a-half times the height of the dog at the withers, with a maximum of not more than six feet.

Broad skull: A skull wide between the ears in relation to the length, as in the golden retriever.

Broke: In hunting breeds, a colloquial term used to refer to a dog that is steady to wing and honors on sight.

Broke dog: In hound events, a dog that will not chase unwanted game.

Broken coat: A thin, wiry, crisp coat.

Broken color: A solid color broken by white and another color.

Broken-down ears: Misshapen ears.

Broken-down pastern: Down in the pastern.

Broken-haired: A rough wire coat.

Broken-up face: A receding nose combined with a deep stop and undershot jaw, such as that found in Pekingese or bulldog.

Bronchial tubes: Passages from the trachea to the lungs.

Bronchioles: The small airways in the lung that branch off the larger bronchus; bronchioles are 1 mm or less in diameter.

Bronchitis: An irritation of the bronchi, which are the narrow airways in the lungs. Can be caused by allergens. Dogs with bronchitis tend to wheeze and have problems breathing.

Bronchoconstriction: Narrowing of the bronchi (air passages) resulting in decreased airflow.

Bronchodilation: Widening of the bronchi, resulting in increased air flow.

Bronchoscope: A tube with a light that is used to examine the air passages.

Bronchoscopy: A method of examining the trachea and bronchi (or even removing a bit of tissue or foreign body).

Bronchospasm: Condition in which the muscles surrounding the air passages to the lungs contract, narrowing the passages.

Bronze: Copper-colored.

Bronzing: Tan color mixed with black hairs.

Brood bitch class: In dog shows, competition based on the quality of at least two of a dam's offspring.

Brood bitch: A female used for breeding.

Brown rice: Unpolished rice before the outer coat has been removed.

Bruce: Dog belonging to Woodrow Wilson.

Brucella titer: A blood test for brucellosis.

Brucellosis (Brucella canis): Bacterial, contagious venereal disease that can cause sterility and abortions in dogs. *Brucella* bacteria can infect several other species, including cattle and human beings.

Brush coat: A natural, short coat standing straight off the body but lying flatter on the limbs.

Brush or brush tail: A heavy, bushy tail.

Brushing: In gaiting, a fault that occurs if the parallel pasterns are set so close that they touch during passing.

Brushwood dog: Shiba inu.

Brussels griffon: Toy dog descended from various Belgian breeds. Weighs less than 12 pounds (usually between 8 and 10). Has a rough, wiry red, beige, or black-and-tan coat.

Brute: A beast or animal. A term sometimes used in law.

BS: Blood sample (veterinary notation).

BSP: Sulfobromophthalein.

BT: Blood test (veterinary notation).

Buck: A device used to "force break" hunting dogs when teaching them to retrieve.

Buddy: Labrador retriever owned by Bill Clinton.

Buff: A color ranging from Irish setter red to a light cream.

Bulging eyes: Protruding eyes.

Bullbaiting: An ancient spectacle in which dogs tormented bulls.

Bulldog: Medium-size (40 to 55 pounds), short-faced dog originally used for bull baiting but now highly docile.

Bullet: German shepherd owned by Roy Rogers.

Bullmastiff: A breed developed by crossing the bulldog and mastiff. It was originally used to guard hunting areas from poachers. Size: 24 to 27 inches, 100 to 130 pounds, with a short red, fawn, or brindle coat.

Bull-neck: Thick, muscular neck, usually short.

Bullous pemphigoid: Rare autoimmune disorder, in which the abnormal response is to a protein in the skin. This results in blisters and ulcers in the skin or mouth. The disease can be serious. Collies are the breed primarily affected.

Bull terrier: Size: 40 to 55 pounds. Descended from the bulldog, other terriers, and dalmatians. Famous for its egg-shaped head. This breed holds records for the most rats killed in minutes, hours, and other time parameters. Also affectionately known as the "white cavalier."

Bump: In pointing breeds, the intentional flushing of a bird by a dog. A serious fault in pointing breeds, since it may occur when the bird is out of shooting range.

Bumper: Canvas training object, two or three inches in diameter, used in place of bird in retrieving breeds. Dummy.

BUN: Blood urea nitrogen.

Burdock root (*Arctium lappa*): Used as a diuretic and also for its cleansing properties.

Burning scent: In foxhunting or similar sports, a scent so strong that the hounds can follow it without hesitation.

Burns: Can be caused by heat, chemical, electric shock, or radiation.

Burr: The inside of the ear.

Bursa: Small, fluid-filled sac lying outside the joint. Produces a lubricating liquid.

Bushdog (*Spetheos venaticus*): Rare wild canid from South America.

Buspar: Brand name for buspirone.

Buspirone: Antianxiety drug, especially helpful in the treatment of phobias.

Bust: A colloquial term for failure to qualify, specifically in a hunting test.

Butorphanol (butorphanol tartrate): Narcotic pain reliever and cough suppressant.

Butterfly lesion: Symmetrical dermatitis over the bridge of the nose.

Butterfly nose: Spotted nose, or nose only partly pigmented.

Button ears: Semi-prick ears where the top part folds forward, as seen in the fox terrier or pug.

Butylated hydroxyanisole: BHA. A chemical preservative.

Butylated hydroxytoluene: BHT. A chemical preservative.

BW: (1) Best of Winners. **(2)** Body weight (veterinary notation).

Bye-Dog: In a pointing breed field trial, a dog not in contention that is chosen to be the bracemate of the last dog picked when an odd number of dogs is entered.

By-products: Animal parts used by the pet food industry not intended for human consumption. They can include organ meats, blood, bone, brain, and tongue.

Byronia: A homeopathic remedy for gastritis, liver disease.

Byronia alba: A homeopathic remedy for pneumonia.

C

C: (1) Cervical (neck) vertebra, usually followed by a number (1 to 17) to mark which one (veterinary notation). **(2)** Cough (veterinary notation). C+ (moderate cough). Cough ++ (severe cough). C- (no cough).

C7d: Recheck in seven days (veterinary notation).

Ca: Calcium.

Cabal: King Arthur's dog.

Cabriole front: See fiddle front.

Cachexia: A condition of emaciation.

Cactus grandiflorus: A homeopathic remedy for heart problems.

Cadaver dog: A dog trained to find human remains.

Ca Eivissenc: Ibizan hound.

Caesarian section: Delivery by incision through the abdominal wall and uterus.

CAFC: Canadian Amateur Field Champion (prefix).

Cage leg: A condition of dogs confined to small crates or pet carriers for long periods. Affected dogs will circle almost continuously and seem unable to walk in a straight line. Many never recover. Head tilting may also appear.

Cairn terrier: Size: 13 to 16 pounds. Shaggy-coated, courageous terrier used to dig out vermin from rocky piles, or cairns. Developed in the Scottish highlands. May be any color except white.

Cal: Calories.

Calcified: The hardening of tissue through the influx of calcium, usually as a result of chronic inflammation.

Calcinosis: Hard lumps of calcium salt deposits in the skin (calcinosis cutis) or other tissues. Frequently accompanies Cushing's disease.

Calcitonin: Polypeptide hormone secreted by the parafollicular cells of the thyroid gland in mammals. Helps regulate calcium.

Calcitrol: A medication representing the activated form of vitamin D.

Calcium: Mineral required for bones and teeth, nerve function, blood clotting, and muscle contraction. Found in milk and bone meal.

Calculolytic food: A food that produces undersaturation of urine with calculogenic minerals to help dissolve uroliths.

Calculus: (1) Stone in the kidney, urinary bladder, or gall bladder, usually composed of mineral salts. **(2)** Mineral salts deposited on tooth surfaces.

California Rescue Dog Association (CARDA): A group of volunteers with specially trained dogs dedicated to assisting in the search for missing persons.

Callback: (1) In retrieving trials, a list provided by dog game judges prior to the next series in an event. This list denotes those who are invited back to continue participating in the event. Those who do not make the "call back" have been disqualified for some reason. **(2)** The return of a dog for judging in a hunting test in a category that was missed in the regular running.

Call-back pen: In pointing breed trials, a wire pen that holds the quail.

Callus: Thickening of the horny layer of the skin in one area due to pressure or friction.

Caloric density: Energy per unit weight of food, usually expressed as kcal per pound.

Calorie: (1) The amount of heat energy needed to raise the temperature of one gram of water from 14.5 to 15.5 degrees Celsius. **(2)** Kilocalorie, when used in nutrition.

Camel back: An arched back.

Campaign: (1) In conformation or field trials, to compete in many dog shows with a Champion of Record (a "Special") in order to obtain national rankings. **(2)** In obedience, to compete in many obedience trials at the Open or Utility level to get in the "Top Ten" list.

Campylobacteriosis: Disease characterized by acute diarrhea in puppies.

CAN. CH.: Canadian Champion.

Canaan dog: Ancient dog of the Middle East, now widely used as a guard dog in Israel. Size: 19 to 24 inches, 35 to 55 pounds, with a medium-length harsh outer coat. Color is either white with mask and possibly body markings, or solid black or brown with or without white trim.

Canadian Kennel Club (CKC): Maintains a system of registering purebred dogs that satisfies the requirements of the Animal Pedigree Act, Agriculture Canada, and the Club members. It maintains a system whereby clubs and associations may hold dog shows, obedience trials, field trials, and other trials, tests, and activities for purebred dogs.

Cancer: Any malignant, cellular tumor of potentially unlimited growth. One out of four dogs gets cancer during its life; 50 percent of dogs over age ten die from cancer or have it when they die. Cancer is largely hereditary. Signs include lumps (especially lumps that continue to grow), sores that don't heal, mouth odor, abnormal discharge from any orifice, loss of appetite, persistent lameness, increased water consumption, wheezing, and coughing.

Cancerinum: A homeopathic remedy for cancer.

Candida: Any member of yeast-like genus of fungi that inhabits the vagina or digestive tract. An infection with *Candida* is called candidiasis.

Candidate gene: A gene that results in a similar disease in another organism or that is thought to be biologically relevant to the canine disease through comparison to other organisms.

Candle flame ears: Wide, large, erect, pointed ears, used in reference to the English toy terrier.

Cane corso: Italian herding and guarding breed. Essentially a working breed. Colors include black, gray, blue, and fawn with a mask. Small white patch on chest, foot tips, or bridge of nose accepted. Size: 22 to 28 inches, 80 to 140 pounds.

Caniche: Poodle.

Canid: Any carnivorous animal of the Canidae family.

Canidae: Family of dogs that includes jackals, coyotes, foxes, wolves, and dogs.

Canidae Pet Foods: Telephone: (800) 398-1600. Web site: www.canidae.com.

Canine: Pertaining to dogs.

Canine adenovirus type 1: Cause of infectious hepatitis. See also adenovirus.

Canine adenovirus type 2: A factor in kennel cough. See adenovirus.

Canine babesiosis: See Babesiosis.

Canine cognitive dysfunction or canine cognitive syndrome: A series of geriatric behavioral signs and problems, not explained by other medical conditions. Signs include: general confusion, inappropriate vocalization, getting day and night mixed up, loss of housetraining, and personality changes. This condition is often treated with Anipryl.

Canine Companions for Independence: A nonprofit organization that provides highly skilled assistance dogs for people with disabilities other than blindness. Web site: www.caninecompanions.org.

Canine coronavirus: See coronavirus.

Canine ehrlichiosis: See ehrlichiosis.

Canine Eye Registry Foundation: A group of board-certified veterinary ophthalmologists who maintain a closed registry of purebred dogs that the ACVO Diplomats (members) examine and have found to be unaffected by major heritable eye disease. Telephone: (317) 494-8179; Located at Purdue University. Web site: www.vet.purdue.edu/~yshen/cerf.html.

Canine Freestyle Federation: 4207 Minot Drive, Fairfax, VA 22032. Web site: www.canine-freestyle.org.

Canine Good Citizen (CGC) program: Established in 1989, CGC is a certification program that is designed to reward dogs that have good manners at home and in the community. To receive the certificate, dogs must pass a ten-part "good manners" test, including accepting a friendly stranger, sitting politely for petting, good appearance and grooming, walking on a loose lead, walking through a crowd, sitting and downing on command, coming when called, reacting politely to another dog, responding appropriately to distractions, and behaving well during a supervised separation from its owner.

Canine Health Foundation: An independent national public foundation established in 1995 by the AKC. It raises money for research grants at veterinary schools, universities, and research institutions for the purpose of advancing canine health.

Canine hepatozoonosis: A protozoan disease transmitted by the brown dog tick.

Canine hip dysplasia: See hip dysplasia.

Canine histiocytic ulcerative colitis: A condition characterized by bloody mucoid diarrhea, resulting in weight loss and continued diarrhea, most common in young boxers.

Canine icthyosis: Congenital disease characterized by rough, scaly, fishlike skin.

Canine juvenile polyarteritis syndrome: a painful condition seen in young laboratory beagles, caused by systemic vasculitis.

Canine leukocyte adhesion deficiency: An inherited abnormality of the immune system due to a missing enzyme, in which the white blood cells are unable to fight infection. Puppies are small and slow to develop and tend to get infections from an early age. A problem in Irish setters and, to a lesser degree, in red-and-white setters.

Canine parvovirus (CPV): See parvovirus.

Canine sprue: Chronic diarrhea, usually accompanied by weight loss.

Canine tooth: The eyetooth, fang, or cuspid, situated between the incisors and premolars.

Canis latrans: Coyote.

Canis lupus familiaris: The domestic dog. Literally, "the familiar wolf."

Canker: Ulceration, usually of the lip, ear, or mouth.

Canned food: Food that has been processed, sterilized, sealed, and packaged in cans.

Canopar (thenium closylate): Dewormer (hookworms).

Canter: A three-beat gait, slower than the gallop.

Cantharis: Homeopathic remedy for bladder stones and kidney problems.

Canthus: The angular junction of the eyelids at either corner of the eyes.

Cão de agua: Portuguese water dog.

Cap: Darkly shaded color patch on the skull of certain breeds, usually covering the top of the head and ears and coming to a point in the center of the forehead.

Cape: Abundant hair enveloping the shoulders.

Capillaries: Tiny blood vessels that carry bright red blood slowly through the tissues. The capillaries also diffuse gases, nutrients, and metabolic waste products.

Captan: Antifungal prescribed for ringworm.

Carbaryl: Insecticide, much stronger than pyrethrin and with more residual activity.

Carbohydrate: A compound of carbon, hydrogen, and oxygen. Carbohydrates are immediate energy sources. They are present in most foods but are primarily in the sugars and starches of plants.

Carbonic-anhydrase inhibitors: Anti-glaucoma medication.

Carcinogen: A substance that can cause cancer.

Carcinoma: A cancer that arises in the epithelium, the tissue that lines the skin and internal organs of the body.

CARDA: California Rescue Dog Association.

Carder: Wire-bristled brush with bent teeth. Used primarily to remove dead hair from the undercoat on shorter-haired dogs.

Cardiac: Relating to the heart.

Cardiac auscultation: Listening to a dog's heart with a stethoscope.

Cardigan Welsh corgi: Ancient Welsh dog used for driving cattle. Low-set, 10 to 12 inches tall, with a dense medium-length coat in all shades of red, sable, and brindle.

Cardio-: Pertaining to the heart.

Cardioangiography: Radiological examination of the heart and blood vessels.

Cardiology: The study of the diseases and functions of the heart.

Cardiomyopathy: Disease of the heart, resulting from the dysfunction of the heart muscle (myocardium) without malformation of the heart or its valves. There is a predisposition to dilated cardiomyopathy in giant breeds, as well as in Doberman pinschers and boxers. Cardiomyopathy can also develop as a result of some toxins or infections. See also dilated cardiomyopathy and hypertrophic cardiomyopathy.

Cardioplasty: Plastic surgery of the esophagus and stomach. It is sometimes used to manage megaesophagus in dogs.

Cardiopulmonary: Relating to the heart and lungs.

Cardiovascular system: Body system that includes the heart and blood vessels; the cardiovascular system pumps and carries blood, which contains oxygen and nutrients, to the rest of the body.

Cardiovascular: Pertaining to the heart and circulation.

CARE: Companion Animal Rescue Effort.

Carlin: Pug.

Carnassial teeth: The shearing tooth, upper fourth premolar, and lower first molar in dogs.

Carnitine: Amino acid prescribed for cardiomyopathy.

Carnivore: An animal whose natural diet includes meat.

Carnivorous: Subsisting primarily upon meat or other animal material.

Carp back: A roach back similar to a camel back, but with a lower arch.

Carpals: A group of seven bones arranged in two rows between the foreleg bones (ulna and radius) and the metacarpal bones in the foot. Corresponds to the wrist in humans.

Carprofen: NSAID (non-steroidal anti-inflammatory drug), prescribed for relief of pain and inflammation, especially arthritis. Also used for post-surgical pain. Rimadyl is the best known.

Carpus: The joint between the paw and forelimb (the wrist in people).

Carriage dog: Dalmatian.

Carrier: Animal that harbors an infectious organism, such as a virus, bacteria, or parasite.

Carrot-shaped tail: A tail characteristic of the Scottish terrier.

Cartilage: The spongy white gristly substance that covers the ends of the bone, certain junctures in the rib, the nasal septum, and other places in the body. Made of water, sugars, and certain proteins, including proteoglycans and collagen. Much of the cartilage found in young dogs changes to bone as the animals mature.

Cartilaginous exotosis: Outgrowths of cartilage from bones throughout the body.

Cartilaginous: Consisting of cartilage.

Carting/drafting: A canine sport in which dogs pull a two- or four-wheeled cart through a course with turns, changes in speed, and halts.

CASA: Community Animal Shelter Association.

Cast: **(1)** The direction and range shown by a dog while searching for game. **(2)** In retriever field trials, a whistle and arm signal given by a handler that tells the dog which direction to take to find a bird or bumper. **(3)** In pointing trials, when a dog runs toward a birdy objective. **(4)** In tracking, to stray or wander off a track by more than three to five feet on either side of the actual track.

Cast refusal: When a dog declines to move in the direction ordered.

Castration: Neutering of a male dog by surgical removal of the testes from the scrotum.

Castro Laboreiro sheepdog: Strong, wolf-like dog native to the mountains of Portugal.

Casts: Solid lumps in the urine created when a proteinaceous material is concentrated in the nephrons.

CAT: Computerized axial tomography, as in CAT scan. An imaging technique using X-rays.

Cat foot: Small, round foot with well-arched toes.

CAT scan: A sectional view of the body constructed by computed axial tomography.

Catabolism: The breaking down of muscle tissue to supply the body with glucose. The opposite of anabolism.

Catalan sheepdog: Hardy working dog. Colors include black, gray, russet, and tan with or without white. Size: 15 to 20 inches, 35 to 46 pounds.

Catalog: In AKC events, a printed catalog containing the names of all dogs and their owners entered in an event. A catalog is mandatory for A-level events, optional for B-level events.

Catalonian sheepdog: Breed originating in the Pyrenees, now used not only as a stock dog but also for police and military work.

Cataracts: Opacities of the lens of the eye, usually characteristic of older dogs. So-called "juvenile cataracts" are hereditary. Eye may be gray, blue, or whitish. Any opaque spot on the lens, no matter how small, is technically a cataract.

Catch dog: A dog that is used to physically catch game, usually referring to wild pig.

Cathartic: A laxative given to quickly purge the dog's bowels.

Catheter: A flexible tube inserted into a body opening or cavity and used to remove or insert fluids.

Catheterization: The process in which a urinary catheter is inserted up the urethra into the bladder to relieve obstructions.

Cation: An ion carrying a positive ion such as sodium (Na+) or potassium (K+).

Catnip/catnip tea: In herbal medicine, used in cases of fever, colic, insomnia, and stress.

Caud: Caudal (veterinary notation).

Cauda equina syndrome: A group of neurological signs resulting from compression of nerves in the lumbosacral region of the spine.

Caudal: (1) Toward the tail. (2) Relating to the tail.

Caudal/inguinal glands: Milk glands nearest the rear of the bitch.

Caudal vertebrae: The approximately twenty vertebrae found in the tail.

CAV: Canine adenovirus.

Cavalier King Charles spaniel: A small dog related to Oriental toy breeds. Size: 12 to 13 inches, 13 to 18 pounds. Originally used for flushing small game; now a companion dog. Origin: England, 1600s. Named after both King Charleses, especially the latter, who was accused of being more interested in his dogs than his country.

Cave canem: Latin for "Beware of the dog."

CBC: Complete blood count (veterinary notation).

CBR: Chesapeake Bay retriever.

CC: (1) Coursing Champion, title awarded by NAOFA. (2) Chief complaint (veterinary notation). (3) Coccygeal vertebra, usually followed by a number to indicate which one (veterinary notation). (4) Cubic centimeter.

CCD: Canine cognitive dysfunction.

CCR: Curly-coated retriever.

CCV: Canine coronavirus.

CD: (1) Companion Dog. Title follows the dog's name. **(2)** Canine distemper.

CDC: Centers for Disease Control and Prevention.

CDRM: Chronic degenerative radiculomyelopathy.

CDV: Canine distemper virus.

CDX: Companion Dog Excellent. The title follows the dog's name.

ce: Clinical examination (veterinary notation).

CEA: Collie eye anomaly.

Cecum: The first portion of the large intestine, a blind sac.

Cell-mediated immunity: The immunity that is the result of either special lymphocytes directly killing the foreign invader, or lymphocytes (T cells) releasing special chemicals that activate macrophages to kill the invader.

Cellulitis: Painful, inflamed skin. Caused by a wound infection or foreign object.

Cellulose: An unbranched, long-chain polysaccharide that is a component of dietary fiber.

Center for Veterinary Acupuncture: 1405 West Silver Spring Drive, Glendale, WI 53209. Telephone: (414) 352-0201.

Center for Veterinary Medicine (CVM): Division of the Food and Drug Administration charged with ensuring the safety of animal feeds.

Centesimal potency: In homeopathy, the scale of dilution of a remedy, each dilution being one in a hundred.

Central nervous system (CNS): The brain and spinal cord.

Central progressive retinal atrophy (CPRA): Degeneration of retinal cells, beginning with those serving the central areas of vision. Most commonly seen in older Labradors, border collies, golden retrievers, Irish setters, and English springer spaniels.

Central proteins: Visceral proteins, including constitutive proteins like albumin and transferrin, and acute-phase proteins like globulins and ferritin.

Cephalexin: Broad-spectrum antibiotic useful in most common and uncomplicated infections. It is especially useful against staphylococcal infections (most skin infections) and is commonly used for long courses (6- to 8-week courses) against deep skin infections (pyodermas). Brand name: Keflex.

Cerberus: Three-headed mythical dog of the underworld.

Cereal: Grains such as barley, rice, rye, sorghum, corn, and wheat.

Cerebellar abiotrophy: Degeneration of brain neurons in the cerebellum, caused by a recessive gene. Ataxia and signs of cerebellar dysfunction appear at an early age.

Cerebellar hypoplasia: Underdevelopment of the back part of the brain.

Cerebellum: The part of the brain responsible for coordination of posture, balance, movement, and regulation of muscle tone. Located at the back of the brain.

Cerebral: Relating to the cerebrum.

Cerebral neoplasia: Brain tumor.

Cerebrospinal fluid (CSF): Fluid surrounding the brain and spinal cord.

Cerebrum: Major portion of the brain.

CERF: Canine Eye Registry Foundation.

Ceroid lipofuscinosis: Metabolic disorder in which ceroid lipofuscin (a waste product) accumulates in the cells, eventually destroying brain cells and leading to blindness and abnormal behavior.

Cerumen: Waxy material secreted by the epithelial cells of the ear canal in response to irritation.

Cervical: Pertaining to the neck.

Cervical spinal instability: Excess movement between the neck vertebrae.

Cervical vertebrae: The seven vertebrae of the neck region.

Cervical vertebral instability (wobblers): Compression of the cervical spinal cord caused by instability or malformation of the cervical vertebrae. Dogs show lack of muscle coordination in the back legs and possibly the neck.

Cervix: Oval-shaped fibrous structure that serves as the opening between the vagina and the uterus.

Cesky: Terrier cross between a Scottish and Sealyham terrier (and possibly the Dandie Dinmont). Colors include gray and light brown. Size: 11 to 14 inches, 15 to 18 pounds.

Cestode: Tapeworm.

CF: Cardiac failure.

CFC: Canadian Field Champion.

CG: Certificate of Gameness (American Working Terrier Association).

CGC: Canine Good Citizen, a certificate offered by the AKC. The title is available to all dogs, even those of mixed ancestry.

Ch: AKC Champion. The title is prefixed to the dog's name.

CH: Certified herbalist.

Chalking: Use of powder or chalk to alter the texture or color of the coat.

Challenge certificate: Awarded by the Kennel Club (England) and many British Commonwealth countries. Certifies that a dog has won a legitimate competition against other purebreds at a sponsored event. Three challenge certificates are required to attain the Champion title.

Chamomile tea: An herbal treatment for gastritis in puppies.

Champion: A conformation a dog that has accumulated fifteen points, including two majors won under two different judges and at least one point won under a third judge.

Champion tracker: Dog that holds all three tracking titles: TD, TDX, and VST. The Champion Tracker title is not a competitively earned title and does not figure into Dual or Triple Champion titles.

Changeover bark: In treeing events, a different type of bark, to indicate a change from trailing to treeing.

Channel, channeling: In retrieving trials, a dog that swims down the center of a narrow body of water lengthwise.

Channel blind: In retrieving trials, a water blind run in an area that, due to the close proximity of the bank on both sides, makes it very tempting for the dog to exit the water and get up on land.

Character: Showing all the most important features of a breed.

Charcoal: See activated charcoal.

Charley: Poodle owned by John Steinbeck, author of *Travels with Charley.*

Charlie: An English toy spaniel.

Chase: When an unsteadied bird dog runs after a flushed bird.

CHD/HD: Canine hip dysplasia/hip dysplasia.

Cheater: In scent hound field trials, a dog that has the trail but does not make claim to it properly, thus not giving the bracemate a chance to move in and move the trail forward.

Cheating: In retrieving trials, when a dog avoids cover or obstacles en route to or returning from an item to be retrieved.

Check: In scent hound field trials, when a hound loses the trail and must work to find it again.

Check chain: Choke chain.

Check cord: A nylon rope twenty to fifty feet long, used to train bird dogs.

Check dog: A broke dog that will come back to the hunter if other dogs are chasing off-game. Used when training pups.

Checkers: Richard Nixon's cocker spaniel (which actually belonged to his daughters).

Check in: When a dog that ranges out looking for a track returns when none is found.

Cheeks: The skin region below the eyes that begins at the lips and reaches back to the area in front of the ears.

Cheeky: Too much fill in the skull cavities, bulging sides of face.

Chelating agent: An agent used in the chemotherapy of metal poisoning.

Chelation: Binding of a substance to a metal, thus helping the body remove it.

Chemical score: See biological score.

Chemotherapeutic: (1) An agent used in conventional medicine to fight bacterial and protozoan infection.**(2)** Anti-cancer agent.

Chemotherapy: Drugs (either oral or injected) used in the treatment of cancer.

Cherry eye: Protrusion or enlargement of the tear gland beyond the third eyelid. Can result from an infection. Can generally be corrected with surgery. See prolapsed gland of the third eyelid.

Chesapeake Bay retriever: Native American breed developed in the nineteenth century or earlier. A wavy-coated breed used for duck hunting. It is famous for its ability to retrieve in cold water. A large, powerful dog. Size: 21 to 26 inches, 55 to 80 pounds. Colors are brown or sedge, which allows the dog to blend in with its surroundings.

Chestnut: A solid, warm brown color.

Chewing: A normal behavior of all puppies and many older dogs, especially hunting and retrieving breeds. Motivations for chewing include teething, exploratory chewing, anxiety, and boredom. To prevent inappropriate chewing, dogs should be supervised and given plenty of their own toys, as well as positive interaction and playtime with human beings.

Chewing-gum fits: The seizures associated with distemper that look as if the dog is chewing gum.

Cheyletiella: A contagious mange mite that causes scaling, intense itching, and hair loss. Also called walking dandruff.

CHF: (1) Congestive heart failure.**(2)** Chronic heart failure.

Chi: In acupuncture, the life energy that circulates along well-defined channels on the skin. Also spelled qi.

Chicken: In dog-food labeling, the clean combination of flesh and skin with or without accompanying bone, derived from the parts or whole carcasses of chickens exclusive of feathers, heads, feet, and entrails.

Chicken (or poultry) by-product: In dog-food labeling, the ground, rendered clean parts of slaughtered chicken (or poultry) such as the necks, feet, undeveloped eggs, and intestines exclusive of feathers (except in such amounts as occur in good rendering practices).

Chicken meal: In dog-food labeling, the dry, ground, rendered product from a combination of flesh and skin with or without accompanying bone, derived from the parts or whole carcasses of chickens, exclusive of feathers, heads, feet, and entrails.

Chien de berger Belge: Belgian sheepdog, Belgian Malinois, or Belgian Tervuren.

Chien de Montagne des Pyrenees: Great Pyrenees.

Chien des Pyrenees: Great Pyrenees.

Chien St. Hubert: Bloodhound.

Chihuahua: Named after a Mexican state, it is the smallest canine in history, weighing as little as one pound. It may be traced to South America, where some believe it is related to the Aztec sacred dog. Others trace it to the Toltecs or Incas.

China eye: Usually a clear blue eye. See also wall eye.

Chinchilla factor: Occurring when the guard hairs are banded with white, producing a silvery effect in double-coated dogs.

Chinese beagle syndrome: A form of familial neuronal abiotrophy (inherited malformation of nerve cells).

Chinese crested: Originally used to hunt vermin, they were widely distributed by 1500. Occurs in two varieties, hairless and powderpuff, that are identical except for their coats. The hairless have long hair on their crests, tails, and feet, while the powderpuffs have a full coat. Size: 11 to 13 inches.

Chinese fighting dog: Chinese shar-pei.

Chinese medicine: One of three traditional therapies: herbal medicine, acupuncture, or food cures.

Chinese shar-pei: Ancient Chinese breed. Size: 18 to 20 inches, 40 to 55 pounds, with a short, harsh coat in a variety of solid colors.

Chippendale front: Feet turned out, pasterns close, and forelegs out at the elbows.

Chips: Part collie and part German shepherd dog, a member of Patton's Third Army.

Chiseled: A clean-cut head between the eyes.

Chiseling: Pertaining to head structure, the outline and smoothness of the facial region

Chlorambucil: Immunosuppressant and anti-cancer drug. Chlorambucil is also used to treat some immune-mediated diseases, such as pemphigus, feline infectious peritonitis, and inflammatory bowel disease. Brand name: Leukeran.

Chloramphenicol: Broad-spectrum antibiotic. Due to its pH, chloramphenicol can easily pass deeply through purulent material to the organisms hiding within, through cell membranes to attack parasites living within, and into organs where other antibiotics cannot go.

Chlorhexidine: Antiseptic prescribed for bacterial and fungal skin infections. Nolvasan is the best-known brand.

Chlorpheniramine: Antihistamine prescribed for itching caused by allergies, snakebite, vaccination reactions, blood transfusions, bee stings, and insect bites. It tends to be more effective in cats than in dogs. Trade name: Clor-Trimeton.

Chylothorax: A buildup of chyle (milky fluid) in the lungs.

Chocolate: A medium brown color.

Choke chain or choke collar: A slip collar made of chain that tightens as the dog pulls on the leash.

Chokebore: A dog with excellent scenting abilities.

Cholangitis: Inflammation of the gall bladder or bile duct.

Choline: Necessary for proper liver function. Found in liver, soybean, and yeast. Related to the B vitamins. It is also part of the neurotransmitter acetylcholine.

Chondro-: Indicates cartilage.

Chondrodyplasia: (1) A disorder of cartilage. **(2)** A type of dwarfism associated with anemia.

Chondrogeneron: Combination of fibrogen (a simple protein commonly found in animal tissues) and a cartilage-regenerating substance called transforming growth factor beta. They can be used together to help treat arthritis.

Chondroitin: A substance that decreases the activity of enzymes that break down cartilage in a joint.

Chondroplasia: Formation of cartilage.

Chondroprotective agent: A nutritional supplement that protects cartilage.

Chop: The foreface of a bulldog.

Chop bark: A series of short, fast barks. Mainly a cur dog trait. Also called chop mouth.

Chops: (1) Jowls. **(2)** In dog training, especially retriever training, good practical skills.

Chorea: Nervous twitching. In dogs, usually applied to conditions arising from distemper infections.

Choroid: The membrane in the eye between the retina and the sclera, containing blood vessels supplying the eye.

Chortaj: A greyhound of the European steppes. It is large, with a thick coat, rose ears, and a long, thin tail.

Chow chow: Chinese breed famous for is black tongue and straight back legs. Stands 17 to 20 inches tall and has either a rough or smooth coat.

Chromatid: Two identical copies of a chromosome replicated during meiosis, each eventually becoming a new chromosome.

Chromosomes: Strands of DNA and protein found in the cell's nucleus that store genetic information.

Chronic: Long-term or recurring.

Chronic active hepatitis: A progressive inflammation of the liver caused by autoimmune or infectious factors such as infectious canine hepatitis, leptospirosis, copper toxicosis, or drug toxicity.

Chronic degenerative radiculomyopathy (CDRM): Inherited progressive deterioration of spinal transmission signals.

Chronic disease: A condition of long standing for which no cure is available.

Chronic non-specific gastritis: Chronic vomiting at varying intervals.

Chronic obstructive pulmonary disease (COPD): A condition in which the lungs are inflamed, resulting in shortness of breath.

Chronic superficial keratitis: A chronic condition of the eye, in which blood vessels grow across the cornea (the clear surface of the eye). The cornea looks hazy and sometimes reddened; it may eventually take on a dark pigment. Also called pannus.

Chrysanthemum dog: Shih tzu.

Chunk: In dog-food labeling, a semimoist food that has been extruded and cut into sausage-like pieces.

CHV: Canine herpes virus.

Chyle: Fluid within the lymphatic system that contains droplets of fat absorbed from the intestine.

Chylomicron: A droplet of lipoproteins responsible for the transport of cholesterol and triglycerides from the small intestine to the tissues.

Chyme: A semi-fluid material produced by the action of gastric juice or ingested food and discharged through the pylorus into the small intestine.

Cicatricial alopecia: A smooth, hairless scar.

Cilia: (1) Eyelashes. **(2)** Hairlike appendages of certain cells, especially in the respiratory tract, that aid in their movement.

Ciliary body: Muscular part of the eye connecting the choroids and the iris.

Ciliary dyskinesia: Abnormality of ciliary movement.

Cimetidine: Histamine antagonist prescribed for GI tract ulcers.

Cinnamon: Dark, rich brownish-red.

Circuit: Convenient string of consecutive shows in one area.

Circular eye: Round eye, as in the smooth fox terrier.

Cirrhosis: Scar tissue on the liver.

Cisapride: Gastrointestinal stimulant. Prescribed as an antiemetic.

Cisplatin: Anti-cancer drug used in chemotherapy.

Citric acid cycle: Series of reactions that convert glucose into carbon dioxide, water, and energy.

CK: Creatine kinase.

CKC: Canadian Kennel Club.

CKCS: Cavalier King Charles spaniel.

CL: (1) Canine leptospirosis. Comes in two forms: hepatitis and nephritis. **(2)** chloride.

CLAD: Canine leukocyte adhesion deficiency.

Clavamox: An antibiotic that is a combination of amoxicillin and clavulanic acid (sodium clavulanate). The clavulanate is able to protect the penicillin structure from destruction by staphylococci. This means that this combined medication can be used against anything for which amoxicillin can be used, plus for staphylococcal infections (usually skin infections). Also called Augmentin.

Clean head: A head free from wrinkles and bony or muscled lumps.

Cleanings: In dog-food manufacturing, the chaff, weed seeds, dust, and other foreign matter removed from cereal grains.

Cleft: A fissure or long opening, usually occurring during fetal development.

Cleft palate: A birth defect in which the palate fails to develop completely, allowing food and water to pass between the oral and nasal cavities. Usually occurs in breeds with short, broad muzzles.

Clemastine: Antihistamine (fumarate) prescribed for itching caused by allergies. Trade name: Tavist.

Clicker: A toy noisemaker used in dog training.

Clicker training: A term used for a training method developed by Karen Pryor. Pryor defines it as a subset of operant conditioning using positive reinforcement, extinction, negative punishment, and an event marker to modify behavior.

Clindamycin: Antibiotic and antiprotozoal drug of the lincosamide class, possessing similar properties to its sister compound lincomycin. Trade name: Antirobe.

Clinical signs: Overt symptomatic signs, visible to the naked eye.

Clipping: A gaiting fault in which the rear feet actually knick the pads of the front feet when in a full trot.

Clitoris: Female sex organ, in some ways analogous to the penis.

Cloddy: Low, thickset, heavy.

Clomipramine: Antianxiety and antidepressant drug.

Close behind: Movement with hocks close together.

Close hunter: A dog that stays close while looking for a scent trail.

Close-coupled: A short loin in comparison to other proportions.

Closed registry: A database containing a repository of health test results, allowing access of information only about normal results.

Closed tunnel: In agility, a rigid tube with a collapsed chute of nylon or canvas at the end. Also called a soft tunnel.

Closed-angle glaucoma: A primary glaucoma characterized by a shallow anterior chamber and a narrow angle that compromises filtration and causes an increase in intraocular pressure.

Closing time/closing date: The time at which entries for a field trial or dog show close; after this, no more entries are accepted.

Clostridium: Anaerobic bacteria present in the soil and in animal feces. Responsible for tetanus and botulism.

Clotrimazole: Antifungal drug.

Clotting factors: A group of thirteen components necessary for blood to clot.

Clumber spaniel: The name comes from the second Duke of Newcastle's Clumber Park, but the breed is probably French. A low, sturdy dog, 17 to 20 inches, 55 to 80 pounds, with a long, dense white coat with lemon or orange markings.

Cluster: A group of consecutive shows held at the same show site.

Cluster seizures: Multiple seizures within a short period of time with only brief periods of consciousness in between.

CM: (1) Courser of Merit, a title awarded by NAOFA. (2) Centimeter.

CMI: Cell-mediated immunity.

CNS: Central nervous system.

Co: Cough (veterinary notation).

CO_2: Carbon dioxide.

Coagulation: Formation of a clot.

Coagulation studies: Studies of the clotting ability of the blood.

Coagulopathy: Any disorder of blood coagulation, usually a defect in blood-clotting ability.

Coarse: Unrefined, inappropriately big-boned.

Coat: The hair covering a dog's skin.

Cobalamin malabsorption of giant schnauzers: A condition in which the animal is unable to absorb vitamin B_{12}. Symptoms include low weight gain, lethargy, and recurrent pulmonary infections.

Coban Kopegi: Anatolian shepherd.

Cobby: Compact, well ribbed-up.

Coccidia: A common parasite of the intestinal tract.

Coccidiosis: Infection with coccidial parasites, resulting in diarrhea. Usually occurs in young dogs.

Cocculus: A homeopathic remedy for travel sickness.

Coccygeal: Pertaining to the tail.

Cochlea: Spiral tube forming part of the inner ear.

Cocked ears: Semi-erect ears, similar to button ears but with only the tip folded.

Cocked-up tail: Tail raised at right angles, as in the cocker spaniel.

Cocker spaniel: (1) Long-haired, silky-coated dog originally developed to hunt birds. In other countries this breed is called the American cocker spaniel. Origin: Possibly Spain, but the breed was developed in England. **(2):** English cocker spaniel (in England). Size: 14 to 15 inches; comes in a variety of colors. The English cocker is a little taller than the American.

Co-dominance: In genetics, when neither gene is dominant and progeny express a trait somewhere between the two parental types. See partial dominance.

Coenzyme Q_{10}: A vitamin-like substance (resembles vitamin K) often used to treat pets with heart disease. Also called ubiquinone. This substance is essential for energy production at the cellular level.

Cofactor: A substance with which another factor must unite in order to function properly. A vitamin is often a cofactor that is needed to make a functional enzyme.

Cognitive dysfunction: A common medical condition in older dogs that results from abnormal brain function. It causes certain behavior changes, such as disorientation, housebreaking problems, and changes in sleeping patterns and interactions with others.

Cold: In retriever training, a term used to define the running of a dog on a concept with which it is familiar, but where the exact placement of the item is new to the dog.

Cold funk: Another name for alopecia X, a cosmetic hair-loss condition.

Cold nose: A dog that can smell an old, nearly scentless track.

Cold trail or line: A faint scent.

Cold trailing: Following an old line or trail.

Colibacillosis: Disease condition caused by the bacteria *E. coli*, which normally resides harmlessly in the gastrointestinal tract.

Colitis: Inflammation of the colon, usually due to parasite infection. Onset may be acute or chronic, disrupting normal bowel habits. Acute colitis occurs most commonly and often responds to one to three weeks of treatment. Chronic colitis can go on for several years or even a lifetime.

Collagen: A fibrous structural protein found in skin, bone, and other connective tissues.

Collapsed nostrils: Stenotic nares.

Collapsed trachea: Respiratory condition seen mostly in toy breeds, resulting in a narrowed air passage.

Collar: (1) A leather, chain, nylon, or cotton apparatus that fits around the dog's neck and is used for control and to hold identification tags. Several types are available, including buckle, slip collar, choker, and prong. **(2)** Marking around the neck. **(3)** In field trials, to hold the dog by the collar after a flush.

Collar-condition: To train a dog to accept an electric collar stimulation as a training aid.

Collie: An ancient, medium-sized herding dog from Scotland. There are two varieties: the rough (longhaired) and smooth (shorthaired). The

name may derive from "colley dog," a name given to the breed by the Scots farmers who used the dogs to herd mountain sheep called colleys. Has an abundant coat of sable and white, blue merle, tricolor, or white. Size: about 26 inches, 50 to 75 pounds.

Collie eye anomaly (CEA): Congenital abnormalities found in posterior part of the eye; they may include a detached retina and optic nerve abnormalities. A condition primarily affecting collies, Shetland sheepdogs, and associated breeds.

Collie nose: Lesions on the bridge of the nose, probably due to sunlight exposure.

Colloidal oatmeal: Used to relieve itching.

Colloidal solution: A stable suspension containing particles that resist settling out.

Colon: Part of the large intestine.

Colonic disease: Disease of the large bowel.

Colonopathy: Any disorder of the colon.

Color class: Divisions created by dog associations to classify certain types of coat colors or patterns, such as parti-color.

Color mutant alopecia: A clinical syndrome in dogs of blue or fawn color, caused by the dilution gene at the D locus. Clinical signs include bacterial folliculitis, scaling and red spots, and hair loss.

Color ribbon: A ribbon given to the best dog in a specific coat color class, such as best tricolor collie.

Colorings: In dog-food manufacturing, a substance added for consistent product appearance or to distinguish between flavors in a multiparticle food.

Colostrum: The dam's first milk; a thick, yellowish substance containing protective antibodies and immunoprotective compounds.

Coltsfoot: In herbal medicine, administered for skin disorders.

Coma: State of unconsciousness.

Come gee: In sledding, a command to U-turn to the right and return to the musher.

Come haw: In sledding, a command to U-turn to the left and return to the musher.

Come-bye/Go-bye: In herding, a command to move the dog clockwise around the livestock or to circle to the left.

Comedo: A plug of keratin blocking a hair follicle; a blackhead.

Comforter: An old nickname for the Maltese.

Commercial dog breeder: One who engages in the propagation and sale of dogs for profit.

Commies: Term used by bird dog people for "common pigeons."

Community Animal Shelter Association: An organization created to help animal shelters make better adoptions; it offers dog training and other help. Telephone: (845) -687-4406. Web site: www.CASA/friends.org.

Companion Animal Rescue Effort (CARE): Organization dedicated to placing homeless animals into safe, loving homes. Web site: www.thesphere.com/CARE.

Companion Dog (CD): AKC title awarded to a dog when three different judges certify that it received qualifying scores in Novice classes at three licensed or member obedience trials. To receive the title, it must compete with at least six dogs in competition, earn scores of 170 or better out of the possible 200, and in each instance must have received at least 50 percent of the allowable score for each individual exercise.

Companion Dog Excellent (CDX): AKC title awarded to a dog

that has been certified by three different judges to have received qualifying scores in Open classes at three licensed or member obedience trials. To win, it must compete with at least six dogs in competition, earn 170 or better out of the possible 200, and in each case must have received at least 50 percent of the value of each individual exercse.

Complete blood count (CBC): Blood test to evaluate red and white blood cells.

Complete fracture: A bone broken all the way through.

Compound fracture: Where a soft-tissue wound is associated with the fracture.

Compulsive disorder: A recurrent obsession severe enough to be time-consuming or cause marked distress or significant impairment; it is the equivalent of human obsessive-compulsive disorder.

Concaveation: When a spayed or virgin female dog acts maternal or produces milk in response to the nursing of a puppy.

Conception: The onset of pregnancy.

Concussion: An unconscious state that kills brain cells.

Conditioned dog: A hunting dog trained to respond to electric stimulation.

Cone-shaped head: A head triangular in outline, as in the dachshund.

Conformation: Physical build or structure of the dog.

Confusion: A possible sign of various conditions, including head trauma, epilepsy, pressure or swelling on the brain, diabetes, distemper, heatstroke, canine cognitive dysfunction, and exposure to toxins.

Congenital disorder: Condition present from birth, but not necessarily inherited.

Congestive heart failure: Chronic heart condition caused by

Congo dog: Basenji.

Congo terrier: Basenji.

Conjugation: Addition of glucuronic acid or other substances to a drug molecule or other foreign toxin to make it more water-soluble and easier to excrete in the urine.

Conjunctiva: Mucous membranes of the eye.

Conjunctivitis: Inflammation of the lining membrane (conjunctiva) that covers the inside of the eyelid; the condition causes watering, redness, and soreness. It is the most common disease of the eye.

Connection points: In acupuncture, points connecting meridians. Also called Luo points.

Conspecific: Belonging to the same species or group.

Constipation: Stool accumulation within the intestine. Can be caused by lack of fiber, insufficient exercise, inadequate water, obesity, or blockage. Holistic treatment includes alumina, baryta carb, and arsenicum alb.

Constituent: A single element that is part of a whole.

Contact dermatitis: Skin condition resulting from contact with an irritant.

Contagious: Transmissible from one animal to another.

Continental toy spaniel: Papillon.

Contraindicated: Not recommended.

Contrast X-ray: An X-ray image produced by using a substance opaque to X-rays, to improve visibility of certain structures.

Controlled break: A dog that tries to break but is called back by the handler. Subject to penalty in some hunting tests and field trial events

Contusion: Bruising, including bruising of the brain.

Convulsion: Seizure or involuntary muscle contraction.

Coomb's test: A blood test to determine autoimmune hemolytic anemia.

COPD: Chronic obstructive pulmonary disease.

Copper: Mineral that helps blood formation. Found in the liver and kidney.

Copper-associated hepatopathy: Overaccumulation of copper in the liver. Common condition in Bedlington terriers.

Copper toxicosis: Accumulation of copper in the liver, resulting in chronic hepatitis. See copper-associated hepatopathy.

Coprophagy or coprophagia: Eating feces. A fairly normal behavior in dogs.

CoQ$_{10}$: Coenzyme Q$_{10}$.

Coquetdale terrier: Old name for the border terrier.

Corded: A coat consisting of twined, ropelike mats. Cords should remain separate. Typical of breeds like the puli.

Core vaccine: Vaccine that should be given to all animals of certain species.

Corky: (1) Active, alert, lively. **(2)** Compact.

Corn: (1) Lump of keratin in the foot pad. **(2)** Maize; a kind of grain.

Corn bran: The outer coating of the corn kernel, without the starchy portion of the germ.

Cornea: Outer, domed, transparent layer of the eyeball.

Corneal dystrophy: Inherited degenerative condition in which the cornea becomes opaque. It appears as gray-white, crystalline, or metallic opacities in both eyes. See corneal opacities.

Corneal erosion: Loss of the outer layers of the cornea. If progressive, can result in a corneal ulcer.

Corneal opacities: Deposits of white or silver spots on the central area of the cornea. Also called corneal dystrophy.

Corneal ulcer: A break in the outer layer or epithelium of the cornea, resulting in a raw area. It is most often associated with trauma. If there are no complications, the ulcers usually heal in a few days with proper care.

Corn germ meal: In dog-food manufacturing, the by-product of the dry-milling process used in the manufacture of corn meal.

Corn gluten: By-product of the wet-milling process used in the manufacture of cornstarch.

Corn gluten meal: The dried residue from corn after the removal of most of the starch and germ and the separation of the bran.

Cornified: Converted to keratinized material.

Cornstarch: Helps prevent chafing when brushed into the skin folds.

Corn syrup: Concentrated juice from corn.

Coronavirus: First recognized in 1971; a cause of infectious enteritis.

Correction: A short, humane signal to a dog that it is doing something wrong.

Cortex: Outer layer of the bone, adrenal gland, or kidney.

Corticosteroids: Hormones produced by the adrenal gland, prescribed for itching, Addison's disease, rheumatoid arthritis, autoimmune diseases, inflammatory bowel disease, and other ailments. There are two types of hormones: glucocorticoids that regulate blood glucose levels and mineralocorticoids that regulate mineral (i.e., sodium and potassium) blood levels.

Cortisol: The principal glucocorticoid hormone produced by the adrenal gland, affecting the function of most organs. Primary functions are to increase blood sugar and to reduce inflammation.

Cortisone: A group of adrenal gland hormones with both glucocorticoid and mineralocorticoid activity.

Cosequin: Anti-arthritis treatment containing glucosamine hydrochloride, chondroitin sulfate, and manganese ascorbate.

Costochondral: Pertaining to the ribs and associated cartilage.

Coton de Tulear: Small white companion dog originating in Madagascar. Size: 8 to 13 pounds.

Coughing: A sign of disease, not a disease in itself. Can indicate an infection (such as kennel cough), bronchitis, or heartworm, among other things. Kennel cough typically produces a dry, hacking cough.

Coumestan: Estrogen-like substance produced by certain plants such as alfalfa; type of phytoestrogen.

Couple: In hound sports, two hounds. Hounds are always counted in couples, not singly. If one has thirteen dogs, then one has six and a half "couples."

Coupling: (1) Area between the shoulders and hips. (2) Loin.

Course: A designated pattern for tracking, herding, agility, and similar performance events.

Course objectives: In field events, variations in the terrain or vegetation that could hamper game.

Coursing: (1) Hunting, usually of hare. (2) Lure coursing.

Cover: Vegetation lying on a hunting field.

Covert: In foxhunting, the area in which there are dens or other places for a fox to hide. (Pronounced "cover.")

Cow-hocked: A condition in which the hocks point toward each other.

Cowlick: A whorl of hair going in a different direction from the rest of the coat.

Coxfemoral luxation: Dislocation of the hip joint.

Coydog: The hybrid offspring of a coyote and a feral dog.

Coyote (Canis latrans): Relative of the domestic dog Size: about 30 pounds.

CP: Canine parvovirus.

CPI: Canine parainfluenza.

CPK: Creatinine phosphokinase.

CPR: Cardiopulmonary resuscitation.

CPRA: Central progressive retinal atrophy. See progressive retinal atrophy.

CPV: Canine parvovirus.

Cr: Cranial (veterinary notation).

Crab: Fictional dog owned by Launce, a character in Shakespeare's *Two Gentlemen of Verona.*

Crabbing (sidewinding): Moving with the body at an angle to the line of travel. A gaiting fault.

Cramp: The involuntary contraction of a muscle.

Cranberry: In herbal medicine, administered for urinary tract health.

Cranial: (1) Toward the head. **(2)** Pertaining to the head.

Cranial nerve: One of the twelve nerves going directly from the brain to organs.

Craniomandibular osteopathy: Abnormal development of the jaw, due to a recessive gene. Occurs mostly in Scottish and West Highland white terriers.

Cranium: Upper part of a dog's skull, not including the mandible.

Crank tail: A crank-shaped tail carried down.

Crataegus tincture: Homeopathic remedy for heart problems, especially coughing caused by arrhythmia.

Crate: Portable indoor kennel or cage, used as a sleeping den or for housetraining purposes. Made of wire mesh, fiberglass, or sturdy plastic.

Cream: (1) Light yellow. **(2)** A semi-solid preparation of oil, water, and a medicinal agent used as a topical medication.

Creatinine: A chemical by-product of muscle exertion. It is excreted in urine by the kidneys; an increase in creatinine levels indicates kidney malfunction.

Creatinine kinase: Enzyme involved in production of energy from food. It is found in three forms: CK1 in the brain, CK2 in the heart, and CK3 in the skeletal muscle.

Creep: In retrieving trials, where a dog moves a short distance in the direction of a mark while the mark is being thrown and before the dog is sent for the retrieve.

Crepitation: The crackling, grating noise heard when arthritic limbs or broken limbs are manipulated.

Crepitus: Crepitation.

Crest: Arched area of neck.

CRF: Chronic renal failure.

CRH: Corticotropin-releasing hormone.

CRI: Chronic renal insufficiency.

Cricopharyngeal dysphagia: A disease condition characterized by regurgitation and nasal reflux after eating. Also called achalasia.

Crimped: Waved.

Croatian sheepdog: Black, long-coated dog with either erect or pendant ears. Tails may be curled, stumpy, or long.

Cropping: Surgical trimming of the ear for cosmetic reasons. Officially banned in many countries, but still permissible in the United States. Many AKC breeds include cropped ears as part of the breed standard.

Cross-bred: A dog with parents of different breeds.

Crossover: (1) In agility, a variation of the dog walk, consisting of a table with a ramp on each side. Also called dog cross or cross walk. **(2)** In conformation, where the legs converge beyond the midline when viewed from the rear during movement.

Crosswind: In a tracking event, a wind not blowing parallel to the track.

Croup: The lower spinal region, just above the hips.

Crown: Highest part of the head.

CRT: Capillary refill time.

Cruciate ligament: Cross-shaped ligament found on the front (anterior) and the back (posterior) of the stifle (knee) joint. The anterior cruciate ligament (ACL) frequently ruptures in strenuous exercise.

Crude: In dog-food manufacturing, the amount of nutrient present in the food. Crude nutrients do not always translate into usable nutrition.

Crude fiber: A method of expressing fiber, as determined by a procedure that represents the organic residue that remains after plant material has been treated with dilute acid and alkali solutions.

Crude protein: Method of expressing protein in a food by a procedure that measures nitrogen.

Crufts: Prestigious British dog show, inaugurated in 1886. It is held outside London every March.

Crust: Scab; an area of fluid or cells on the skin. The fluid may have been blood, serum, pus, or medication.

Cry: The baying of hounds.

Cryosurgery: Removal of tissue by freezing with liquid nitrogen or carbon dioxide.

Cryptorchid: A dog with one or two undescended testicles.

Crystalluria: The excretion of crystals in the urine.

CS: (1) Clinical signs (veterinary notation). **(2)** Corticosteroids.

CSF: Cerebrospinal fluid.

CT: Champion tracker. An AKC title that is prefixed to the dog's name.

CTP: Thrombocytopenia.

CT scan: Computed tomography (using X-rays to scan the body).

Cu: (1) Copper. **(2)** Cubic.

Cub hunting: Informal training period where young foxhounds are worked with experienced hounds in chasing yearling foxes from their mother's territory.

Cue: A voice, gesture, or other stimulus from the handler used as a signal or reminder.

Culottes: Longer hair on the backs of the thighs, such as in the schipperke.

Culture: A process by which specimens are collected and incubated in a laboratory medium and evaluated for bacterial, viral, or fungal growth.

Cur: (1) A mongrel or crossbred dog. A pejorative term. **(2)** A dog that hunts like a hound but is not a hound.

Curly-coated retriever: Powerful gun, guard, and retriever dog developed in the nineteenth century or earlier. Possibly descended from an ancient European breed known as the water dog. Size: 23 to 27 inches, usually either solid black or liver in color.

Cushing's syndrome or disease (hyperadrenocorticism): An endocrine hormonal disease normally occurring in middle-aged and older dogs. It is usually caused by a problem with the adrenal gland or by a pituitary tumor, which results in the overproduction of corticosteroids, especially the hormone cortisol. Too much cortisol causes excessive drinking, eating, and urinating, as well as loss of hair. May also occur in any dog that is being treated with excessive amounts of glucocorticoids. Cushing's syndrome is more common in certain breeds and in dogs that are six years of age or older.

Cushion: Fullness or thickness of upper lips.

Cut: In the show ring, the dogs that the judge wishes to consider further for placements are said to have made the cut; others are usually dismissed from further consideration.

Cutaneous asthenia: Ehlers-Danlos syndrome.

Cutaneous: Relating to the skin.

Cv: Cardiovascular (veterinary notation).

CVA: (1) Cerebrovascular accident, a blood clot on the brain. **(2)** Cardiovascular accident. **(3)** Certified veterinary acupuncturist.

CVH: Canine viral hepatitis.

CVT: Certified veterinary technician.

Cx: See Cc.

Cyanosis: A condition in which the blood is not carrying enough oxygen (reduced hemoglobin). A dog with cyanosis may have a bluish nose or skin.

Cyclic neutropenia: Cyclic interruption in bone marrow production of white blood cells.

Cyclophosphamide: Immunosuppressant and anti-cancer drug.

Cynophobia: Fear of dogs.

Cynotherapy: Healing therapy by use of dogs.

Cyproheptadine: Antihistamine prescribed for allergies and Cushing's disease.

Cyst: An abnormal smooth sac or lump, usually slow-growing, filled with fluid or solid center produced by the cells lining the cyst's wall.

Cysteine: An amino acid.

Cystic endometrial hyperplasia: Pyometra.

Cystinuria: A kidney defect that causes excessive cysteine secretion into the urine, leading to bladder stone formation.

Cystitis: Inflammation of the urinary bladder, usually caused by a bacterial infection.

Cystocentesis: Removing urinary bladder contents with a needle or aspirator.

Cystogram: A radiograph that directly evaluates the size and contour of the urinary bladder.

Cystoscopy: The examination of the bladder using an instrument inserted through the urethra.

Cystotomy: A surgical opening of the bladder.

Cytokines: Compounds produced by certain cells, which act as messengers to control the action of lymphocytes and other cells in an immune response.

Cytology: (1) Study of the function and structure of the cells. **(2)** Examining cells under a microscope.

Cytoplasm: Substances that make up the inside of a cell and surround the nucleus of the cell, which contains the genetic material.

Cytostatic: Capable of halting cell growth.

D

D: (1) Day (veterinary notation). **(2)** D: diarrhea (veterinary notation); d-: Diarrhea absent or lessened (veterinary notation); d+ (diarrhea increased); d++ (diarrhea marked), d+++ (diarrhea severe).

Dachshund: Originally developed in Europe to hunt badgers. Comes in two sizes (standard and miniature), three coat types (smooth, long, and wirehaired), and a variety of colors. Standards weigh between 16 and 32 pounds, miniatures less than 11 pounds.

Dacryocystitis: Inflammation of the lacrimal sac.

Dacryocystorhinography: X-ray of the skull after injection of contrast material into the nasolacrimal duct.

Daffy: A powdered pigment that enhances dogs' colors or markings, often used with terriers.

Daisy: Gray dog owned by the

Bumsteads of cartoon fame.

Dalmatian: This highly active dog has played many roles, including drafting, herding, and hunting. Size: 19 to 23 inches, about 55 pounds. Has a distinctive white coat with black spots.

Dam: Mother dog.

Damp hay itch (Pelodera dermatitis): The larva of a nematode (*P.strongyloides*) living in damp marsh hay infiltrates the skin on a dog's chest (usually a retriever's) and raises pustules.

Danazole: Synthetic male hormone prescribed for hemolytic anemia.

Dandelion: In herbal medicine, used to stimulate the liver and as a powerful diuretic. Helps in cases of poisoning.

Dandie Dinmont terrier: Developed in the seventeenth century or earlier. Size: 8 to 11 inches, 18 to 24 pounds. The coat is 2 inches long, composed of a mixture of soft and harsh hair.

Dandruff: Flaky, scaly skin caused by dry skin, poor diet, infrequent bathing or grooming, or thyroid disease. Regular grooming and adequate fats in the diet correct most cases. Dogs with thyroid disease may need a thyroid supplement.

Dapple: Mottled or variegated color pattern. No one color predominates. The dapple gene is also called the merle gene.

Daylight: The light showing underneath the body.

DC: (1) Dual champion. (2) Doctor of Chiropractic.

DCM: Dilated cardiomyopathy.

DD: Differential diagnosis.

Dead bird: In retrieving trials, a cue used to indicate to the dog that a blind should be retrieved.

Dead ear: A limp, immobile ear, characteristic of beagles and other hounds.

Dead heat: An exact tie in a greyhound race.

Deadgrass: Straw color to bracken color.

Deafness: Inability to hear in one or both ears. Can be tested with a BAER test.

Debride: To remove dead tissue and debris or contaminated tissue from a wound or sore.

Decimal potency: In homeopathy, scale of dilution of a remedy, each dilution being one in ten.

Deep-set eyes: Eyes placed deep in the head, as in the chow chow.

Deerhound: Scottish deerhound.

Deer tick: Tick (*Ixodes scapularis* or *Ixodes dammini*) primarily responsible for the transmission of Lyme disease in the northeastern and midwestern United States.

Defecate: To move the bowels.

Degenerative joint disease (DJD): A condition caused by the breakdown of a joint component, such as the cartilage. Also called arthritis or osteoarthritis.

Degenerative myelopathy: Any degenerative disease or condition of the spinal cord.

Dehiscence: Separation of the incision layer after surgery.

Dehydration: Loss of normal body fluid.

Delayed chase: In field events, running in the direction of flushed game after either pointing, honoring, or stopping to flush instead of obeying the handler's command to cast off in a different direction.

Delta Society: Therapy Dog Association. 580 Naches Avenue SW, Suite 101, P. O. Box 1080. Renton, WA 98057. Telephone: (425) 226-7357. Web site: www.deltasociety.org.

Demodectic mange: Skin disease caused by mange mites. Most commonly affects dogs under one year, although all dogs carry demodectic mange mites (*De-*

modex canis) in their hair follicles. Usually found on front legs and face. When older dogs get a clinical case, it usually indicates that something is awry with the immune system. This kind of mange is not transmissible to other pets or the owner. Treatment involves dipping the pet every week or so in Mitaban (amitraz). Often, several treatments are required. If the infection is only on a small part of the pet's body, treatment with benzoyl peroxide may be sufficient.

Demodicosis: A disease caused by the mange mite. See demodectic mange.

Demulcent: A soothing agent.

Dental caries: Tooth cavities.

Dentition: The order and arrangement of the dog's teeth.

Deoxyribonucleic acid (DNA): The genetic building block, a nucleic acid made up of nucleotides and transmitted from generation to generation.

Deprenyl: Selegine. Brand name Anipryl. Used to treat canine cognitive dysfunction.

Deracoxib: Member of the class of drugs known as NSAIDs (non-steroidal anti-inflammatory drugs). The chief use for such drugs in the dog has been pain relief, usually for joint or post-surgical relief. Trade name: Deramaxx.

Deramaxx: Brand name for deracoxib.

Derby: Competition for dogs who are over six months of age and are not yet two years of age. The tests are the easiest of any that are required in official stakes.

Derby class or stakes: A juvenile stake in the AKC Pointing Breed Field Trials or stakes held by the FDSB. Each organization has slightly different rules about the age.

Dermacentor: A genus of ticks.

Dermal: Pertaining to the skin.

Dermatitis: Inflammation of the skin; skin disease.

Dermatology: Study and treatment of diseases of the skin.

Dermatomyositis: Systemic connective tissue disease causing inflammation of skin, subcutaneous tissue, and muscles.

Dermatophyte: Fungi that cause ringworm; includes Trichophyton, Microsporum, and Epidermophtyon.

Dermatophytosis: Ringworm, a fungal infection of the hair follicles.

Dermis: Inner layer of skin positioned just above the subcutaneous tissue.

Dermoid: Indicates a skinlike condition.

Dermoid cyst: A benign skinlike growth, usually appearing on the back and covered with hair. Most common in boxers and Rhodesian ridgebacks. Also an area or fold of normal skin that forms in an abnormal area, usually on the eyelid of one or both eyes, often causing irritation.

Dermoid sinus: Abnormal tubular indentation from the skin into the back, even into the spinal canal.

DES: Diethylstilbestrol.

Descemet's membrane: Thin attachment of the cornea to the fluid in the eye below.

Desensitization: Gradually increasing dog's exposure and tolerance to an object of fear, such as a vacuum cleaner or hairdryer, by slowly increasing the time the stimulus is present.

Desiccation: Drying up.

Desmopressin: Antidiuretic hormone prescribed for diabetes and von Willebrand's disease.

Deutsche dogge: Great Dane.

Deutscher: German shorthaired pointer.

Deutscher drahthaariger: German wirehaired pointer.

Deutscher schaferhund: German shepherd dog.

Developmental orthopedic disease: Bone and joint disease caused by alteration in endochondral ossification during growth.

Dewclaws: Functionless remnant of the first digit on each paw. Some dogs have missing dewclaws on front, back, or both. Dewclaws can catch on fabric or underbrush and are frequently removed in puppies.

Dewlap: Loose, pendulous skin under the jaws and on the throat. Much looser in some breeds than in others.

Dewormer (anthelmintic): Medication given to expel intestinal parasites.

Dexamethasone: Member of the glucocorticoid class of hormones; used as an anti-inflammatory

Dexamethasone suppression test: Test measuring levels of cortisol in the blood. Used in the diagnosis of Cushing's disease.

Dextromethorphan: Cough suppressant.

Dextrose: An old name for glucose that is still used when referring to IV solutions.

DHG: Dog Handler's Guild.

DHLPP: Multivalent vaccine for distemper, hepatitis, leptospirosis, parainfluenza, and parvovirus.

Dhokhi apso: Tibetan terrier.

Dhole (Cuon alpoinus): Asian wild dog.

DI: Diabetes insipidus.

Diabetes: Any of a variety of chronic conditions characterized by the production of excessive urine.

Diabetes insipidus: Endocrine disease, a metabolic disorder in which deficient amounts of the pituitary antidiuretic hormone (ADH or vasopressin) is released, resulting in failure of kidney tubular reabsorption of water. It may be acquired, inherited, or idiopathic.

Diabetes mellitus: Endocrine disease of the pancreas in which insufficient insulin is produced, resulting in abnormally high blood sugar (glucose) levels. Signs include polydipsia and polyuria. May require insulin injections, or may be controlled with diet. May be acquired or possibly inherited. Breeds at increased risk include the keeshond, Alaskan malamute, chow chow, Doberman pinscher, English springer spaniel, Finnish spitz, golden retriever, Labrador retriever, miniature schnauzer, Old English sheepdog, poodle, schipperke, and West Highland white terrier. Also called sugar diabetes.

Diabetic ketoacidosis: Life-threatening acidity in the blood; the result of untreated diabetes.

Diamond eye: Also known as macropalpebral fissure (an abnormally large palpebral fissure). Can occur in brachycephalic breeds from the protrusion of the eyeball or in other breeds from overlong eyelid margins.

Diapedesis: Seepage of red blood cells and serum out of the capillaries.

Diaphragm: Thin sheet of muscle separating the chest cavity from the abdomen.

Diaphragmatic hernia: Rupture of the diaphragm, the muscle that separates the chest cavity from the abdomen.

Diaphysis: Central shaft of the long bones.

Diarrhea: Abnormally liquid feces.

Diathesis: (1) In homeopathy, a condition predisposing the body to a certain type of disease reaction. **(2)** A predisposition to a particular disease.

Diazepam: Anti-anxiety medication, occasionally used as a muscle relaxant and seizure control drug. The injectable form is often used in anesthetic protocols. Trade name: Valium.

DIC: Disseminated intravascular coagulation.

Dichlorophen: Dewormer for roundworm, hookworm, and tapeworm.

Dichlorvos: Dewormer for roundworm and hookworm.

Diestrus: The phase in the estrous cycle when progesterone levels are high and estrogen levels are low. Most conducive state to implantation.

Dietary indiscretion: Eating inappropriate material.

Dietary therapy: Using the diet or food intake as a method of treating or preventing a disease.

Dietary thermogenesis: The energy needed to digest, absorb, and assimilate nutrients. Also called specific dynamic action of food.

Diethylcarbamazine: Heartworm and roundworm preventative.

Diethylstilbestrol: Used to treat urinary incontinence by improving sphincter tone. Usually abbreviated DES.

Digest: In dog-food labeling, the liquefied or powdered fats and animal tissue sprayed on dry dog food to enhance palatability.

Digestibility coefficient: The proportion of the consumed nutrient that is actually available for absorption and use.

Digestible energy: The actual amount of energy that can be obtained from food that can be digested and absorbed.

Digestive enzymes: Natural chemicals produced by the body to break down food into nutrients.

Digestive system: Includes oral cavity, esophagus, stomach, small intestine, cecum, large intestine, rectum, anus, pancreas, liver, and gall bladder. The digestive system digests and absorbs food and also eliminates solid waste from the body.

Digging: A natural behavior, especially pronounced in some breeds (such as terriers, dachshunds, and huskies). Can also indicate boredom, desire to escape, or lack of exercise.

Digitalis: Homeopathic remedy for heart problems, especially valvular insufficiency.

Digitalis glycosides: Class of drugs including digitoxin and digoxin, which are drugs derived from the purple foxglove (*Digitalis purpurea*) plant, and used in the treatment of congestive heart failure.

Digoxin: Medication prescribed for congestive heart failure, dilated cardiomyopathy, and abnormal heart rhythms. It is derived from the purple foxglove (*Digitalis purpurea*).

Dilated cardiomyopathy: Most common type of cardiomyopathy, in which there is enlargement of the chambers of the ventricles and some increase (hypertrophy) in the heart muscle mass, accompanied by a loss of the normal contracting abilities of the ventricles.

Diltiazem: Calcium channel blocker prescribed for heart failure and abnormal heart rhythms.

Dilution: In homeopathic medicine, a way to potentize the remedy. Preparations are alternately succussed and diluted.

Dimenhydrinate: Antiemetic (Dramamine) prescribed for motion sickness.

Dimethylglycine: Metabolic enhancer used to improve performance.

Dimethyl sulfoxide (DMSO): Anti-inflammatory analgesic and a vehicle to enhance the penetration of other drugs through the skin; prescribed for heatstroke, pain and inflammation, swelling from acute trauma, arthritis, acute kidney failure, and inflammatory bowel disease, among other conditions.

Dingo (*Canis dingo*): Australian wild dog. It is believed that the dingo was brought by ancient people as a semi-domesticated feral dog. Often interbreeds with domestic dogs.

Dioctophyma renale: Parasitic worm that destroys the kidneys.

Diphenhydramine: Antihistamine, cough suppressant, antiemetic; prescribed for allergies, nausea, and coughing.

Diphenylhydantoin: Phenytoin.

Dipylidium caninum: Most common dog tapeworm, occurring in the small intestine. Segments look like grains of rice.

Direct diagnostic test: A diagnostic test that is based on examining for the presence of actual disease-producing genetic mutations.

Direct heartworm test: A test wherein the blood is smeared on a slide and examined for heartworm larvae or filaria. Not always accurate, since the filaria may not be active.

Directly to hand: In pointing breed events, the return of the bird by the dog straight to the handler, without the handler leaving the spot.

Disaccharide: Simple carbohydrate consisting of two linked monosaccharides such as table sugar (sucrose).

Disal: A brand name for furosemide, a diuretic prescribed for pulmonary edema, congestive heart failure, and similar conditions.

Disaster dog: A dog trained to locate humans trapped under rubble or collapsed buildings. These dogs can discriminate between living and dead persons.

Disc competition: A sport in which dogs race after and attempt to catch a plastic disc thrown by the owner.

Discoid lupus erythematosus: Autoimmune skin disease confined to the face resulting in reddened, ulcerated skin and in a butterfly shaped hair loss between the nostrils and eyes.

Discolored teeth: Yellow-stained dentition that may result from the administration of certain antibiotics during the pregnancy of the dam.

Dish-faced: A slightly concave foreface, such as in the pointer.

Dishing: Crossover.

Dislocation: Separation of the bones forming a joint. Also see luxation.

Disophenol: Dewormer for hookworms.

Disqualification: An insufficient score, below five in a hunting test.

Disseminated intravascular coagulation: Widespread formation of blood clots, primarily within the capillaries.

Distal: Farther away from a point of reference; usually toward the rear.

Distemper: Highly infectious viral disease of dogs, affecting a number of body systems, including the respiratory, gastrointestinal, and nervous systems. The causative agent is similar to the one that causes measles in people. Early signs include fever, loss of appetite and eye inflammation. Later signs include coughing, breathing problems, mucus discharges, vomiting, diarrhea, blindness, seizures ("chewing-gum fits"), and other neurological impairment. There is no specific cure, but the disease can be prevented by vaccination.

Distemper teeth: Teeth yellowed or pitted by distemper.

Distichiasis: A congenital condition in which an extra row of eyelashes grows from the eyelids and rubs against the cornea.

Diuresis: The process by which the body eliminates waste in the urine.

Diuretic: A substance used to increase urinary output. Often prescribed for congestive heart failure.

Divergent hocks: Hocks that turn outward when in a natural stance.

Diversion: In field trials, a distraction of some sort, including but not limited to a bird, a shot, or a person moving, talking, yelling, or walking. Done in dog games to test against switching, or dropping. Diversions in dog games are commonly a thrown bird as the dog returns from a retrieve. Sometimes these become part of a delayed mark.

Divided find: In pointing breed events, when two dogs point the same bird independently and it is not possible to discern which dog found it first.

DJ: Directed jumping.

DJD: Degenerative joint disease.

Dl or dL: Deciliter.

DLE: Discoid lupus erythematosus.

DM: Diabetes mellitus.

DMG: Dimethylglycine.

DMSO: Dimethyl sulfoxide.

DNA: Deoxyribonucleic acid.

DNA profile: A genetic "fingerprint" or composite of a set of highly polymorphic genetic markers that uniquely characterizes an individual.

DNP: Disophenol.

do: "Days old" followed by a number (veterinary notation).

DO: Drain out or remove surgical drain (veterinary notation).

DOA: Dead on arrival.

Doberman: Doberman pinscher.

Doberman pinscher: Developed in Germany and used as a fighting dog in World War I. Size: 24 to 26 inches, 60 to 75 pounds, with a short black, blue, red, or fawn coat.

Docking: The amputation of the tail or part of the tail. Sometimes done to prevent trauma in hunting dogs while working in thickets. Also done for cosmetic reasons.

DOCP: Desoxycorticosterone pivilate, an injectable mineralocorticoid used to replace aldosterone in Addison's disease patients.

Dog: (1) A domestic canine (*Canis lupus familiaris*). **(2)** A male canine.

Dog-cheap: A linguistic distortion of the Old English godchepe (a good bargain).

Dog Collar Museum: Private collection of antique and valuable collars. Located at Leeds Castle in Kent, England.

Dog days: The hot days of July and August, when the dogstar, Sirius, rises. The Romans gave this period (July 3 to August 11) its name, caniculares dies. According to their theory, Sirius added significantly to the heat of the sun.

Dog-ear: To turn a page corner down to mark a place in a book.

Dog-fall: In wrestling, when both wrestlers fall together.

Dog game: An organized off-season dog activity.

Dogged: Determined, like a dog.

Dog Genome Project: A collaborative study aimed at producing a map of all of the chromosomes in dogs.

Doggy: Female dog showing male characteristics, especially size and weight.

Dog in basket: In sledding, a tired or injured dog carried in the sled.

Dog Latin: Pretend or "mongrel" Latin. Not as well organized as pig Latin.

Dogo Argentino: A twentieth-century breed originally developed as a fighting dog.

Dog-rose: A wild rose so named because was supposed to cure the bite of a mad dog.

Dogs for the Deaf: 10175 Wheeler Road, Central Point, OR 97502. Telephone (voice/TDD): (541) 826-9220. Web site: www.dogsforthedeaf.org.

Dog show: Officially, an event sanctioned by the national kennel club (of whatever specified country).

Dog sleep: A fake sleep, so named because many dogs seem to sleep with one or both eyes open, although one would think this would be a false "awake."

Dog's-nose: Gin and beer.

Dog star: Sirius. The brightest star (nonplanet) in the night sky.

Dog tick (*Dermacentor variabilis*): Common disease-bearing tick afflicting dogs and other mammals.

Dogue de Bordeaux: Also known as the French mastiff and Bordeaux bulldog; it is an ancient French breed. Formerly used to hunt bears, boars, and wolves.

Dog walk: In agility, a catwalk 4 to 4.5 feet high, consisting of three narrow 12-foot planks going up, across, and then down. Also known as the balance beam.

Dog-watch: A linguistic corruption of dodgewatch. Two short evening watches on a ship, one from four o'clock to six o'clock, and the other from six o'clock to eight o'clock, introduced to dodge the routine.

Dog Writers Association of America: 173 Union Road, Coatesville, PA 19320. Telephone: (610) 384-2436.

Dolichocephalic: A long, narrow skull, such as that found in collies and borzois. Extreme cases are related to a loss of intelligence.

Domed: Evenly rounded, convex top skull.

Domestic animal: An animal that has been housed and fed by humans for generations and has little fear of people as a result.

Dominant: In genetics, when the presence of only one copy of a gene results in the inheritance of an observable trait or disease.

Dominant gene: The gene that overrides a recessive gene so its characteristics are evident in the offspring.

Domino: (1) A reverse facial mask. (2) Character in *101 Dalmatians* and *102 Dalmatians*.

DOR: Drop on recall.

Dors: Dorsal (veterinary notation).

Dorsal: Toward the back, spinal column, or ceiling.

Dorsal recumbence: Lying on its back.

Dot: Rutherford B. Hayes's cocker spaniel.

Double: In retrieving trials, two marks or two blinds. Items are not thrown at the same time. A double tests the dog's memory, as the animal must pick up one item, return to its handler, then go get the other item and bring it back.

Double coat: Coat with an outer, weather-resistant layer, and a soft inner layer.

Double handling: The handling of a dog by another person in addition to the designated handler.

Double lead: In sledding, two dogs who lead the team side by side.

Dowel: In retriever training, a wooden item not larger than one-half inch in diameter used to teach the dog the *hold* command. The dog should hold the dowel gently but firmly.

Down: obedience command instructing the dog to lie down.

Down-faced: A muzzle that inclines downward from the top of the skull to the tip of the nose, as in the bull terrier.

Down in pastern: Weak, excessively sloping pastern.

Downwind: In tracking, wind blowing at the dog's back.

Doxorubicin: Anti-cancer drug used in chemotherapy.

Doxycycline: A member of the tetracycline antibiotic family, providing broad antibacterial protection by inhibiting bacterial protein synthesis. Can penetrate biological barriers that other members of its class cannot. Often prescribed for *Borrelia bergdorferi* (an agent of Lyme disease), *Ehrlichia* (another tick-borne infection), Mycoplasma (urinary and upper respiratory infections),and prostate gland infections.

Dragback: In field trials,a scent left in the field by a dog returning to the line from a mark or blind.

Drahthaar: German wirehaired pointer.

Drawing: In foxhunting,the plan by which hounds search a covert for fox.

Dressing the dogs: In sledding, harnessing the team.

Drive: Strong, powerful thrust from the hindquarters during movement.

Driving: In herding, moving the stock away from the handler.

Droncit (Praziquantel): Dewormer (tapeworms).

Drool: Lots of dripping saliva. Normal in certain loose-skinned breeds, such as bassets, bloodhounds, boxers, mastiffs, Newfoundlands,and Saint Bernards. Can be a sign of distress,such as bloat, poison, or an object lodged in the mouth of dogs if it appears in a dog that doesn't usually drool.

Drop ear: An ear folded forward.

Drop on recall: In open obedience classes,an action in which a dog sits at one end of the ring and the handler goes to the other end and calls the dog, dropping him on a signal from the judge. He then calls the dog in as in the regular recall.

Dropped Dog: In sledding,a dog that has been dropped from its team at a checkpoint during the race.

Drotszoru Magyar vizsla: Vizsla.

Drs. Foster and Smith: Suppliers of dog-related items. 2253 Air Park Road, P. O. Box 100, Rhinelander, WI 54501-0100.

Telephone: (800) 826-7206.Web site: www.drsfostersmith.com.

Dry eye (keratoconjunctivitis sicca): A condition in which the eye is unable to manufacture enough tears. Often an autoimmune disease that may lead to ulceration. Veterinary treatment is available, but it is expensive and must continue throughout the life of the dog.

Dry head: See clean head.

Dry matter: Food residue after heating to a constant weight and removing all of the water.

Dry matter basis: Expression of nutrient content of food on a moisture-free basis.

Dry neck: A taut,unwrinkled neck. Opposite of wet neck.

Dry pop: In retrieving field trials,a shot that is fired without throwing the bird.

Dual champion: Any dog awarded the title Champion of Record (Ch.) and Field Champion or Herding Champion (HC).

Dudley nose: Liver- or flesh- colored nose. A disqualification in many breeds.

Duke: Common name for dogs, including Jed Clampett's dog in the Beverly Hillbillies, the dog in Swiss Family Robinson, and the dog in Booth Tarkington's Penrod, among others.

Dummy: See Bumper.

Dummy collar: A collar that is the exact duplicate of an electronic collar in size,shape,and weight but that cannot produce electrical stimulation.

Dumped: Colloquial term used for a dog that lost,especially when said dog was expected to win.

Duodenum: Portion of the small intestine directly attached to the stomach, extending from the pylorus to the jejunum.

Duragesic patch: Post-surgical pain patch containing fentanyl.

Duration of immunity: Length of time an animal is protected from a disease.

Dutch shepherd dog or Dutch sheepdog: Derived from the Belgian sheepdog, a breed that is not well known outside Holland.

Dx: Diagnosis (veterinary notation).

Dye studies: The injection of a dye into a part of the body before taking a radiograph to view abnormalities.

Dyschezia: Painful or difficult defecation.

Dysmetria: A neurological disorder characterized by an inability to regulate the rate, range, and force of movement.

Dysmyelination: (1) Reduced amount of myelin. **(2)** Abnormal layer of myelin around the central nervous system, causing rear limb weakness.

Dysphagia: Difficulty in eating and swallowing.

Dysplasia: An abnormal development of bone, organs, or tissue. Common in dogs.

Dysplastic: The state of having dysplasia.

Dyspnea: (1) Difficulty in breathing, shortness of breath. **(2)** Labored breathing.

Dystocia: Difficult birthing.

Dystrophic: Disorder caused by incorrect nutrition.

Dysuria: Difficulty urinating.

E

E & A: Euthanasia and aftercare (veterinary notation).

E collar: Electronic collar; a collar worn by the dog that enables the trainer to make an instant correction from a distance through the use of small amounts of electricity.

EAC, EAC-V, EAC-JH: Elite Standard, Veterans, Junior Handler (NADAC).

EAG: Express anal gland (veterinary notation).

Eagle Pet Products: Telephone (800) 255-5959. Web site: www.eaglepack.com.

Ear canal: The tube that connects the external ear with the eardrum.

Ear cancer: Rare in most dogs, but occurs occasionally in cocker spaniels.

Ear carriage: How the ears are held against the head, either permanently or as an indication of mood.

Ear clamps: Templates or patterns attached to an anesthetized dog's ears to outline where the surgical cropping cut is to be made.

Eardrum: The membrane that divides the outer ear from the inner ear, where the mechanism of hearing takes place. The membrane prevents infection from reaching the inner ear, as well as vibrating to amplify sounds.

Ear infections: Can be caused by bacterial or fungal agent; are most common in floppy-eared dogs such as basset hounds, spaniels, and setters. Ears are frequently the site of such infections because they are warm, moist, and oily (three prime conditions for the development of infection). Infected ears cause head-shaking and pawing and are usually malodorous. In fact, the smell can give you a clue as to the source of the infection. Bacterial infections smell strong and "sour," while yeast infections smell yeasty. Mild infections can be treated with a good cleaning of the ears with a 50-50 mixture of vinegar and water; this changes the acidity (pH) of the ear and makes an unwelcome environment for the infection. The cleaning should be followed by a good non-alcohol drying agent. (Alcohol is too painful for many dogs.) If that does not work, see a vet.

Ear mites: Several species of white, crablike parasites feeding on skin flakes inside a dog's ears, mostly in the ear canal, and producing intense itching. While the mites themselves are hard to see, they leave a crusty, reddish-brown discharge. Many can be killed with over-the-counter medication, although ear mites that migrate to the base of the tail in times of trouble can return later. Regular cleaning of the ears with vinegar and water helps discourage ear mites. Powdering the ears with any drying powder will also help kill mites by clogging their breathing holes.

Ear set: Describing where on the head the ears are attached.

East-west front: A condition in which the forefeet point out to the sides, away from each other.

EBT: English bull terrier.

Eccrine sweat glands: Exocrine sweat glands in the footpads. Primarily used for territorial marking, not thermoregulation.

ECFVG: Educational Commission for Foreign Veterinarian Graduates.

ECG: Electrocardiogram, a printout of an analysis of the electrical activity in the heart.

Echinacea: In herbal medicine, used as an immune stimulant and for disorders of the lymphatic system.

Echocardiography: An ultrasound examination of the heart using sound waves bounced off the interior and exterior of the heart.

Eclampsia: Also called lactation or puerperal tetany, a condition that occurs in bitches just before giving birth or within three weeks afterward. It occurs when, during lactation, the bitch's dietary calcium is inadequate and she cannot utilize her bone reserves of calcium quickly enough. When this happens, the body drains calcium directly from the bloodstream. Can be life-threatening; signs in-

clude muscle spasms, tremors, and seizures. It tends to be more common in toy breeds with larger-than-usual litters.

Ectoparasites: Parasites living outside the dog, such as fleas and ticks.

Ectopic ureter: A birth defect in which the entrance to the urethra is in an abnormal location.

Ectopic: Nonmalignant tissue growing in an unusual location.

Eczema: Inflammatory dermatitis that may be acute or chronic.

ED: Elbow dysplasia

ED+: Eating and drinking normally (veterinary notation).

Eddie: Stage name of the Jack Russell Terrier that starred on *Frasier.* Real name: Moose.

Edema: Excessive accumulation of fluid in body tissue. See anasarca.

Educational Commission for Foreign Veterinarian Graduates: Board enabling graduates of a foreign school of veterinary medicine to sit for the National Board Examination.

EDUD: Eating, drinking, urinating, defecating (veterinary notation).

EEG: Electroencephalogram.

EFA: Essential fatty acids.

EGC, EGC-V, ECG-JH: Elite Gamblers, Veterans, Junior Handlers (NADAC).

Egg-shaped head: A head that tapers toward the nose, as in the bull terrier.

Ehlers-Danlos syndrome: A condition in which the connective tissue of the skin tears easily. Also called cutis hyperelasticity and cutaneous asthenia.

Ehrlichiosis: Noncontagious chronic infection. Also known as canine typhus. Caused by the rickettsia *Ehrlichia canis* and transmitted by the brown dog tick.

EIA: Enzyme immunoassay.

Eicosanoids: Biologically active metabolites of 20-carbon fatty acids, including prostaglandins, leukotrienes, prostacyclins, and thromboxanes.

EJC, EJC-V, EJCJH: Elite Jumpers, Veterans, Junior Handlers (NADAC).

EKG: Electrocardiogram. Also called ECG. A printout of the electrical activity of the heart.

Elavil: Brand name for amitriptyline, an antidepressant that has been helpful for animal patients with obsessive grooming, inappropriate urination, and separation anxiety.

Elbow: The joint at the top of the forearm between the humerus and the radius and ulna.

Elbow dysplasia: Collective name for a group of conditions for various kinds of deformed elbows, such as fragmented medial coronoid process, ununited anconeal process, and osteochondrosis of the medial condyle of the humerus. Primarily affects large and giant breeds. Causes differ for each form, but may include trauma, genetics, joint abnormalities, or metabolic disease.

Elbowing out: The elbows outturned, away from body

Elective surgery: Surgery not rendered necessary by disease or illness. Elective surgeries include spaying, neutering, ear cropping, tail docking, and dewclaw removal.

Electro-acupuncture: Acupuncture technique in which electrodes are attached to the needles and a slight electric current is passed into the acupuncture point. Practitioners believe it aids the healing effect.

Electrocardiography or electrocardiogram (EKG or ECG): Noninvasive, relatively cheap way to discover heart arrhythmias and enlargement by measuring electrical activity traversing the heart.

Electrocautery: A procedure in which a sharp-tipped instrument, heated by electricity, is applied to a tissue. Electrocautery may be used to make an incision, remove a mass, or stop bleeding.

Electroencephalogram (EEG): A method to evaluate brain function by measuring electrical activity.

Electrolyte: A substance that splits into ions when put into solution, becoming capable of conducting electricity. Electrolytes include sodium, potassium, calcium, chloride, and bicarbonate.

Electrolyte solution: A mixture of water, electrolytes (salts), or dextrose prescribed for dehydration, vomiting, diarrhea, shock, and other conditions.

Electroretinography: The recording of electrical changes in the retina of the eye in response to stimulation by light.

Electrosurgery: The use of an electrical impulse to cut tissue.

Element points: Horary points; an acupuncture term.

ELISA: Enzyme-linked immunosorbent assay, used to detect levels of antibodies or antigens.

Elixir: A liquid (usually water and alcohol) containing sweetening, flavoring, and a medicinal preparation.

Elizabethan collar: Funnel-shaped plastic or cardboard headpiece, designed to keep a dog from biting or licking a wound or stitches. Named for the high, ruffed necks popular in the time of Elizabeth I.

Elkhound: Norwegian elkhound.

Elongated soft palate: Abnormal extension of the palate that interferes with breathing.

EM: Electron microscopy.

Emaciation: Severe weight loss.

Embolic parasitic pneumonia: Pneumonia usually secondary to heartworm infestation in the side of the heart.

Embolus: A clot or plug originating in a larger blood vessel and traveling to a smaller one.

Emesis: Vomiting.

Emetic: Substance that induces vomiting.

EMG: Electromyogram.

Emollient: A soothing agent, such as an ointment applied to irritated skin.

Emphysema: A lung disease characterized by an increase in size and overall expansion of the alveoli.

Empyema: Accumulation of pus in a body cavity.

Emulsifier: In dog-food manufacturing, a material that causes fats and oils to remain in suspension.

Emulsion: A medicinal preparation of oily substances dispersed in an aqueous medium, with an additive to stabilize it.

Enalapril: An angiotensin-converting enzyme (ACE) inhibitor, prescribed for heart failure and related conditions.

Enamel hypoplasia: Lack of normal protective covering on tooth surfaces. Occurs in puppies stricken with distemper at an early age.

Encephalitis: Inflammation of the brain, usually due to infection.

Encephalo-: Pertaining to the brain.

Encephalopathy: Any degenerative disease of the brain. Causes include liver disease (resulting in the buildup of toxic by-products of metabolism), heavy metal (e.g., lead) poisoning, and loss of blood supply.

Endemic: Adjective to describe a disease widely or constantly present over a long period.

Endocrine: Pertaining to the secretion of hormones.

Endocrine glands: Glands that secrete hormones into the blood.

Endocrine pancreas: The part of the pancreas that produces insulin; the islets of Langerhans.

Endocrine system: The body system that produces hormones; composed of numerous ductless glands including the thyroid, parathyroids, adrenals, and part of the pancreas. The endocrine system integrates the activities of other body systems.

Endocrinology: Study of the endocrine glands and their hormones.

Endogenous: Originating from causes inside the body.

Endometritis: Inflammation of the uterine lining, usually due to infection.

Endometrium: Mucous membrane lining the uterus.

Endoparasites: Parasites living inside a dog, such as worms.

Endoscope: A rigid or flexible fiberoptic device that can be inserted into openings in the body to view or treat internal problems.

Endoscopy: Examination of the gastrointestinal tract by use of a special instrument (endoscope) designed for that purpose.

Endotoxemia: Blood poisoning.

Endotracheal tube: A tube placed into the animal's trachea (windpipe) to allow oxygen and gases to be breathed into the lungs.

Energy density: The number of calories provided by a pet food in a given weight or volume.

Energy imbalance: A condition in which the daily food consumption does not equal the energy spent.

English beagle: Beagle.

English bulldog: Bulldog.

English bull terrier: Bull terrier.

English coach dog: Dalmatian.

English cocker spaniel: Medium-sized spaniel. The word cocker refers to woodcock, a bird for which this breed was particularly trained. Once known as the Norfolk spaniel, since the Duke of Norfolk has a kennel of them.

English coonhound: Hunting breed.

English mastiff: Mastiff.

English pointer: Pointer.

English setter: Bird-pointing and retrieving breed, developed mainly for work on the moors. It is the smallest of the setters, and is known for its silky coat and friendly disposition. The first English setters appeared about 400 years ago. Size: 24 to 25 inches, 60 to 70 pounds. Has a white coat mixed with orange and/or blue.

English springer spaniel: Large land spaniel developed in the early eighteenth century. Size: 19 to 20 inches, 40 to 50 pounds. Medium to long coat, usually black or liver with white.

English toy spaniel: Toy breed related to the cavalier King Charles spaniel. Known for its domed head, short nose, and friendly attitude. The breed was developed in the late seventeenth century. Size: about 10 inches, 8 to 14 pounds.

English toy terrier: Toy Manchester terrier.

Enrofloxacin: Antibiotic of the fluoroquinolone class, similar to ciprofloxacin, useful against a wide spectrum of aerobic bacteria. Used to combat different types of infections, especially those involving *Pseudomonas.* Enrofloxacin is also active against *Staphylococci,* and thus is commonly used for infections of the skin. Brand name: Baytril.

Enteral feeding: A method of feeding in which a tube is placed through the body wall into the intestine and a nutritious liquid is forced through the tube into the intestine.

Enteritis: Inflammation of the lining of the small intestine, often resulting in diarrhea.

Entero-: Pertaining to the intestines.

Enterohepatic: Pertaining to the intestines and liver.

Enterohepatic cycling: The process by which a substance undergoes recirculation between the intestine and liver via the bile.

Enteropathy: A disease condition of the intestine characterized by diarrhea, weight loss, and enteritis.

Enterotoxemia: A disease condition characterized by toxins in the blood produced in the intestines.

Entire: Unaltered male.

Entropion: Inverted eyelids, in which the eyelashes irritate the eyeball. Some pups grow out of it; in others it must be surgically corrected. Entropion is a common hereditary disorder.

Enuresis: (1) Incontinence. **(2)** Involuntary discharge of urine while sleeping.

Enzyme: A special protein that makes a chemical reaction proceed faster. Nearly all bodily functions are facilitated by enzymes.

EOD: Every other day (veterinary notation).

Eosinophil: A white blood cell with a bilobate nucleus, which stains with eosin dye. Allergic dogs show increased numbers of these cells.

Eosinophilic myositis: Inflammation of the jaw muscles.

Epagneul Breton: Old name for the Brittany.

Épagneul Nain: Papillon.

EPG: Eggs per gram (of feces).

Ephedra: In herbal medicine, given as a circulatory stimulant.

EPI: Exocrine pancreatic insufficiency.

Epidermal metabolic dermatopathy: A potentially fatal liver disease involving an imbalance of amino acids, fats, and zinc. Also known as superficial necrolytic dermatitis and glucagonoma syndrome.

Epidermis: Outer, nonvascular layer of skin.

Epidermoid carcinoma: A malignant, squamous cell tumor that appears as a cauliflower-shaped lump or a hard, flat, grayish ulcer, usually on the legs or feet. Dogs may lick the area and cause hair loss.

Epididymitis: Inflammation of the epididymus.

Epididymus: Elongated mass of tubes used to store, develop, and move sperm at the back of the testis.

Epilepsy: Seizures caused by

abnormal nerve discharges in the brain. Can be inherited or idiopathic.

Epiphora: Tears streaming from the eyes; watery eyes, usually causing staining. The reddish-brown color is caused by a protein, lactoferrin, which binds to iron.

Epiphysis: The enlarged end of a long bone that forms part of a joint.

Episcleritis: Inflammation of the sclera, or white of the eye, giving the whole eye a red look.

Episodal dyscontrol: Seizure-related aggression. See rage syndrome.

Epistatic effect: When genes at one locus influence the expression of gene at another locus.

Epistaxis: See nosebleed.

Epithelial cells: Cells forming the epithelium.

Epithelium: The tissue that covers the internal and external surfaces of the body.

EPO: Erythropoietin.

Epsiprantel: A dewormer; prescribed for tapeworms.

Epsom salts: Magnesium sulfate. Used to clean and soak wounds and to alleviates hot spots. Also acts as a powerful laxative.

Epulis: Gingival hyperplasia, a common benign proliferation of the gum tissue within the mouth. It attaches the root of the tooth to the jaw bone.

ERG: Electroretinography.

Erosion: A shallow defect in the skin.

Erythema: Redness of the skin caused by congestion of the capillaries.

Erythema multiforme: An acute eruption of the skin and mucous membranes.

Erythrocyte: Red blood cell.

Erythrocyte sedimentation rate: The speed at which red blood cells settle out when the blood is left to stand. Often elevated during an inflammatory process.

Erythromycin: A broad-spectrum antibiotic prescribed for Campylobacter (which causes diarrhea) and certain skin infections. At low doses it can be an antiemetic.

Erythropoiesis: The production of red blood cells.

Erythropoietin: Hormone that stimulates red blood cell production by the bone marrow. Prescribed for anemia caused by kidney failure.

Escape turn: In greyhound racing, the first turn of the racetrack after the front stretch.

Escherichia coli: An aerobic, gram-negative bacteria that causes severe gastrointestinal problems.

Esophageal: Pertaining to the esophagus.

Esophageal achalasia: Failure of the walls of the esophagus to relax sufficiently to allow food to pass into the stomach.

Esophageal disorders: Usually manifested as a problem in swallowing.

Esophageal hypomobility: A condition in which the esophagus fails to push food into the stomach. Characterized by regurgitation, weight loss, and recurrent respiratory infections.

Esophageal obstruction: A blockage that can include tumor, infection, structure, or ingestion of a foreign object.

Esophageal reflux: Condition in which stomach contents move backward into the esophagus.

Esophagitis: Inflammation occurring in the esophagus.

Esophagus: Muscular tube leading from the mouth to the stomach.

ESR: Erythrocyte sedimentation rate.

Essential amino acid: One of the ten amino acids that cannot be produced in the body and so must be supplied in the diet.

Essential fatty acids: Fatty

acids that cannot by synthesized by the body and must be supplied by the diet.

Essential nutrients: Nutrients that cannot be synthesized by the body in the amount needed.

Essiac tea: Herbal remedy consisting of burdock root, sheep sorrel, slippery-elm bark, and turkey rhubarb root. Essiac is Caisse spelled backward; it is named for Rene Caisse, a nurse who developed the formula.

Est: Estimate (veterinary notation).

Estrogen: Steroid hormones produced by the ovary. Prescribed for estrogen-responsive urinary incontinence in spayed female dogs.

Estrous cycle: The breeding cycle. It lasts from six to eight months and contains four phases: anestrus, proestrus, estrus, and metestrus. Bitches can become pregnant only during the week or two of the estrus phase.

Estrus: The recurring "heat" period of a female dog, during which she can become pregnant. Often indicated by the leaving of small blood spots. The blood is from the vagina, not the urinary tract.

E/t: Endo-tracheal (veterinary notation).

Ethology: Scientific study of animal behavior.

Etiology: The cause of a disease.

Etogesic: Nonsteroidal anti-inflammatory drug.

EUA: Examine under anesthetic (veterinary notation).

Eucalyptus: Aromatherapy treatment for pneumonia.

Euth: Euthanize (veterinary notation).

Euthanasia: The act of painlessly putting to death a sick, injured, or unwanted animal.

Euthyroid: Normal thyroid gland.

Even bite: When the front teeth of the upper and lower jaws meet with no overlap.

Evening primrose: In herbal medicine, prescribed for obesity.

Evidence dog: A dog trained to search a small area intensely and indicate evidence like clothing, weapons, or blood.

Ewe neck: A neck like that of a lamb, whose top is concave.

Ex: External (veterinary notation).

Ex lap: Exploratory laparoscopy (veterinary notation).

Excellent Agility Jumper: Title awarded to a dog that earns three qualifying scores in Excellent A Jumpers with Weaves class under at least two different judges.

Excise: Cut out or remove surgically.

Exclusion diagnosis: The process of making a diagnosis by ruling out everything else.

Exclusion diet: A diet that excludes all components of any previous diet, usually consisting of new sources of protein, fat, and carbohydrates.

Exfoliation: Scaling off or peeling in thin layers.

Exhibitor: One who brings a dog to a dog show and shows it. Owner of the show dog.

Exocrine gland: A gland that secretes its products through a duct.

Exocrine pancreas: The portion of the pancreas that produces digestive enzymes.

Exocrine pancreatic insufficiency (EPI): Pancreatic exocrine insufficiency.

Exogenous: Originating outside the body.

Exogenous cortisone: Supplemental cortisone.

Exophthalmos: Protrusion of the eyeball.

Expanded: In dog-food manufacturing, a dry food composed of small, porous nuggets.

Ex-pen: An exercise pen.

Exploratory surgery: Surgery to find the cause of a disease.

Exposure keratopathy syndrome: A syndrome in which there is chronic irritation of the surface of the eye (cornea) because of increased evaporation of tears and increased corneal exposure. This is a result of a combination of anatomic features.

Expression: General appearance of all the features of the head as viewed from the front.

Expulsion: The final phase of the birthing process, in which the placenta is expelled. A greenish fluid may accompany the birth; this is normal.

Extension: In a veterinary exam, increasing the angle of a joint, as when straightening the knee.

Extensor rigidity: A condition in which muscles contract and tend to straighten the limb, prevent it from relaxing.

Extinction: The weakening of a specific behavior through non-reinforcement.

Extinction burst: A temporary increase in behavior in response to the removal of reinforcing stimuli.

Extra eyelashes: See distichia.

Extrahepatic: Outside the liver.

Extra-label use: Used for purposes not indicated on the label.

Extravasion: (1) A discharge of blood from vessels into the tissues, or a similar process. **(2)** Leakage of fluid into the tissues.

Extrudate: Doughlike material in dog-food manufacturing cooked in an extruder under pressure, before forming and cutting.

Extruded: In dog-food manufacturing, a blended dry food forced through an extruder.

Extruder: Cooking machine in the manufacture of dry and semi-moist dog foods.

Exudate: Fluid that has escaped from blood vessels and has been deposited in or on the tissues.

Exudation: Leakage of fluid or cellular debris from blood vessels, usually into the tissues.

Eye shadow: In malamutes, dark color under the eyes that is less intense in appearance than the goggles.

Eyebright (euphrasia): Herb used to treat eye inflammations, corneal ulcers, and infections.

Eyebrows: Projection of the frontal bones over the eyes.

Eyeteeth: Upper canines.

F

F: Female (veterinary notation).

F1/4: Forequarters (veterinary notation).

F1: First generation of a cross between breeds.

F8: Figure eight. Term used in obedience tests.

FA: Fatty acid.

F.A.I.R.: Forensically appropriate indication response.

F.Ch.: (1) Field Champion, a title awarded by the American Sighthound Field Association. **(2)** An AKC prefix (lure coursing).

Factor II deficiency: Lack of a blood-clotting-factor, leading to mild bleeding.

Factor VIII deficiency: Lack of a blood-clotting factor; it causes hemophilia, which results in bleeding gums and nosebleeds. Surgery is dangerous in these dogs.

Factor XI deficiency: A deficiency of a clotting factor in the blood.

FAD: Flea allergy dermatitis.

Fading puppy syndrome: An occurrence in which a seemingly normal puppy weakens and dies within a week or two of birth. Not a specific disorder, but usually related to an infection.

Fainting: Temporary loss of consciousness. Causes can include heart disease, airway obstruction, chemical fumes, and trauma.

Faking: Changing the appearance of a dog in order to deceive.

Fala: Franklin Roosevelt's Scottish terrier.

Fall: (1) In retriever training, the

spot on the ground or water where the item to be retrieved fell. **(2)** The long overhanging hair covering the face of a Yorkshire terrier.

Fallaway: The slope of the croup.

Fallow: Light red or yellowish brown.

False negative: In diagnostic tests, a negative result when the animal tested actually does have the condition.

False positive: A diagnostic test result in which the subject falsely tests positive because of complicating factors or the limits of the test.

False pregnancy: Condition in which bitches show signs of pregnancy or nursing, even those that have not been mated or have failed to conceive. Also called pseudopregnancy.

Familial: Occurring within a particular lineage.

Familial nephropathy: Hereditary impaired kidney function.

Familial neuronal abiotrophy: Inherited malformation of nerve cells.

Famotidine: Drug used to treat Helicobacter infection, inflammatory bowel disease, canine parvovirus, ingestion of a toxin that could be ulcerating (overdose of aspirin, for example), any disease involving protracted vomiting, or used in combination with medications that may have stomach-irritating properties. Brand name: Pepcid AC.

Fancier: One especially interested, and usually participating, in dog events.

Fanconi's syndrome: Kidney tubule defects. An inherited condition in basenjis.

Fancy: Group of people interested in breeding or showing a particular breed or dogs as a whole.

Faou: One of the five varieties of Languedoc sheepdogs.

Far turn: In greyhound racing, the third turn of the racetrack.

Farnum Companies, Inc: Providers of dog medical supplies. 301 West Osborn, Phoenix, AZ 85013. Telephone: (800) 825-2555. Web site: www.farnumpet.com.

Fat: (1) The adipose or fatty tissue of the body. **(2)** Concentrated energy source.

Fat++: Obese (veterinary notation).

Fat-soluble vitamins: Vitamins A, D, E, and K.

Fatty acids: The building blocks of dietary lipids. As a supplement, sometimes prescribed for allergies, inflammation, dermatitis, and similar conditions.

Fatty tumor: Also called lipoma. Ugly, benign, fatty growth. If fatty tumors grow very large or impede movement, they can be surgically removed.

Fault: Any trait that conflicts with the relevant breed standard.

Fault judging: A system of judging based on penalizing a dog's weak points rather than comparing the dog to the overall breed standard.

Fawn: Light brown.

FC: Field trial champion. The title is prefixed to the dog's name and indicates great field ability. In four breeds (German shorthaired pointer, German wirehaired pointer, weimaraner, vizsla), it indicates retrieving ability. In two breeds (German wirehaired pointer, weimaraner), it indicates water-retrieving ability.

FCI: Federation Cynologique International.

FCR: Flat-coated retriever.

FD: (1) Flyball dog. **(2)** Field Dog (pointing, CKC).

FDA: The Food and Drug Administration.

FDCh: Flyball champion.

FDJ: Field Dog Junior (pointing, CKC).

FDSB: Field Dog Stud Book, a

registry of pointing dogs published by the American Field Publishing Company.

FDX: (1) Flyball Dog Excellent. **(2)** Field Dog Excellent (pointing, CKC).

Fe: (1) Female, unspayed (veterinary notation). **(2)** Iron.

Feathering: Long hair on the legs, the tail, and the ends of ears.

Febantel: Dewormer prescribed for roundworm and whipworm.

Febrile: Having a fever.

Feces: Stool; solid waste product.

Federation Cynologique Internationale: European show organization, not a breed registry.

Feed efficiency: The rate at which animals convert feed into tissue.

Feeding oatmeal: In dog-food labeling, a by-product derived during the manufacture of rolled oats or rolled oat grouts.

Felted: Matted, as applied to the coat.

Femoral Head Ostectomy: A surgical procedure for hip dysplasia that consists of removing the ball-like joint at the head of the femur bone.

Femur: Thigh bone; main bone in the rear leg.

Fenbendazole: Dewormer (Panacur) prescribed for roundworm, whipworm, hookworm, tapeworm, lungworm, and lung fluke.

Fennec: Small African desert fox.

Fennel (*Foeniculum vulgare*): In herbal medicine, used to enhance milk flow.

Fenris: In Norse myth, the wolf, son of Loki.

Fentanyl: Narcotic analgesic prescribed for post-operative pain. Often used in a patch.

Feral: A domestic dog that has reverted to the wild.

Fetch: (1) In sporting dogs, the retrieve command, or simply to reach for, pick up, and carry the bird. **(2)** In herding dogs, to move the stock toward the handler.

Fever: A temperature elevation that is usually a sign of viral or bacterial infection, or more rarely, hyperthermia. It is a sign of disease, not a disease in itself.

FGDCh: Flyball Grand Champion. Received after attaining 30,000 points.

FH: In schutzhund, an advanced tracking title (comparable to TDX).

Fibroma: A non-malignant tumor of connective tissue. Compare to fibrosarcoma.

Fibronil: An effective chemical against fleas. Found in Frontline and some other medications. Usually applied as a liquid to the back of the neck, so the dog can't lick it off. It spreads through the oil layer of the skin and travels from one hair follicle to the next. Active for thirty to ninety days.

Fibrosarcoma: A malignant tumor arising from collagen-producing fibroblasts (immature fiber-producing cells of connective tissue). Compare to fibroma.

Fibula: Smaller of the two bones of the lower hind leg. Lies between the patella and the tarsal bones.

Fiddle-front: A combination of an east-west front and bowed legs. From the front, the feet and legs outline a fiddle.

Fido: Formerly, a common dog name, meaning "I am faithful." Abraham Lincoln's family had a dog named Fido.

Field Dog Stud Book (FDSB): The registry of hunting dogs maintained by the American Field organization. Although it registers all sporting breeds, it specializes as a bird dog registry. 542 South Dearborn Street, Chicago, IL 60605. Telephone: (312) 663-9797.

Field spaniel: Sporting dog developed from the cocker spaniel during the nineteenth century with a black, liver, golden liver, or roan coat. Size: 17 to 18 inches, 35 to 50 pounds.

Field trial: A competitive field event for hounds and sporting breeds, evaluating the skills of dogs against each other.

Field Trial Champion: A championship awarded to pointing breeds, scent and sight hounds, and retrievers for winning in various hunting trials.

Field Trial Club: An organization that holds field trials conducted under the AKC or FDSB rules.

Field work: Retriever training; the training is generally conducted away from the area around the kennel. Includes concept work or marks and blinds.

Filbert ears: Rounded, triangular ears, used in reference to the Bedlington terrier.

Fill: Fullness between the eyes, the opposite of chiseled.

Filter heartworm test: A blood sample is passed though filters to isolate the larvae. Somewhat more accurate than the direct test, but not as accurate as the occult test.

Fin: Finish this treatment (veterinary notation).

Find: In pointing breed events, a bird that a dog has found and pointed.

Fine needle aspirate: A procedure in which suction is applied to a hollow needle that has been inserted into tissue and a core of the tissue is withdrawn to culture and/or examine microscopically.

Fines: In dog-food manufacturing any materials that pass through a filtering screen.

Finished: (1) A dog that has completed a championship. **(2)** A dog that is fully trained to run the desired game only.

Finnish spitz: The national dog of Finland, originally used for hunting. Size: 15 to 20 inches, 25 to 30 pounds. Has a long,

harsh outer coat in various shades of golden-red.

Finsk spets: Finnish spitz.

Fipronil: Gamma aminobutyric acid (GABA) inhibitor (Frontline), an insecticide and ascaricide prescribed for killing ticks and fleas.

Fire house dog: Dalmatian.

First cross: The F1 generation; the first generation of crosses between animals of two pure breeds.

Fish eye: Wall eye.

Fish meal: The clean, dried, ground tissue of fresh whole fish or fish cuttings.

Fish scale disease: Ichthyosis.

Fistula: An abnormal opening or passage between two organs or tissues. May be created surgically to facilitate drainage.

Fit: Seizure.

Fixed formula dog food: A food in which ingredients do not change in response to market prices.

FL: Front legs (veterinary notation).

Flag: (1) Long hair on the tail. **(2)** In dog-food labeling, the part of the principal display panel designed to highlight information. **(3)** Wagging the tail while on point, indicating a lack of staunchness. **(4)** Well-fringed tail, carried almost horizontally, as in the setter.

Flagpole tail: A long tail carried erect, as in the beagle.

Flakes: In dog-food manufacturing, an ingredient rolled or cut into flat pieces.

Flanged rib: A ridge near the bottom of the cage on one or both sides. The ribcage slants inward at the "flange."

Flank: The side of the dog between the last rib and the hip.

Flanking: In herding dogs, circling the stock to keep them in a group or change their direction.

Flare: A blaze that widens toward the skull.

Flared nostrils: Wide, open nostrils, as in the Bouvier des Flandres.

Flaring ear: Ears that widen out from the base.

Flashpoint: In pointing breed events, a brief point, followed by the dog's releasing to flush the bird. Not acceptable for Derby classes.

Flashy Sir Award: Given each year to the country's top distance (3/8-mile) greyhound by the NGA; named for an outstanding distance greyhound of the mid-1940s.

Flat bones: Bones found in the skull and ribs.

Flat catcher: A flashy dog whose faults are disguised by its flashiness. British usage.

Flat-coated retriever: Gundog descended from the Labrador retriever and Newfoundland; developed in the nineteenth century. Originally called the wavy-coated retriever. Size: 22 to 24 inches, 60 to 70 pounds. This breed can be either solid black or liver-colored.

Flat croup: A croup with insufficient slope or taper from the hip bones to the root of the tail.

Flat-sided: Insufficiently rounded ribs.

Flat skull: A skull that is flat from ear to ear and from stop to occiput, as in the pointer.

Flat throw: In retrieving trials, a mark thrown at a 90-degree angle from the starting line.

Flattie: Affectionate name for a flat-coated retriever.

Flatulence: Passing excess gas. Normally occurs when food is not completely digested. Highly fermentable foods such as soybeans, often part of a commercial diet, tend to produce flatulence in dogs. Worms can also cause flatulence, as can eating too quickly and gulping air, and more rarely pancreatic disease. Adding fiber, digestive enzymes like CurTail, or acidophilus to the diet may help,

as will exercise and encouraging the dog to eat more slowly.

Flatus: Gas expelled through the anus.

Flavor: In dog-food labeling, "flavor" on the label means that the food contains enough of the named flavor to be recognized by the dog.

Flea: The most common parasite of dogs. The flea that bothers dogs the most is the cat flea (*Ctenocephalides felis*). Causes itching and scratching along the back, tail, and hindquarters.

Flea allergy dermatitis: Fleabite sensitivity.

Fleabite dermatitis: A skin condition resulting from sensitivity to flea saliva. Flea allergy dermatitis.

Fleabite sensitivity: Also called flea allergy dermatitis. Causes severe itching and papules, especially on the back, flank, and legs. The dog is reacting to a protein contained in flea saliva.

Flea collar: Special collar impregnated with chemicals to kill fleas.

Flea dip: A solution made to kill fleas, applied to an animal and not rinsed off, to allow it to have residual action.

Flecked: Coat lightly ticked with another color, but not spotted or roan.

Flesh-colored nose: An even, light-colored nose, as in the pharaoh hound.

Flews: Pendulous upper lip.

Flewsy: Too much flews.

Flexi-lead: A retractable leash.

Flexion: In a veterinary exam, increasing the angle of a joint, as when a knee is bent.

Flight zone: In herding events, an invisible ring around a herd or flock into which a dog cannot penetrate without causing the stock to feel threatened and attempt to escape.

Floating rib: The last, or thirteenth, rib, which is unattached to the other ribs.

Flocked: A coat with the texture of cotton wool.

Flocking: The instinctive tendency of some stock to instinctively cluster together for mutual protection.

Florinef: Brand name for fludrocortisone, a medication given as an oral replacement for aldosterone; it is given to Addison's disease patients.

Flower Essence Society: P.O.Box 1769, Nevada City, CA 95959. Telephone: (800) 548-0075.

Flower essences: Similar to homeopathic remedies, but used to treat behavioral problems.

Flower pot marks: In retrieving trials, two marks thrown from the same gun station in different directions. Also called a "momma-poppa."

Fluconazole: Antifungal drug prescribed for deep (systemic) fungal infections, including ringworm and Candida (yeasts).

Fludrocortisone: Synthetic adrenal corticosteroid prescribed to prevent the circulation crisis associated with adrenocortical insufficiency (Addison's disease). Brand name: Florinef.

Fluffy: A dog whose coat should be of medium length but is too long, with exaggerated feathering.

Fluke: Small, flat parasites (Trematoda) that inhabit the liver or lungs of infected dogs.

Fluoroscopy: Type of radiograph (X-ray) in which motion can be seen.

Fluoxetine: Psychotropic medication (Prozac, a serotonin inhibitor) prescribed for compulsive behaviors, anxiety, and fears.

Flush and stop: When a bird dog flushes a bird rather than pointing it, and then stops, pretending it just happened. A serious fault.

Flush: In pointing breed events, the flight of a bird from cover.

Fly strikes: Areas of the ear that have been continually bitten by flies.

Flyball: A relay race with teams of four dogs that individually run over four hurdles placed ten feet apart and then retrieve a tennis ball after triggering a box. The dog must then return back over the jumps with the tennis ball in its mouth. Once the dog has crossed the finish line, the next dog goes.

Flyball Dog Excellent: Awarded to a flyball dog that has earned one hundred points.

Flyer: In sporting dog field trials, a live bird shot for dogs to retrieve.

Flying ears: Drop or semi-prick ears that stand out or "fly." Often used for breeds that should not have erect ears.

Flying trot: A fast trot in which all four feet are off the ground for a moment. Also called the suspended trot.

Fly-snapping: Repeated snapping at invisible flies. It has been associated with partial seizures, ear infections, and even food allergies. Medication is usually the most effective treatment.

FM: Flyball Master.

FMCH: Flyball Master Champion.

FMX: Flyball Master Excellent.

Fn: Female, spayed (veterinary notation).

FNA: Fine needle aspirate.

Fold dermatitis: Skin fold dermatitis.

Folded ears: Ears that hang down in folds (like a bloodhound's ears) rather than lying flat.

Folic acid: Essential for blood cell formation and fertility. Found in organ meats and green, leafy vegetables.

Follicle: The group of cells in the skin in which a hair develops.

Follicle-stimulating hormone (FSH): Hormone that stimulates ovarian follicle growth in females and spermatogenesis in males.

Follicular dysplasia of the Siberian husky: Another name for alopecia X, a cosmetic hair-loss condition.

Folliculitis: Inflammation of the hair follicles. Characterized by pimply bumps or blackheads along the back and sides of the body.

Food allergy: A reaction to ingredients or preservatives in food. It is a comparatively rare allergy in dogs. Most likely culprits are beef, chicken, eggs, fish, wheat, soy, and corn, all common in processed pet foods. Signs can include itching, especially around the face, and more rarely, gastrointestinal problems. Testing for a food allergy is by an elimination or hypoallergenic diet for two to four months.

Food and Drug Administration (FDA): Agency that regulates the development and approval of animal drugs and feed additives through its Center of Veterinary Medicine.

Food enzymes: Natural chemicals, present in all fresh foods, that contribute to fermentation.

Food spike: A rise in blood glucose levels following a meal.

Force breaking: A training program for sporting dogs in which a trainer teaches a dog to retrieve mechanically.

Force fetch: A training technique that teaches a dog to fetch, hold, and release on command. Generally accomplished after the adult teeth are in place in the six- -to-eight-month age range. Also called FF, forcing, force breaking, conditioned retrieving.

Forechest: The front part of the chest.

Foreign expression: Expression not typical of the breed.

Forelegs: Front legs.

Forensically Appropriate Indication Response (F.A.I.R.): In search and rescue, a term describing a non-interventionist indication that is given by a forensics dog. The dog will merely sit down, not dig or disturb the area.

Forensics dog: A sub-type of cadaver dog, able to detect subtle crime scene evidence as well as decomposing bodies and skeletal remains.

Forging: Pulling ahead on the leash.

Fort Dodge Animal Health: 800 Fifth Street N.W., P.O. Box 518, Fort Dodge, IA 50501. Telephone: (515) 955-4600. Web site: www.ahp.com/fort-dodge.htm.

Fouled track or field: In tracking, a course that has been compromised by an unplanned scent.

Foundation bitch: A bitch used for starting a breeder's line.

Four-square: A dog standing in such a way that a square could be drawn between its paws.

Fox: Group of wild canids in four genera (vulpine, South American, Arctic, and bat-eared) and twenty-one species.

Foxhound: English foxhound. Developed in the early eighteenth century by Lord Fairfax. Usually hunt in packs. Comes in any hound color.

Foxtail: A grass awn with cylindrical spike and stiff bristles that can easily migrate through the skin and tissues.

Fox terrier: Comes in two coat types, smooth and wire, recognized as separate breeds by the AKC. Males of both varieties are about 15 inches tall, weighing about 18 pounds. Females are somewhat smaller. Both are mostly white in color.

Foxy or foxlike head: Sharp, pointed ears and triangular face, as in the spitz breeds.

Fracture: Broken bone.

Fragmented coronoid process: Developmental flaw where a fragment of the ulna never fuses.

Free baiting: Using a treat in such a way that the dog poses itself, rather than being stacked.

Free choice: See ad libitum.

Free radicals: Unstable oxygen-containing molecules produced during metabolism that may damage tissues or cellular components.

Free stack: A show dog's natural show pose without being touched by the handler.

Freestyle obedience: A canine sport that combines dancing and obedience.

Freeze brand: In hunting, a way to permanently mark with desired letters or design for identification. Done by shaving the hair and using a brand that has been placed in alcohol and dry ice to lower the temperature, then placed onto the shaved area. Changes the hair color to white.

Freezing: When a dog refuses to release a bird to the handler.

Freki: In Norse myth, a dog, along with Geri, that accompanied Odin into battle.

French bulldog: Developed in France in the nineteenth century. Weighs less than 28 pounds. Has a short, smooth coat of any color. Known for its bat ears.

French front: Fiddle front.

Frill: See apron.

Fringe: In tracking, the immediate area on either side of the primary track.

Frogface: Extended nose and receding, often overshot jaw.

Front-trailing: In pointing breeds, when a bird dog follows its brace-mate but stays ahead of it. A fault, showing lack of independence.

Frostbite: Body parts that freeze upon exposure to extreme cold. Most commonly affects toes, ears, and scrotum.

Frosting: White hair intermingling with base color around the muzzle.

Froufrou: See pompom.

FSH: Follicle-stimulating hormone.

Full cry: Sound made by a hound that is hot on a scent trail.

Full mask: In malamutes, the combination of bar, goggles, and cap.

Fully open: While on a scent trail, barking freely.

Fun match: Very informal, small show held outside AKC control.

Fungicide: A drug that kills fungi.

FUO: Fever of unknown origin (veterinary notation).

Furnished: Profusely coated.

Furnishings: Long hairs on legs and tails of some breeds.

Furosemide: Diuretic prescribed for pulmonary edema, congestive heart failure, and similar conditions. Furosemide acts on the kidneys to increase the body's loss of water and assorted minerals and electrolytes. Brand names: Lasix, Disal.

Furrow: A slight indentation or median line from stop to occiput.

Futurity: In dog shows, competition for puppies. The litter must be entered before birth or when very young.

Fx: Fracture (veterinary notation).

G

G (g): grams.

G6PD: Glucose-6-phosphate dehydrogenase. An enzyme in red blood cells; a deficiency leads to hemolytic anemia.

GA: General anesthetic (veterinary notation).

GABA: Gamma-aminobutyric acid. An inhibitory neurotransmitter found in the CNS.

Gabble retchets: Gabriel hounds.

Gabriel hounds: Pack of spectral hounds from British folklore. Also known as Gabble retchets.

Gait: A dog's way of movement.

Galactagogue: A substance that stimulates milk production.

Gallery: Human observers of a field event.

Gallop: Fastest dog gait, wherein the paws touch the ground in a four-beat rhythm, and usually with a period of suspension in which all four feet are in the air.

Gambler: An agility course with no predetermined route and where each obstacle is assigned a point value. The handler seeks to accumulate points by performing the obstacles of his/her own choice in the time allotted.

Game bird: Any bird that can be hunted.

Gameness: A powerful desire to succeed despite obstacles, including injury or fatigue.

Gametes: Sperm cells and ova.

Gangline: In sledding, the central line to which all dogs are attached.

Garden: Slang for Madison Square Garden, traditional site of the Westminster Dog Show.

Garm: In Norse myth, a four-eyed dog that guarded Helheim.

Gaskin: Second or lower thigh.

Gastric: Pertaining to the stomach.

Gastric bloat: Swelling of the stomach from excess gas, usually followed by gastric torsion.

Gastric dilatation: Stomach torsion.

Gastric dilatation-volvulus complex (GDV): Also called bloat; a life-threatening disorder of the gastrointestinal system. Large, deep-chested breeds such as Great Danes are at greatest risk. Signs include excessive salivation and drooling, extreme restlessness, attempts to vomit and defecate, and evidence of abdominal pain and abdominal swelling. If your dog is able to belch or vomit, quite likely the condition is not caused by a twisting of the stomach. GDV is an emergency condition.

Gastric lavage: Pumping or flushing out the stomach.

Gastric stasis: Reduced stomach motility, leading to retention of gastric products.

Gastric torsion (gastric dilation-volvulus): Twisting of the stomach. Also called bloat.

Gastric tumor: Tumor in the dog's stomach.

Gastrin: A hormone secreted by the mucous lining of the stomach; it stimulates the secretion of gastric acid.

Gastrinoma: Tumor (either benign or malignant) developed in the pancreas; it secretes the hormone gastrin.

Gastritis: Inflammation of the stomach, especially the mucous membrane.

Gastro-: Pertaining to the stomach.

Gastroenteritis: Infection or inflammation of the membrane lining a dog's stomach and intestines, causing vomiting and diarrhea.

Gastroenterology: Study of diseases of the stomach, intestines, liver, and pancreas.

Gastroesophageal junction: Region where the esophagus enters the stomach.

Gastrointestinal: Pertaining to the stomach and intestines.

Gay tail: A tail carried above the horizontal.

Gaze hound: Breed that hunts by sight, such as a greyhound. Also called a sight hound or long dog.

Gazelle hound: Saluki.

GBE: Ginkgo biloba extract.

GD: Great Dane.

GDC: Institute for Genetic Disease Control.

GDSC: Gundog stake champion. The title is prefixed to the dog's name.

GDV: Gastric dilatation-volvulus; bloat.

Gee: In sledding, a command to turn right.

Gelsemium: A homeopathic remedy administered for nervousness and timidity.

Gene: A functional hereditary unit (a segment of DNA) occupying a fixed location on a chromosome, by which hereditary characteristics are determined and transmitted.

General committee: Governing body of the Kennel Club (UK).

Generic drug: Drug sold under a common name rather than a brand name.

Genetic disease: A medical condition transmitted in the genes.

Genetic heterogeneity: When mutations in different genes produce a clinically similar picture within a breed.

Genetic plasticity: Exhibiting a high degree of variation in the genetic material of a species. (Dogs are a good example.)

Genetic variance: The statistical description of the variability of a given population attributable to differences in genetics.

Genital discharge: Usually the sign of a urinary tract, prostate, or uterine infection (pyometra), or miscarriage. Genital discharge is a sign of a serious problem and should be attended to immediately.

Genitourinary: Pertaining to the genital and urinary organs.

Genotype: The genetic composition of the organism.

Geri: In Norse mythology, the wolf companion that accompanied Odin into battle

Germ: Seed embryo.

German mastiff: Great Dane.

German shepherd dog: Versatile dog used for sheep-herding, guide, guard, rescue, and police. The modern breed was developed in the late nineteenth century. Size: 22 to 26 inches, 75 to 85 pounds, with a medium-length coat of various rich colors.

German shorthaired pointer: Powerful gundog famous for both pointing and retrieving. Size: 21 to 25 inches, 45 to 70 pounds. Color: liver, either solid or combined with white. Has a docked tail. Probably developed from the old Spanish pointer.

German spaniel: Gundog.

German wirehaired pointer: All-purpose, all-weather gundog. Size: 22 to 26 inches, 60 to 70 pounds. Color liver and white. Originated in Germany around the nineteenth century.

Gestation: Pregnancy. The gestation period of dogs ranges from fifty-nine to sixty-five days; the average is sixty-three days. Pregnancy can be confirmed by ultrasound as early as twenty-eight days.

Get: Dog's offspring.

Get back: In sheepdog trials, a command to move away from the stock.

GFC: Grand Field Champion. The title is prefixed to the name of the dog.

GH: Growth hormone.

Ghost trailing: In a hound field trial, following a trail that does not exist.

GI: Gastrointestinal.

Giant breeds: Breeds weighing more than one hundred pounds.

Giant schnauzer: Bred up from the standard schnauzer, and originally used as a drover's dog, perhaps as early as the fifteenth century. A large, strong dog with a harsh black or salt-and-pepper coat. Size: 75 to 80 pounds, 23 to 27 inches.

Giardia: Microscopic parasite that causes diarrhea and irritable bowels, found in lining of cells at the beginning of the small intestine. It is dangerous to nearly all warm-blooded animals; puppies are especially susceptible. See Giardiasis.

Giardiasis: Disease caused by a protozoan of the Giardia species. Giardia damages the bowels, and the resultant infection can prevent the absorption of essential nutrients and vitamins. If left untreated, Giardia can cause severe illness in both dogs and people.

Ginger (Zingiber officinale): In herbal medicine, given for motion sickness.

Gingiva: Gums.

Gingival: Pertaining to the gums.

Gingivitis: Red, inflamed gums resulting from accumulation of tartar, receding gums, and invading bacteria.

Giving tongue: Barking or baying of hounds.

GLA: Gamma-linolenic acid, an 18 carbon essential fatty acid produced in animals by the desaturation of linolenic acid.

Gland: An aggregation of cells that are specialized to secrete or excrete substance unrelated to their ordinary metabolic needs.

Glans penis: The tip of the penis.

Glaucoma: Eye disease characterized by increased, painful intraocular pressure (IOP) on the retina from excess fluid in the eyeball. Often due to an abnormality in the drainage of aqueous fluid from the eye. If untreated, causes partial or total loss of vision.

Glipizide: Antidiabetic medication prescribed for diabetes mellitus.

Globoid cell leukodystrophy: Gradual destruction of white matter in the brain, eventually fatal. Most common in cairn and West Highland white terriers.

Globular: Round and slightly prominent.

Glomerulonephritis: Inflammatory disease of the glomerulus, part of the kidney. May lead to complete loss of kidney function.

Glomerulosclerosis: Fibrosis and scarring in the renal glomeruli.

Glomerulus: Microscopic functional unit of the kidney that makes urine by filtering waste products and excess nutrients from the blood.

Glossal: Word indicating tongue.

Glossitis: Inflammation of the tongue.

Glossy: Shining.

Glove beagle: See pocket beagle.

Glucagon: Hormone secreted by the pancreas islet cells that releases glucose stored in the liver and large muscles.

Glucagonoma: A tumor that secretes glucagon.

Glucocorticoids: Anti-inflammatory steroids, mostly cortisol, produced by the adrenal gland. A general term for drugs that act like the hormone cortisol.

Gluconeogenesis: The formation of glucose from substances that are not carbohydrates, such as amino acids.

Glucosamine: A derivative of glucose found in many glycoproteins and mucopolysaccharides. One of the building blocks the body uses to build new cartilage.

Glucose: A simple sugar appearing in certain foods, especially fruit, and in normal blood; the major source of energy for most organisms.

Glucosuria: The presence of glucose in the urine.

Glutamine: An amino acid that plays an important role in the citric acid cycle and in regulating ammonia concentration in the blood.

Glutathione peroxidase: An enzyme sometimes used to treat allergic conditions. It breaks down various chemicals involved in provoking allergic reactions.

Gluteal: Indicates the buttocks.

Gluten: The protein portion of wheat, barley, and other cereal grains. It remains when the grain is washed to remove the starch.

Glutinous: Sticky.

Glycemia: The presence of glucose in the blood.

Glycerol: (1) Glycerin. **(2)** Part of a triglyceride (fat) molecule.

Glycogen: The stored form of glucose, similar to starch, found in the liver and muscle.

Glycogen storage disease: Deficiency of enzymes required for normal glycogen metabolism.

Glycolysis: First step in the conversion of glucose into carbon dioxide, water, and energy. Acts in the absence of oxygen.

Glycosaminoglycan supplements: Nutraceuticals designed to protect against and help heal arthritis.

GM: (1) Gram. **(2)** Gambler Master (USDAA title).

GMHR: Grand Master Hunting Retriever, a hunting test title from NAHRA.

Gnathostoma: Intestinal parasite infecting fish and the animals that eat them, including dogs.

GNCH: Grand nite champion.

Go bird: In retriever training, the last item the dog sees thrown. In a multiple mark situation, it is generally the first item a dog will pick up.

Go by: In sledding, a command to the dog to go straight on without paying attention to a distraction.

Goggles: A mask of dark color, especially in malamutes.

Gold compounds: Prescribed for immune-mediated arthritis, rheumatoid arthritis, and pemphigus.

Golden retriever: Developed in Scotland in the early nineteenth century. Used for hunting and field and obedience trials. Size: 21 to 23 inches, 55 to 75 pounds. Has a dense water-repellent coat in various shades of gold, usually solid with little white included.

Gonadotropin: Hormone that stimulates the ovaries or testes.

Gone to ground: Expression used to indicate that a rabbit has gone into the earth or other shelter underground.

Goniodysgenesis: Form of glaucoma characterized by an abnormal sheet of tissue in the angle where drainage normally occurs.

Good Samaritan: In law, a licensed veterinarian who renders treatment out of concern (not by contract) for an animal. A "Good Samaritan" veterinarian may not be held liable for a bad result or a mistake.

Goose neck: Long, skinny neck.

Goose rump: Too steep a croup.

Goose-stepping: Movement characterized by exaggerated lift of the forelegs, similar to a hackney gait, but coupled with full extension of the front pasterns and feet before placing them in contact with the ground. The dog has an apparent good reach, but in fact the front foot contact with the ground is delayed. Incorrect in all breeds.

Gordie: Affectionate name for the Gordon setter.

Gordon setter: Black-and-tan gundog developed by the Scottish Duke of Gordon. Most heavily built of all the setters. They were developed for hunting upland game birds, like pheasant and quail. Daniel Webster imported the breed to America in 1842. Size: 23 to 27 inches, 45 to 80 pounds. Dogs from hunting lines tend to be smaller.

GR: (1) Golden retriever **(2)** Grain (in pharmacy).

Grade: In greyhound racing, the designation of how a dog rates in comparison to other greyhounds at the track. Grades range from Grade AA, down through Grades A, B, C, and D. Each time a greyhound wins, it advances one grade until reaching AA. Greyhounds are lowered in grade after posting three consecutive finishes of fourth or lower.

Grain: The seed of cereal plants.

Gram-negative: A classification of bacteria based upon their lack of retention of a certain stain in the laboratory. This laboratory staining method was developed by Hans Gram in 1884.

Gram-positive: A classification of bacteria based upon their uptake of a certain stain in the laboratory. The staining quality is based on the structure of the cell wall surrounding the bacteria. This structure of the cell wall influences which antibiotics will kill the bacteria.

Grand field champion: A coonhound field champion with three First Lines or First Trees in three Final Lines or Final Trees at three different trials with competition.

Grand mal seizure: Severe convulsive seizure, often accompanied by loss of bowel and bladder control, tongue swallowing, jaw snapping, feet paddling, and back arches.

Grand nite champion: A dog that has earned three first place wins as a Nite Champion in AKC licensed Nite Hunts.

Grand water race champion: A dog that has won three First Lines or First Trees in three Final Lines or Final Trees at three different water races with competition. At least one of the three wins must include both Final Line and Final Tree in the same event on the same date with competition. If a hound wins both First Line and First Tree in the Final Line or Final Tree in the same race, it counts as only one win toward a Grand Water Race Champion title.

Granulocyte: A kind of white blood cell.

Granuloma: A mass resulting from infection, irritation, or some unknown cause.

Granulomatous meningoencephalomyelitis (GME): A disease of the nervous system; the precise cause is unknown.

GRAS: "Generally regarded as safe."

Gravy: In dog-food labeling, liquid dressing containing several components, designed to add flavoring.

Gray: Unit of radiation resulting from exposure to X-rays.

Gray matter: Brain tissue that contains mainly cell bodies of neurons lacking myelin.

Gray wolf (*Canis lupus*): Species found in North America, Europe, Asia, and the Middle East.

Great Dane: Developed in Germany in the nineteenth century, although similar dogs appeared much earlier. Once used to hunt boar. Has a short fawn, brindle, black, or harlequin coat. Size: 120 to 150 pounds.

Great Pyrenees: Ancient breed native to the mountains between France and Spain. Used as a guard dog. Size: 25 to 32 inches, 85 to 100 pounds, with a long weather-resistant coat usually white or white marked with various shades of gray, red, or tan.

Great Swiss cattle dog: Greater Swiss mountain dog.

Greater Swiss mountain dog: A large, powerful dog resembling the Bernese mountain dog but with shorter hair.

Green Book: A list of all animal drug products that have been approved by the FDA for safety and effectiveness.

Green-broke: A dog recently trained to be steady to wing and shot.

Green foods: Barley grass, spirulina, alfalfa, wheat grass, and certain algae.

Greenstick fracture: An incomplete fracture that goes through only one side of the bone.

Greyfriar's Bobby: Edinburgh Skye terrier of the nineteenth century, famous for his loyalty to his master.

Greyhound: Ancient breed of hunting dog remarkable for its speed and eyesight. Size: 27 to

31 inches, 60 to 70 pounds, with a short, smooth coat of any color.

Greyhound Project: 261 Robbins Street, Milton, MA 02186. Telephone: (617) 333-4982, (617) 527-8842. An organization that promotes the adoption of retired racing dogs.

GRHRCH: Grand Hunting Retriever Champion. A UKC/HRC title denoting that a retriever has qualified in the annual HRC Grand event.

Griffon: Type of dog resembling a terrier.

Griffon Belge: Brussels griffon.

Griffon Bruxellois: Brussels griffon.

Griffon D'aArrêt à poil dur: Wirehaired pointing griffon.

Gripping: In sheepdog trials, when a dog unnecessarily bites the sheep.

Griseofulvin: Medication used to treat ringworm, a fungal infection of the skin involving fungi called dermatophytes. Griseofulvin is produced by Penicillium bacteria. Brand name: Fulvicin.

Grizzle: A roan pattern, usually a mixture of black, gray, or red.

Groenendael: Belgian sheepdog.

Grooming: A practice of brushing, clipping, and caring for the coat.

Gross energy: The total energy included in a food. Not all gross energy is usable by the animal.

Grosser Schweizer sennenhund: Greater Swiss mountain dog.

Ground pattern: A bird dog's way of covering the ground while hunting.

Group show: A show for dogs belonging to one of the seven AKC groups: hounds, sporting dogs, herding, non-sporting, toy, working, or terrier.

Growth-hormone-responsive dermatosis: A condition in which there are skin changes due to a lack of growth hormone (somatotropin), a hormone secreted by the pituitary gland that is necessary for hair growth and the maintenance of normal elasticity of the skin. Affected dogs have varying degrees of hair loss and darkening of the skin, but are otherwise healthy.

Gruff expression: A tough, hard expression.

GSD: German shepherd dog.

GSHP: German shorthaired pointer.

GSP: German shorthaired pointer.

GU: Genitourinary.

Guaranteed analysis: On commercial dog food labels, the minimum levels of nutrients in the food.

Guard dog: A dog used for sentry duty or to guard sheep.

Guard hairs: Stiff, longer hairs growing through the undercoat. They help keep water away from the dog's body.

Guide dog: A specially trained and licensed dog whose expertise allows it to guide its blind master, even into places from which dogs are normally excluded.

Gun barrel front: A front in which the forelegs and pasterns are straight, parallel, and vertical to the ground.

Gun shy: A dog that reacts negatively to gunfire.

Gun station: Location of one or more gunners in the field who throw or shoot a mark.

Gundog stake champion: A dog that has won first place in a stake that has been designated as an Open Gun Dog Championship stake.

Gundog stake: A field trial with more restricted range than an all-age stakes.

Gundog: (1) Dog trained to find and retrieve shot game. (2) A dog used more for hunting than for field trials.

Gunner: One who shoots or throws dead birds at a stake or field trial.

GWCH: Grand Water Race

champion. The title is prefixed to the dog's name.

GWP: German wirehaired pointer.

Gwyllgi: Legendary dog from Wales and parts of Great Britain. Also known as the Dog of Darkness, Mauthe Doog, or Barghest.

Gyp: In hunting hounds, a young female dog, usually one who has not been bred.

H

H and E: Hematoxylin and eosin (stain).

H+: (1) History (veterinary notation). (2) Hydrogen ion.

H1/4: Hindquarters (veterinary notation).

HAC: Hyperadrenocorticism.

Hacking: In field events, loud and repeated commands to a dog. Overhandling.

Hackles: Hairs on the neck and back that raise involuntarily in fright or anger.

Hackney: High-stepping front movement. Correct for a miniature pinscher, generally a fault in other breeds.

Hahnemann, Samuel: The founder of homeopathy.

Hair pore infection: See folliculitis.

Halitosis: Bad breath, often caused by periodontal or dental disease.

Hall's Heeler: Australian cattle dog.

Haloes: Dark pigmentation around or over eyes.

Halothane: An inhalant anesthetic with a quick recovery time.

Halti head collar: Nylon headpiece similar to the kind of halter used for foals. The point of control is under the chin.

Ham: Muscular development of the hind leg over the stifle.

Handler: One who takes the dog through its paces either in competition or in training. Some owners hire professional handlers for performance events.

Handler's draw or handler's show: A show that draws many professional handlers.

Hand-pluck: To pick out hairs with the fingers.

Hardiness: Ability to cope with stress and discomfort.

Hard-knuckled: Tight foot with prominent arches in each of the toes.

Hard-mouthed: In retrieving breeds, a dog that leaves tooth marks on the game, rendering it unfit for the table.

Hard pad: An old name for distemper, so called because the pads of the feet are thickened by the disease.

Hare foot: A foot in which the two center toes are considerably longer than the outer and inner toes.

Hare lip: Fissure of the upper lip.

Harking in: Joining the hound that declares the scent line left by prey.

Harlequin: Spotted color (black or blue on a white background); used for Great Danes.

Harrier: Small hound developed in antiquity. Size: 19 to 21 inches, 45 to 55 pounds, with a short, dense coat of any color.

Harvest mites: Parasites that appear in autumn and cause skin irritation. Also called chiggers or grain mites.

Haunch: Rump or buttock; the region rising above the hip.

Havanese: Ancient breed developed in the Mediterranean region. Easily trained; excels at obedience. Size: 8 to 12 inches, 7 to 11 pounds, with a long, soft, profuse coat in any color.

Haw: (1) Exposed third eyelid (nictitating membrane). (2) In sledding, a command to turn left.

Haw-eyed: Eyes with a good deal of conjunctival membrane visible (as in the bloodhound), due to the pouching lower eyelid from heavy, loose skin on the face.

Haw's syndrome: Protruding third eyelid.

Hazel: Light brown eye color.

HBB: Hit by bullet (veterinary notation).

HBC: Hit by car (veterinary notation).

HBT: Hit by truck (veterinary notation).

HC: AKC herding champion. The title is prefixed to the name.

HCH: Herding Champion. This AKC title is prefixed to the name.

HCl: Hydrochloride.

HCM: Hypertrophic cardiomyopathy.

HCT: (1) Hematocrit. (2) Herding Capable Tested (AHBA title).

HD: Hip dysplasia (veterinary notation). Sometimes CHD.

Head halter: A device similar to a horse's halter, in which the animal is controlled by the head instead of the neck.

Head shaking: Possible sign of ear infection, ear mites, and obstructions in the ear, or of allergies, bites, or wounds. Check the ears carefully.

Healing crisis: See aggravation.

Heart: Hollow, muscular organ that serves as a pump to move blood through the veins and arteries. Located near the center of the thoracic cavity.

Heart block: A condition in which the electrical impulses of the heart are not properly conducted from the atria (chambers that receive the blood) to the ventricles (chambers that pump the blood).

Heart disease: Can be detected by clinical signs, X-rays, ultrasound, or electrocardiogram findings. Most cases of heart disease are nonreversible.

Heart failure: Syndrome in which the heart no longer functions effectively. Fluid accumulation in the lungs or abdomen and a lack of blood to vital organs commonly accompany heart failure. Signs include coughing, breathing problems (especially during exercise), loss of weight, abdom-

inal distension, and weakness.

Heart murmur: Usually the earliest sign of a congenital heart disorder; it may appear before the dog exhibits any other symptoms. Often indicates a leaky heart valve.

Heart rate: The normal resting rate in adult dogs is 75 to 120 beats per minute. If consistently higher than 120, consult a veterinarian.

Heart-shaped ears: Ears like that of a Pekingese.

Heartworm (*Dirofilaria immitis*): Parasites, the larvae of which are carried by mosquitoes. They live in the heart (primarily the right side) and lungs, and they block vessels and damage tissues. The longer dogs have heartworm, the harder it is to treat. The condition is potentially fatal. Signs vary according to the number of worms present, stage of life cycle, and age and health of the dog.

Heat: Estrus. The period during which female dogs can mate.

Heatstroke: Increased body temperature due to muscle exertion combined with high environmental temperature and humidity, or by exposure to a super-heated environment like a parked car. Most commonly affects short-snouted breeds, such as Pekingese and pugs, which have short air passages that limit the ability of the body to expel heat by panting. This is an emergency situation that requires immediate treatment.

Heavy stock: In herding events, stock that requires a great deal of pressure from the dog in order to be moved.

Hecla Lava: Homeopathic remedy for generalized arthritis.

Heel: (1) A command to a dog to keep close beside its handler, usually on the left side. (2) Rear part of paw.

Heel free: When a dog heels without a leash.

Height: Usually the height of the dog at the shoulder.

Heimlich maneuver: A lifesaving technique to expel objects stuck in the throat. Stand behind the dog and wrap your arms around the lower abdomen, behind the ribcage. Lift the hindquarters, and squeeze the abdomen, giving a gentle shake. Small dogs can be lifted up completely; large dogs can be maneuvered like a wheelbarrow. Do not be afraid to use firm, even sharp pressure to expel the object.

Heinz bodies: Inclusions in the red blood cells resulting from oxidative injury to the hemoglobin.

Heinz body anemia: A hemolytic anemia resulting from oxidation of hemoglobin and formation of Heinz bodies. Commonly caused by eating onions.

Heinz Pet Products: Telephone: (800) 843-4008. Web site: www.naturesrecipe.com.

Helix: The external flap of the ear; the pinna.

Helminth: Parasitic worm, including nematodes, cestodes, and trematodes.

Hemangiosarcoma: Aggressive cancer of the blood vessels; tumors often appear in the spleen, liver, heart, and skin. Prognosis is poor.

Hematochezia: The presence of bright red blood in the bowel movements (feces).

Hematocrit: The ratio of red blood cell volume to the total blood volume. Also called packed cell volume.

Hematology: The study of blood.

Hematoma: Localized hemorrhage, bruise, or swelling, usually in the earflap.

Hematopoietic system: Blood-forming system that includes the bone marrow, which is located inside the bones. Three types of blood cells are made in the bone marrow: white blood cells that fight infection, red blood cells that carry oxygen, and platelets that are part of the blood-clotting system.

Hematopoietic tumor: Liquid tumor of the blood-forming elements.

Hematuria: Passing blood in the urine.

Heme: Part of hemoglobin, the oxygen-carrying molecules of the blood cells.

Hemicellulose: A group of branched-chain polysaccharides that help form the matrix of plant cells.

Hemivertebra: Partially formed, wedge-shaped vertebra. Often found in bulldogs, pugs, and Boston terriers.

Hemodialysis: A process used to remove waste products from the blood.

Hemoglobin: The substance in red blood cells that carries oxygen to the body.

Hemolysis: The breakdown of red blood cells.

Hemolytic anemia: Anemia (decrease in red blood cell count) resulting from the fragmentation of red blood cells.

Hemophilia: A sex-linked condition in which the blood lacks clotting factors, causing a strong tendency to bleed without stopping. Type A is due to a factor VIII deficiency; type B is due to a factor IX deficiency. Occurs almost exclusively in males.

Hemorrhage: Profuse bleeding, either internal or external.

Hemorrhagic diathesis: Disease syndrome in which spontaneous bleeding occurs.

Hemorrhagic enteritis: See hemorrhagic gastroenteritis.

Hemorrhagic gastroenteritis: Inflammatory disease of the stomach and intestinal tract, leading to a sudden onset of bloody diarrhea in a previously healthy dog. Vomiting, anorexia, and lethargy are also possible. Emergency condition; the exact cause of this disease is unknown.

Hemostat: A surgical instrument used to pinch small blood vessels to stop bleeding. It may also be used in nonsurgical procedures, such as plucking hair from the ear canals.

Heparin: Anticoagulant drug prescribed for conditions in which there is excessive clotting.

Hepatic: Relating to the liver.

Hepatic cirrhosis: Scar tissue on the liver that replaces normal cells.

Hepatic cysts: Cysts on the liver.

Hepatic encephalopathy: Neurological or behavioral disturbances related to decreased liver function and the resulting accumulation of ammonia in the brain.

Hepatic lipidosis: Abnormal, severe accumulation of fats in the liver. More clinically important in cats than in dogs.

Hepatitis: Inflammation of the liver, either chronic or infectious. Signs for infectious canine hepatitis are fever, lethargy, vomiting, depression, and anorexia. Severely affected dogs may have abdominal tenderness, increased thirst and urination, coughing, and bloody diarrhea. The disease can be fatal.

Hepatitis blue eye: Clouding of the cornea; it results from a viral infection that usually affects the liver, also possibly from a vaccine. Usually temporary.

Hepato-: Pertaining to the liver.

Hepatocytes: Liver cells.

Hepatomegaly: Enlargement of the liver.

Hepatopathy: Any disease of the liver.

Herding Advanced Course A (ducks, sheep, cattle): Title that became available after January 1, 2000. Three qualifying scores in the Advanced Course A classes using ducks (HXAd), sheep (HXAs), or cattle (HXAc) from three different judges at three different trials.

Herding Advanced Course B (ducks, sheep, cattle): Title that became available after January 1, 2000. Three qualifying scores in the Advanced Course B classes using ducks (HXBd), sheep (HXBs), or cattle (HXBc) from three different judges at three different trials.

Herding Advanced Course C (sheep): Title that became available after January 1, 2000. Three qualifying scores in the Advanced Course C classes using sheep (HIAs) from three different judges at three different trials

Herding Champion: A dog who has earned fifteen points with at least two firsts carrying championship points, one of which must be for three or more points.

Herding Excellent: Title not available after January 1, 2000. Three qualifying scores in the Advanced classes from three different judges at three different trials.

Herding Group: An AKC group traditionally used to herd livestock.

Herding Intermediate: Title awarded to a dog that scored three qualifying scores in the Intermediate classes from three different judges at three different trials.

Herding Intermediate Course A: (ducks, sheep, cattle): Three qualifying scores in the Intermediate Course A classes using ducks (HIAd), sheep (HIAs), or cattle (HIAc) from three different judges at three different trials.

Herding Intermediate Course B (ducks, sheep, cattle): Three qualifying scores in the Intermediate Course B classes using ducks (HIBd), sheep (HIBs), or cattle (HIBc) from three different judges at three different trials.

Herding Intermediate Course C (sheep): Three qualifying scores in the Intermediate Course C classes using sheep (HICs) from three different judges at three different trials.

Herding Started: Three qualifying scores in the Started classes from three different judges at three different trials. Title not available after January 1, 2000.

Herding Started Course A (ducks, sheep, cattle): Title that became available after January 1, 2000. Three qualifying scores in the Started Course A classes using ducks (HSAd), sheep (HSAs), or cattle (HSAc) from three different judges at three different trials.

Herding Started Course B (ducks, sheep, cattle): Title that became available after January 1, 2000. Three qualifying scores in the Started Course B classes using ducks (HSBd), sheep (HSBs), or cattle (HSBc) from three different judges at three different trials.

Herding Started Course C (sheep): Title that became available after January 1, 2000. Three qualifying scores in the Started Course C classes using sheep (HSCs) from three different judges at three different trials.

Herding Tested: A dog must qualify twice under two different judges. Dog may qualify twice in one day at the same event, provided that it is judged by different judges.

Hereditary: A condition present at birth that can be traced back to ancestors.

Hereditary disorder: Condition passed down genetically through the generations.

Heritability: An estimate of how much of a role environmental factors play in the expression of the inherited genes.

Hernia: A protrusion of organs through a weak spot or abnormal opening, usually in the abdominal or groin area. Some puppies are born with hernias.

Herniated disk: Rupture of a spinal disk.

Herring gutted: (1) Gradual slope from a rather shallow chest to the tuck up. **(2)** Flat-sided.

Heterochromia: Irises of two different colors.

Heteropathy: A homeopathic term for allopathy or conventional medicine.

Heterozygote: An organism receiving two different alleles at a given genetic locus.

Heterozygous: Cell having two different genes for the same characteristic.

Hgb: Hemoglobin.

HGE: Hemorrhagic gastroenteritis.

HI: (1) Hemagglutination inhibition. **(2)** Herding Intermediate. Title follows the dog's name. Title not available after January 1, 2000.

HIAdsc: Herding Intermediate Course A (ducks, sheep, cattle). Title follows the dog's name. Title became available after January 1, 2000.

Hiatal hernia: A condition where the stomach obtrudes partially into the chest cavity through a hole in the diaphragm. Signs include regurgitation, hypersalivaton, and dyspnea.

HIBdsc: Herding Intermediate Course B (ducks, sheep cattle). Title follows the dog's name. Title became available after January 1, 2000.

HICs: Herding Intermediate Course C. Title follows the dog's name. Title became available after January 1, 2000.

Hie-on: A command to a bird dog to go out farther ahead, usually to correct a dog that seems to pottering.

High-dose dexamethasone suppression (HDDS) test: A test to distinguish between cases of adrenal-dependant and pi-tuitary-dependent HAC.

High in rear: A dog higher at the croup than at the withers.

High-set ears: Ears perched high on the skull.

High-stationed: A tall, long, legged, rangy dog.

High titer vaccine: A modified live vaccine that contains a higher number of virus particles than the average vaccine. High titer vaccines can generally elicit an immune system response in young animals that have a maternal antibody level that would prevent them from responding to an average vaccine.

Hike: The command to sledding dogs to move forward. "Mush!" in movie language.

Hill's Pet Nutrition: Telephone: (800) 445-5777. Web site: www.sciencediet.com.

Him and Her: Lyndon Johnson's beagles.

Hip dysplasia: A chronic malformation of the hip joint, resulting in an unstable joint that allows excess movement, followed by calcium deposits, inflammation, pain, and degeneration of the hip socket tissues. Dogs are not born with this condition; it develops as a dog grows, but can manifest itself as early as four months. Most common in large breeds.

Histamine: Histamine is an inflammatory biochemical that causes skin redness, swelling, pain, increased heart rate, and blood pressure drop when it binds to one of many "H1" receptors throughout the body.

Histiocyte: Large phagocytic cell. Also called a macrophage.

Histiocytoma: Raised, reddish, "buttons" of rough tissue. Most disappear without treatment; however, these tumors need to be examined by a veterinarian. Usually occur in young dogs.

Histiocytosis: The appearance of histiocytes in the blood; this is usually a sign of inflammation and may indicate a rapidly progressing cancer.

Histoplasmosis: Fungal lung disease causing mild respiratory problems. Results from inhaling organisms found in the soil (mostly in the eastern United States and midwestern United States).

HIT: High in Trial winning.

HL: Hind legs (veterinary notation).

Hobby breeder: A breeder who does not rely on dog-breeding for a living, and who breeds dogs for the love of the breed.

Hock: The true heel of the dog; the tarsus.

Hocking out: Hocks turned out.

Hocks well let down: Hock joints close to the ground.

HOD: Hypertrophic osteodystrophy.

Hokkaido: Also called the Ainu dog, this is the most ancient of the Japanese breeds. Originally developed to hunt bears.

Holders: Canine teeth.

Hold hard: In foxhunting, a command from the Huntsman or Whip for the riders to stop immediately.

Holding blind: In retriever field trials, a screen placed to hide a retired gun or to prevent a dog from viewing a test before he has run.

Holding pen: In herding events, the enclosure outside the course where the stock are kept before and after their use in the trial.

Holistic: Study of the whole body and mind.

Holt: Fox or other animal den.

Homeopathic remedy: In homeopathy, a medicine prepared according to homeopathic methods—succussion and dilution.

Homeopathy: Treating disease with small doses of substances that, in large doses, can cause symptoms similar to the disease.

Homeostasis: Maintenance of stability in the body's internal environment.

Homologous: Corresponding parts in a different species.

Homozygote: An organism receiving two identical alleles at a given genetic locus.

Homozygous: Presence of identical genes (alleles) at a given locus on homologous chromosomes. Thus the cell would have two sets of identical genes for a specific characteristic.

Honor: In pointing breed events, where a second dog points at a dog already pointing at a bird.

Honorable scars: Scars from injuries received during work.

Hooded ears: Upright ear whose edges curve forward and somewhat towards each other, as in the basenji.

Hook tail: A tail that is carried down but that curves up on the end.

Hookworm: Small ($\frac{1}{4}$ to $\frac{1}{2}$ inch), thin parasites (*Ancylostoma uncinaria* and other genera) of the small intestine. They hook onto the intestinal wall and can consume a great deal of blood. Can cause black, tarry stools. Can also affect human beings.

Hookworm dermatitis: Hookworm larvae infesting the skin, resulting in inflammation.

Horary point: In acupuncture, a point along the meridian matching one of the five traditional Chinese elements. Also called element points.

Horizontal tail: Straight-out tail carriage typical of the bull terrier. A bee-sting tail.

Hormone: A substance produced by an endocrine organ that moves around the body in the blood, affecting organs distant from its point of origin.

Horn: Toenail.

Horner's syndrome: Collection of facial symptoms due to damage to the sympathetic portion of the involuntary nerve supply.

Horse coat: Very short, harsh coat, standing off from the body and lying flatter on the limbs.

Horseshoe front: A front with straight forelegs wider apart at the chest, as in the Bedlington terrier.

Host: Animal in which a parasite lives.

Host-specific parasite: Parasite that lives upon only one host.

Hot nose: Term used to describe a dog that will work only a fresh track that was recently made.

Hot spot: A bald, circular patch of red and inflamed skin. It is a secondary reaction to another condition, such a fleabite or tight knot of hair. Hot spots need to be clipped, cleaned, and dried. Antibiotics are sometimes necessary. See acute moist dermatitis.

Hound: A dog that pursues game by sight or scent. Hounds include dachshunds, coonhounds, and Afghans.

Hound coat: A hard, short/ medium-length coat.

Hound-colored or hound-marked: Black, brown, and tan with a saddle.

Hound fashion tail carriage: Tail carried at about 90 degrees to the back when the dog is moving.

Hound glove: A mitt with short bristles, used to a give a "polish" to short-haired dogs.

Housebreaking: Training a dog to eliminate outside.

House soiling: Inappropriate elimination that can be caused by any one or a combination of the following: incorrect housetraining or no housetraining, separation anxiety, marking behavior, submissive behavior, urinary tract infection, sickness, incontinence caused by age.

Hovawart: German breed used for guarding. Can be gold, or black and gold.

HQ: Hindquarters.

HR: (1) Hunting Retriever, a UKC title. **(2)** Heart rate (veterinary notation).

HRC: Hunting Retriever Club.

HRCH: Hunting Retriever Champion, a UKC Hunt title.

HS: Herding Started. This title not available after January 1, 2000. Title follows the dog's name.

HSAdsc: Herding Started Course A (ducks, sheep, cattle). Title became available after January 1, 2000. Title follows the dog's name.

HSBdsc: Herding Started Course B (ducks, sheep, cattle). Title became available after January 1, 2000. Title follows the dog's name.

HSCs: Herding Started Course C (sheep). Title became available after January 1, 2000.

HSUS: Humane Society of the United States.

HSV: Herpes simplex virus.

HT: Herding tested. Title follows the dog's name.

HTD1: Herding trial dog, first level (AHBA title).

HTD2: Herding trial dog, second level (AHBA title).

HTD3: Herding trial dog, third level (AHBA title).

Hucklebones: Tops of the hip bones.

Humane: Showing kindness and compassion.

Humane Society of the United States (HSUS): 2100 L Street, NW, Washington DC 20037.

Humerus: Largest bone in the front legs.

Humor: Certain fluid materials in the body (e.g., aqueous and vitreous humor).

Humoral immunity: The immunity that is the result of antibody production by B cells.

Hump back: Camel back.

Hund: German word for "dog."

Hungarian kuvasz: Kuvasz.

Hungarian pointer: Vizsla.

Hungarian puli: Puli.

Hungarian vizsla: Vizsla.

Hungarian water dog: Puli.

Huntaway: A barking sheepdog used in New Zealand; not a specific breed, but usually an Airedale cross. Unlike most sheepdogs, this dog is used to drive flocks away from the shepherd, rather than bringing them back in.

Hunter: A dog with perfect construction for the hunt, usually a relatively short body coupled with maximum length of stride.

Hunting dead: The process of a retriever finding a killed bird.

Hunting Retriever Club, Inc.: United Kennel Club's hunt test organization.

Hunting test: A noncompetitive event conducted under AKC rules. There are three levels of increasing difficulty (Junior, Senior, and Master).

Hup: Command meaning either "sit" (used by hunters or field trailers) or "jump" (used by handlers in agility).

Husky: A term, derived from derogatory slang referring to Eskimos, for any of several northern breeds.

HX: (1) Herding Excellent. This title not available after January1, 2000. Title follows the dog's name. **(2)** History (veterinary notation).

HXAdsc: Herding Advanced Course A (ducks, sheep, cattle). Title follows the dog's name.

HXBdsc: Herding Advanced Course B (ducks, sheep, cattle): Title follows the dog's name.

HXCs: Herding Advanced Course C (sheep): Title follows the dog's name.

Hybrid: Offspring that result from breeding animals of different varieties or breeds.

Hybrid vigor: Enhanced health as a result of increased numbers of heterozygous gene pairs.

Hydrocephalus: The accumulation of fluid in the ventricles of the brain and spinal cord, causing the head to become large and dome-shaped. Many toy breeds have a degree of hydrocephalus that is considered normal for that breed. Severe hydrocephalous damages brain tissue.

Hydrochloride: Elements of hydrochloric acid (HCl), often added to a drug or nutritional supplement to make it more water-soluble. The added hydrochloride does not otherwise affect what it is added to.

Hydrocodone: Narcotic cough suppressant prescribed for dry, non-productive cough.

Hydrocortisone: Short-acting (eight to twelve hours) glucocorticoid.

Hydrogen peroxide: Topical antiseptic and emetic, used to induce vomiting in poisoning cases. Usually available as a 3 percent solution.

Hydrolysis: Chemical reaction that splits a drug molecule or other compound by the addition of water.

Hydrophobia: An antiquated term for rabies. Literally, "fear of water."

Hydroxyapatite: An inorganic compound made of calcium and phosphorous, found in the matrix of teeth and bones.

Hydroxyzine: Antihistamine used to treat skin allergies.

Hygroma: A thick-walled, fluid-filled sac, usually appearing on the elbows.

Hyper-: Prefix denoting "abnormally high."

Hyperadrenocorticism: An excess production of cortisol. Cushing's disease.

Hypercalcemia: An abnormally high concentration of calcium in the blood.

Hyperesthesia: Abnormal sensitivity to touch, pain, or other sensory stimuli.

Hyperextension of the hock: To extend the hock so that the hock angle is greater than normal.

Hyperglycemia: Elevated levels of sugar in the blood.

Hypericum: Homeopathic remedy for tender areas that resulted from animal bites.

Hyperkalemia: Excess potassium in the blood.

Hyperkeratosis: Excess growth in the outer layer of the skin.

Hyperlipidemia: Elevated concentrations of triglycerides or cholesterol in the plasma of fasted dogs.

Hyperparathyroidism: Hyperactivity in one of the four parathyroid glands located in the dog's neck.

Hyperphagia: Overeating.

Hyperphosphatemia: Excess phosphorus in the blood.

Hyperplasia: Increase in cell number; thickening or enlargement of a tissue.

Hyperreactive: Producing an exaggerated, or greater than normal, response to a stimulus.

Hypersensitivity: An exaggerated immune response.

Hypersialism (hypersialosis): Overproduction of saliva. Drooling.

HyperT4: Hyperthyroidism (veterinary notation).

Hypertension: Persistently high blood pressure.

Hyperthermia: Abnormally elevated body temperature.

Hyperthyroidism: Overactive functioning of the thyroid gland.

Hypertrophic: A thickening or enlargement of an organism.

Hypertrophic arthritis: A condition characterized by extra growth or spurs on the joints.

Hypertrophic cardiomyopathy: An unusual form cardiomyopathy in which there is a great increase in the mass of the heart muscle in the ventricles, plus decrease in chamber size. No breed predisposition has been identified.

Hypertrophic osteodystrophy (HOD): Inflammation of the growth plates, or "bone scurvy," most often seen in giant breeds, characterized by pain and swelling around the growth plates of the long bones. Possibly caused by oversupplementation of vitamin D.

Hypertrophy: Increased size of an organ or cell, often due to excessive use.

Hyperventilation: An increase in the rate and/or depth of respiration such that the body loses too much carbon dioxide.

Hypervitaminosis A: Condition caused by too much vitamin A. Less common in dogs than in cats and reptiles.

Hypo-: Decreased, deficiency, lower than normal.

Hypoadrenocorticism: Addison's disease.

Hypoallergenic diet: Diet designed to have very low levels of potential allergy-causing foods.

Hypoestrinism: Estrogen deficiency, found mostly in spayed females.

Hypoglycemia: Low blood sugar (low blood glucose level). It can be caused by overproduction of insulin or too much exercise if the dog is not fit. Hypoglycemia can cause weakness, incoordination, and coma, especially in young puppies.

Hypokalemia: Abnormally low potassium concentration in the blood.

Hypomyelination: Abnormally low amount of myelin in peripheral nerves, resulting in weakness of limbs.

Hypophosphatemia: Decreased phosphorous concentration in the blood.

Hypophysis: Pituitary gland.

Hypoplasia: Inadequate development of tissue.

Hypoproteinemia: Low protein in the blood, due to poor diet, poor digestion, or absorption of dietary protein in the intestines, or loss of protein through urine or feces.

Hyposensitization: A method of treating allergies using injections of diluted allergens. Also called antigen therapy or allergy shots.

Hypospadias: Abnormal location of the male urinary orifice.

HypoT4: Hypothyroidism (veterinary notation).

Hypotension: Persistent low blood pressure.

Hypothalamus: A portion of the brain that controls part of the pituitary gland as well as many of the autonomic functions of the body.

Hypothermia: Abnormally low body temperature, most likely to occur when a dog is wet. Holistic treatment includes aconite and arnica together.

Hypothyroidism: Decreased thyroid activity resulting in decreased metabolic activity, probably the most commonly diagnosed endocrine disease in dogs. It is generally considered to be an autoimmune disease, in which the dog forms antibodies against its own thyroid gland. It has a great many (and variable) signs. Breeds with increased incidence of hypothyroidism include the Afghan hound, Airedale terrier, boxer, Chinese shar pei, chow chow, cocker spaniel, dachshund, Doberman pinscher, bulldog, golden retriever, Great Dane, Irish setter, and miniature schnauzer.

Hypovitaminosis A: A condition produced from insufficient amounts of vitamin A. Less common in dogs than in birds and retiles.

Hypoxia: A deficiency of oxygen in the tissues.

I

I: (1) Incisor, followed by a number to indicate which one (veterinary notation). **(2)** Chemical symbol for iodine.

IA: Intra-arterial.

Iams Dog Food Company: Telephone: (800) 525-4267. Web site: www.iams.com.

Iatrogenic: Caused by the veterinarian, or as side effect of medication.

IBD: Inflammatory bowel disease.

Ibizan hound: May have been developed in ancient Egypt, as a statue of a similar dog was found in Tutankhamen's tomb. Size: 22 to 27 inches, 45 to 50 pounds. Comes in short and wirehaired varieties. Red or white or the two colors in combination.

IC: Intracardiac.

Iceland sheepdog: Spitz breed used as a sheepdog.

ICH: Infectious canine hepatitis.

Ichthyosis: A congenital condition that produces rough, scaly skin that worsens with age.

Icterus: Jaundice (an abnormal yellow color) of the skin and mucous membranes, due to accumulation of pigments normally metabolized by the liver.

Ictus: The seizure in epilepsy, characterized by sudden increase in tone of all muscle groups.

ID: (1) Intradermal. **(2)** Identification.

I/D: Interdigital (veterinary notation).

IDDM: Insulin-dependent diabetes mellitus (IDDM): A form of diabetes in which so little insulin is produced that supplemental insulin must be given for the animal to live. Also called Type I diabetes mellitus.

Idiopathic: Self-originated or of unknown cause.

Idiopathic disease: A disease for which there is no known cause.

Idiopathic epilepsy: Seizures of no known cause. Sometimes called inherited epilepsy.

Idiopathic vestibular syndrome: Inflammation of the inner ear, where balance is regulated. Cause is uncertain.

Idiosyncratic drug reaction: Unusual or unexpected reaction to a drug.

Iditarod: A Gold Rush city of Alaska; also the 1,049-mile sled race from Anchorage to Nome each March.

IDST: Intradermal skin test.

IFN: Interferon.

Ig: Immunoglobulin (with class following: A, D, E, G, M).

IgA: Class of antibody present in secretions such as saliva.

IgA deficiency: Immune system deficiency, resulting in respiratory, skin, and ear infections.

Igloo: Wire fox terrier belonging to Admiral Richard Byrd. The dog flew with him over both the North and South poles.

IGR: Insect growth regulator.

IHA: Indirect hemagglutination antibody.

iid: Once a day (veterinary notation).

Ileum: Distal part of the small intestine. Not to be confused with ilium.

Ileus: A condition in which there is an absence of muscular contractions of the intestine that normally move the food through the system; can result in an intestinal obstruction.

Ilium: One of the three bony components of the pelvic girdle. Not to be confused with ileum.

Ill dog: One that frequently fights with other dogs. Used in scent hound circles.

ILP: Indefinite listing privilege.

IM: Intramuscular.

IMHA: Autoimmune hemolytic anemia.

Imidacloprid: Pesticide medication (Advantage) used to prevent and treat flea infestations.

Immune-mediated: When the immune system attacks normal parts of the body, such as red blood cells. A condition caused by an over-reaction of the nervous system.

Immune-mediated hemolytic anemia (IMHA): Anemia resulting from immune-mediated destruction of the red blood cells.

Immune system: The body's defense system that recognizes infectious agents and other foreign compounds and works to destroy them.

Immunization: An injection of vaccination serum to provide protection from a disease.

Immunodeficiency: Reduced function of the immune system of an animal, making it more susceptible to infectious disease.

Immunoglobulin A (IgA): First line of defense of the immune system.

Immunoglobulins: Class of proteins including antibodies.

Immunostimulant: A compound that stimulates the immune system to work more effectively to kill bacteria, viruses, or cancer cells.

Immunosuppressant: Substance that reduces the function of the immune system of an animal.

Immunosuppressed: Referring to a diminished immune system responsiveness.

Imperforate lacrimal punctum: Watering of the eyes, due to malformed duct.

Impetigo: Also known as "puppy pyoderma" or "puppy acne." Characterized by white pimples on the chin and abdomen. Common in toy and miniature poodles.

Impounding officer: An agent of the government authorized to take control of abandoned or abused animals.

Impr: Improved (veterinary notation).

IN: Intranasal.

Inappetence: Loss of the appetite.

Inbreeding: The mating of closely related animals, such as mother and son or brother and sister.

Incisors: The six upper and six lower front teeth between the canines.

Incontinence: Involuntary passing of urine or feces.

Incoordination: Staggering.

Incubation period: The time between infection and the onset of disease signs.

Indefinite listing privilege: AKC registration for obviously purebred dogs who have no proof of breeding. Such a listing allows dogs to compete in most AKC events with the exception of conformation.

Indent: In retriever trials, a term used to identify the placement of a shorter mark in relation to the other marks in the field.

Index of bone: Circumference of metacarpals ×100 divided by height.

Index of format: Oblique length of dog ×100 divided by height at withers.

Index of leg height: Measure of forearm to elbow ×100 divided by height at withers.

Indian dog: In sledding, an Alaskan husky from a Native American village.

Indole: A compound produced by the decomposition of tryptophan in the intestine. Indole has a role in giving feces its odor.

Indolent ulcer: Cloudy patch on the eye not caused by injury. Also called refractory ulcer. Common in boxers.

Inductive training: Positive reinforcement.

Inf: (1) Inferior (veterinary notation). (2) Infection (veterinary notation).

Infection: Multiplication of organisms such as bacteria within the body, usually leading to disease.

Infectious: Capable of being spread from one animal to another.

Infectious agents: Agents that cause disease.

Infectious canine hepatitis (CAV-I): Also called canine adenovirus. A highly contagious, but rare, viral disease. Most dogs are vaccinated against it as part of routine care.

Infectious tracheobronchitis: Kennel cough, a highly contagious disease that can spread rapidly through a kennel.

Infestation: Invasion of parasites.

Infield: In greyhound racing, the area surrounded by the oval track.

Inflamed eyelids: See blepharitis.

Inflammation: Redness and swelling, often in response to trauma or infection.

Inflammatory bowel disease (IBD): A special type of enteritis, characterized by an increase in a certain type of inflammatory cell.

Inflammatory bowel syndrome: General term referring to chronic inflammation of the digestive tract.

Inflammatory carcinoma: Tumor characterized by aggressive growth, severe tissue swelling, and discoloration.

Information panel: Part of the dog-food label that includes the guaranteed analysis, list of ingredients, nutritional adequacy statement, feeding guidelines, and manufacturer information.

Ingest: Eat, devour.

Ingredient list: On commercial foods, the list of components, usually listed from the highest concentration to the lowest.

Inguinal: Pertaining to the groin region.

Inguinal hernia: A protrusion of abdominal contents through the inguinal canal. Appears as a lump just beneath the skin located in the groin (upper inner thigh) area. Often more serious than an umbilical hernia; should be surgically repaired as soon as detected.

Inhalant allergic dermatitis: Canine atopic dermatitis; atopy.

Inj: Injection (veterinary notation).

Insect growth regulator (IGR): Substance designed to prevent the larva or egg from developing into an adult. Used for flea control.

Insect stings: Usually cause painful swelling at the site of the sting or bite.

Insoluble carbohydrate: Fiber that resists enzymatic digestion in the small intestine.

Institute for Genetic Disease Control: An open registry reporting orthopedic and ophthalmologic evaluation reports, tumor, epilepsy, heart registry, and some other breed-specific health information. Web site: www.vetmed.ucdavis.edu/gdc/gdc.html.

Insulin: Hormone that regulates blood glucose levels, prescribed for diabetes mellitus.

Insulin-dependent diabetes mellitus (IDDM): Type of diabetes that can be controlled with insulin.

Insulinoma: Insulin-producing tumor of the pancreas; the increased production and blood level of insulin resulting from these tumors can cause low blood sugar (hypoglycemia).

Int: Internal (veterinary notation).

Integument: Skin.

Integumentary system: This system includes the skin and fur. The skin protects the underlying organs, while the hair helps insulate against heat loss.

Intensity: The rigidity of a dog frozen on point. Staunchness.

Interbreeding: Mating of dogs of different breeds.

Interdigital: Between the toes.

Interference: In field events, when a dog impedes, pays too much attention to, or hinders his bracemate.

Intermediate exercise: Exercise that lasts a few minutes to a few hours.

Intermediate host: Animal upon which a parasite passes some or all of its larval stages.

International Association for Veterinary Homeopathy: 334 Knollwood Lane, Woodstock, GA 30188. Telephone: (404) 516-5954.

International Disc Dog Handlers Association: 1690 Julius Bridge Road, Ball Ground, GA 30107. Telephone: (770) 735-6200. Web site: www.iddha.com.

International Foundation for Homeopathy: 2366 Eastlake Avenue E., Suite 301, Seattle, WA 98102. Telephone: (206) 324-8230.

International Sled Dog Racing Association. Web site: www.isdra.org.

International Veterinary Acupuncture Society (IVAS):

Nonprofit organization dedicated to promoting excellence in the practice of veterinary acupuncture as an integral part of the total veterinary health-care delivery system. IVAS seeks to integrate veterinary acupuncture and the practice of western veterinary science. It runs educational programs and an accreditation examination. P.O. Box 271395, Ft. Collins, CO 80527-1395. Telephone: (970) 266-0666. Web site: www.ivas.org/main.cfm.

International Weight Pull Association: A nonprofit association that promotes the sport of dog pulling through well-organized, sanctioned events. 1406 East Sterns Road, Erie, MI 48133. Telephone: (734) 848-8636. Web site: www.iwpa.net.

Interstitial: Between parts or within the spaces of tissue.

Intervertebral disk disease (IVDD): Displacement of the center of a vertebral disk, resulting in pain and often paralysis. Most common in dachshunds, bassets, and beagles.

Intervertebral disks: Soft, cartilaginous structures between the spinal vertebrae.

Intestine: The gut, whose function is to absorb nutrients and water and to eliminate wastes. Includes the small intestine, large intestine, colon, and rectum.

Intra-arterial: Injection into an artery.

Intracellular: Within the cell.

Intralesional: Inside a lesion or sore.

Intramuscular: Into the muscle.

Intranasal: Through the nose.

Intraocular: Within the eye.

Intraperitoneal: (1) Within the peritoneal cavity. (2) An injection, usually of antibiotics, directly into the peritoneal cavity.

Intrauterine: (1) Within the uterus. (2) Occurring in the uterus before birth.

Intravenous fluids: Fluids given via a catheter directly into a vein.

Intravenous pyelogram (IVP): An X-ray to study the kidney, bladder, and uterus after injection of a contrast medium.

Intussusception: A life-threatening condition in which the intestine telescopes on itself, causing a blockage.

In utero: In the uterus; before birth.

Involution: (1) The return of a reproduction organ to normal after delivery. (2) Degeneration associated with aging.

Iodine/Iodide: (1) Disinfectant and antiseptic. (2) A nutrient required for thyroid function.

Iodum: A homeopathic remedy for a variety of conditions, especially glandular conditions.

IOP: Intraocular pressure.

IP: Intraperitoneal injection.

Ipecac: (1) An emetic. (2) Homeopathic remedy prescribed for diarrhea.

Iris: The flat, colored membrane within the eye.

Iris coloboma: Pits in the iris of the eye.

Iris cyst: Cyst located on the iris, characterized by small dark spots that are not firmly attached.

Iris versicolor: A homeopathic remedy for diabetes mellitus and pancreatitis.

Irish: A color pattern term, referring to a dog with white chest and white on face, feet, neck, and tail tip. Found in many breeds, from Siberian huskies to Great Danes.

Irish blue terrier: Kerry blue terrier.

Irish red-and-white setter: A red-and-white version of the Irish setter, recognized by the Kennel Club in the UK.

Irish red terrier: Irish terrier.

Irish setter: Silky-coated, solid red gundog; oldest of the setting breeds. Origin: nineteenth-century Ireland. Size: 25 to 27 inches, 60 to 70 pounds.

Irish terrier: May be the oldest of the terriers. Used to hunt vermin and even retrieve in water. Size: 18 inches, 25 to 27 pounds. Usually a solid color in some shade of red or wheaten.

Irish water spaniel: Tallest of the spaniels, this ancient breed is remarkable for its solid liver-colored coat of tight curls. Size: 21 to 24 inches, 45 to 65 pounds.

Irish wolfhound: Tall, rangy sight hound of ancient origin. Size: 30 to 35 inches, often weighing 120 pounds or more. The dogs are often gray but come in many colors.

Iritis: Inflammation of the iris.

Iron: Mineral necessary for the formation of red blood cells, the circulation of oxygen to the tissues, and the metabolism of sugar to make energy. Found in liver, meat, and soybeans.

Irregular bite: A bite in which some of the incisors have erupted abnormally.

Irritable bowel syndrome: Soft, watery feces, often with mucus. Associated with stress. See colitis.

Isabella: Fawn or light color.

Ischial tuberosity: The rear of the pelvis.

Ischium: The rearmost hipbone.

ISDRA: International Sled Dog Racing Association.

Islets of Langerhans: Endocrine pancreas that secretes insulin.

Isoflurane: Anesthetic gas with a rapid recovery. A good anesthetic for older dogs.

Isopathy: In homeopathy, treatment of disease by the identical agent of the disease.

Italian greyhound: A toy version of the greyhound, developed in antiquity. Size: 13 to 15 inches, 10 to 11 pounds.

Italian spinone: Spinone Italiano.

Iterative process: Repetitive process.

-itis: A suffix denoting "inflammation of."

Itraconazole: Antifungal medication prescribed for deep (systemic) fungal infections, such as those caused by ringworm and Candida (yeast).

IU: International units. A measure of the effectiveness of a preparation rather than the actual weight. Often used with fat-soluble vitamins.

IV: Intravenous; an injection given directly into a vein.

IVAS: International Veterinary Acupuncture Society.

IVD: Intervertebral disk.

IVDD: Intervertebral disk disease.

Ivermectin: Medication (Heartguard and other products) to provide monthly protection against heartworm and other kinds of worms, including most intestinal worms (except tapeworm). It is also effective against most mites, and some lice. It is not effective against fleas, ticks, flies, or flukes. It is effective against larval heartworms (the "microfilariae" that circulate in the blood) but not against adult heartworms (which live in the heart and pulmonary arteries). This drug should not be used on collies, Old English sheepdogs, or related breeds, as they may show fatal interactions with it.

IVP: Intravenous pyelogram.

J

Jabot: The apron of the schipperke.

Jackal: Group of wild canids comprising four separate species: the gold jackal (*Canis aureus*), the black-backed (*Canis mesomelas*), the simien (*Canis simiensis*), and the side-striped (*Canis adustus*).

Jacket: Coat.

Jackpot: In dog training, a huge reward given after a tremendous effort.

Jack Russell terrier: Parson Russell terrier.

Jamthund: Also known as the Swedish elkhound; an ancient hunting breed.

Japanese Akita: Akita.

Japanese chin: Despite the name, this breed originated in China. It was once the court dog of Japan. Size: 8 to 11 inches, about 7 pounds with an abundant black-and-white or red-and-white silky coat. May have tan points.

Japanese small-size dog: Shiba inu.

Japanese spaniel: Japanese chin.

JAR: "Just ain't right" (veterinary notation).

Jasper: Color patches, usually red, brown, or yellow.

Jaundice: Yellow skin or mucous membranes, due to the accumulation of abnormal amounts of bilirubin. Jaundice is seen in non-haired parts of the body: white parts of the eyes, inside the mouth and ears, and on the belly. Also called icterus.

JC: Junior Courser (AKC suffix).

JE: Junior Earthdog (AKC suffix).

Jejunum: The middle portion of the small intestine that extends beyond the duodenum to the ileum. It is the longest part of the small intestinal tract.

Jewel eye: Whole eye tinged with red. Also walleye.

JH: Junior Hunter (AKC suffix).

JHD: Junior Herd Dog (AHBA title).

Jindo: Aboriginal wild dog from Jindo Island in Korea; it is internationally protected as a natural treasure. Also known as the Chindo, or Jindo Gae.

Jip: Mongrel owned by Abraham Lincoln, who had found the dog shivering in the snow on a battlefield.

JM: Jumpers Master (USDAA title).

Joint capsule: Sometimes called the synovial sac, the joint capsule is a sealed fibrous structure that contains the end of the bone and its cartilage. The joint capsule helps stabilize the joint and keeps the cartilage bathed in synovial fluid. The outside of the capsule consists of ligaments that anchor the bone.

Joint fluid analysis: Examination of the lubricating fluid from a joint.

Joint laxity: A term that refers to the looseness of a joint.

Jowls: Flesh of lips and jaws.

Jt: Joint (veterinary notation).

Judge: Person designated to pick the winner in a dog show. To become an AKC judge, the applicant must have at least ten years experience in a breed, have bred four litters, and have finished two champion dogs. In addition, they must have had "practice" by judging matches and sweepstakes and have been a steward at several shows. They must pass an interview and, finally, be approved by the AKC.

Judging schedule: A brief publication offered by the superintendent or show secretary that lists when and where each breed will be judged that day, and by whom.

Jugular: A large vein on the bottom surface of the neck that may be used to collect blood samples or to place catheters.

Junior: A person between the ages of ten and eighteen who competes with other juniors of similar age/experience levels in exhibiting his or her dog-handling skills, ring conduct, and sportsmanship.

Junior Courser: A hound running alone shall receive certification from a judge on one date, and a second certification from a different judge at a later date, stating that the hound completed a 600-yard course with a minimum of four turns. The hound must complete the course with enthusiasm and without interruption. The two runs can be on the same date at or in conjunction with a National Breed Specialty.

Junior Earthdog: A dog must

have a record of having qualified in the Junior Earthdog test in two AKC licensed or member club tests under two different judges.

Junior handling: Competitive classes in which Juniors exhibit their handling skills. The AKC and CKC offer classes for two age groups, each divided by skill: Novice Junior, Novice Senior, Open Junior, and Open Senior.

Junior Hunter: For a title, dog must receive qualifying scores at four licensed or member tests.

Junior testing level: The lowest level in AKC hunting tests.

Junk game: Unwanted game.

Juvenile hyperparathyroidism: A condition in which the parathyroid glands, which are important in the regulation of calcium and phosphorus, are abnormally active. The disease causes problems in the bones and kidneys. The German shepherd is most commonly affected.

Juvenile vaginitis: Inflammation of the vagina seen in puppies six to twelve weeks old, characterized by vulvar discharge.

K

K: Potassium.

K9: Police colloquial term for canine.

Kai: Also called the Kai-tora; a southern Japanese breed used for hunting.

Kangal dog: Anatolian shepherd.

Kaopectate: Soothes stomach upsets and treats diarrhea. Give one teaspoon for every ten pounds of your dog's weight.

Kara bas: Anatolian shepherd.

Karabash dog: Anatolian shepherd.

Karelian bear dog: Named for a province in Finland.

Karyotype: Arrangement of the chromosomes in the nucleus.

Kasbec: Afghan owned by Pablo Picasso.

Kava kava: In herbal medicine, given for nervousness and insomnia.

KC: Kennel Club (Great Britain).

Kcal: Kilocalorie.

KCS: Keratoconjunctivitis sicca, or dry eye.

Keel: The rounded outline of the lower chest, prominent in the dachshund and basset hound.

Keen: Penetrating expression.

Keeshond: A medium-sized spitz-type breed from the Netherlands. Size: 17 to 18 inches, 55 to 65 pounds, with an abundant coat dramatically marked with gray, black, and cream.

Keflex: Brand name for cephalexin, an antibiotic.

Kelb tal-Fenek: Pharaoh hound.

Kelev K'naani: Canaan dog.

Kelp: In herbal medicine, given for constipation and stress.

Kennel blindness: Colloquial term for owner/breeders who are unable to see faults in their own dogs.

Kennel cough (infectious tracheobronchitis): A highly contagious upper respiratory infection. The most common cause is the bacterium *Bordetella bronchiseptica*, for which there is a vaccine (good for about six months). However, a variety of viral, bacterial, or fungal infections may also be involved. Kennel cough is most serious in young puppies and is most common in areas where a number of dogs live in close confinement, as in a kennel. It is characterized by a dry, hacking cough. In most cases, kennel cough resolves itself in seven to ten days. It can be soothed with cough syrup designed for humans. For some cases, antibiotics are needed.

Kennel run: Enclosed outdoor living area.

Keratin: Tough, fibrous structural protein that makes up the hair and nails.

Keratinization: The development or conversion into keratin.

Keratitis: Inflammation of the clear part of the eye, the cornea.

Keratoconjunctivitis sicca (KCS): Dry eye caused by decreased tear production. May lead to ulceration.

Keratolytic: Scale-removing.

Kernel: Whole grain.

Kerry blue terrier: Developed in County Kerry, Ireland. Used for hunting small game and for retrieving from land and water. Size: 17 to 19 inches, 30 to 40 pounds. Has a soft, dense, wavy coat in any shade of blue-gray.

Ketoacidosis: A serious form of diabetes mellitus in which the pet has increased amounts of acids in the blood.

Ketoconazole: Antifungal medication used to treat deep (systemic) fungal infections, including those caused by ringworm and yeast. It also reduces levels of cortisol and can be used for patients with Cushing's disease.

Ketones: By-products formed during the metabolism of fat to glucose.

Ketonuria: The presence of ketones in the urine.

Kg: Kilograms.

Kibble: Dry dog food manufactured in small pieces.

Kidney disease: Any condition in which the kidneys lose function and can no longer clear the blood of urea and creatinine. Acute failure can be caused by leptospirosis, antifreeze, and rat poison. In acute failure, there will be dehydration, a stiff gait, and little or no urine production. Chronic kidney disease (the most common) is one of the most common causes of death in older dogs; some breeds, like cockers, Samoyeds, and bull terriers, are genetically predisposed. Signs include increased thirst and urination, weight loss, weakness, and a tendency to bruise or bleed easily.

Kidney worm: A parasite (*Dioc-tophyme renale*) that can be ingested in a diet of raw fish.

Killed vaccine: Vaccine made by taking the real, disease-causing viruses (or bacteria), killing them, and putting them into a liquid base.

Kilocalorie: Unit of energy equal to the amount needed to raise the temperature of one kilogram of water one degree Celsius. Often referred to as a calorie when discussing nutritional needs.

Kindling: In epilepsy, a mechanism by which epileptic neurons in the brain "recruit" normal neurons into the original seizure focus, enlarging the area of the brain that can produce seizures and lowering the seizure threshold.

Kinesiology: The study of body movement.

King Charles spaniel: English toy spaniel.

King Timahoe: Irish setter owned by Richard Nixon.

King Tut: Dog owned by Herbert Hoover.

Kink tail: A bent tail. Usually caused by a malformation of the caudal vertebrae.

Kishu: Ancient Japanese breed of medium size. Originally developed to hunt deer and boar.

Kiss of Allah: A small snip of differing color on the center of the top of the skull.

Kiss spots: Markings on the coat over the eyes and on the cheeks.

Knee: Term sometimes applied to the joint between the forearm and fore pastern. May also refer to the stifle.

Knitting: See crossover.

Knock: See bump.

Knuckled over: Steep pastern, or one with a reverse slope. Here the carpal (wrist) bones flex forward under the weight of the dog's standing. This is a faulty structure in all breeds.

Knuckled up: Strongly arched; said of the toes.

Koban copek: Anatolian shepherd.

Komondor: A large sheep guard dog with a white-corded coat. Developed in Hungary more than 1,000 years ago. Size: 25 to 27 inches, 80 to 100 pounds.

Kooikerhondje: Duck-hunting dog indigenous to Holland.

Korthals griffon: Wirehaired pointing griffon.

Kurzhaar: German shorthaired pointer.

Kurzhaariger Vortsehund: German shorthaired pointer.

Kuvasz: Guard dog and sheep-dog developed in Hungary in the fifteenth century or earlier. Has a thick white coat. Size: 26 to 30 inches, 70 to 115 pounds.

L

L: (1) Lumbar vertebrae, usually followed by a number to denote which one (veterinary notation). **(2)** Left (veterinary notation). **(3)** Abbreviation for liter.

LA: Local anesthetic (veterinary notation).

Labia: External folds of the vulva.

Labor: Middle stage of birthing process. Signs include straining, contractions, and the appearance of the placental sac and puppy. Many puppies are born "feet-first."

Labrador retriever: A compact, strongly built dog originally from Newfoundland named by the Earl of Malmsbury. The Labrador comes in black, yellow, and chocolate. Size: 21 to 24 inches, 55 to 80 pounds.

Laceration: Cut.

Lacrimal (lachrymal): pertaining to tears.

Lacrimal duct disease: Malformation of the duct that drains tears from the eye.

Lacrimal gland: The tear-producing gland in the inner corner of the eye.

Lacroix operation: A surgical procedure that drains the external ear canal.

Lactation: Production of milk.

Lactation tetany: Eclampsia.

Lactic acid: An end product of glycolysis. Excess accumulation in muscle leads to pain and cramps.

Lactoferrin: A protein with antibiotic properties involved in protecting the eye from infection. May produce tear-staining in some breeds.

Lactulose: Osmotic stool softener and laxative; prescribed for constipation. Also reduces the amount of ammonia in the blood of dogs with liver failure.

Laddie Boy: Airedale owned by Warren Harding.

The Lady and the Tramp: 1955 feature-length cartoon by Walt Disney.

Laelaps: A legendary dog that never failed to catch what he was hunting. A gift from Zeus to Europa.

Lagophthalmos: Inability to close the eyelids completely.

Laika: (1) Russian breed. **(2)** The first dog in space. Laika was aboard the Soviet satellite Sputnik 2 in 1957.

Lakeland terrier: An old breed developed in northern England. Noted for its courage and tenacity. Size: 14 to 15 inches, 15 to 17 pounds. Has a soft undercoat and a harsh outer coat in a variety of colors.

Lamppost disease: Leptospirosis. So called because dogs can pick it up by sniffing the urine of other dogs.

Land blind: A bird or dummy hidden where the dog can be directed to it mostly by land.

Landseer: (1) Black-and-white Newfoundland dog. **(2)** Painter known for his dog paintings.

Languedoc: Any of five breeds of small to medium-sized sheepdogs from the province of

Languedoc. Also called the Bergers du Languedoc.

Languishing eye: A mournful, appealing look.

Laparoscopy: Examination of the abdominal cavity with a special viewing instrument.

Laparotomy: A surgical procedure to open the abdominal cavity.

Lapland Sheepdog: Finnish breed of medium size with erect ears and a long tail.

Lara: James Buchanan's Newfoundland.

Lard: Rendered fat of swine.

Large intestine: The lower part of the intestinal tract, including the colon, cecum, and rectum. Bacteria that live harmlessly in the large intestine help to digest complex carbohydrates.

Large Munsterlander: All-around hunting, retrieving, watch, and guard dog "bred up" from the small Munsterlander.

Larva: Immature life stage of some insects.

Laryngeal hemiplagia: Paralysis of one side of the larynx, due to malfunction of the nerve that supplies the vocal cords on that side.

Laryngeal paralysis: A failure of the laryngeal cartilages to open during inspiration, creating a partial or complete upper airway obstruction, leading to difficult breathing. It is usually caused by dysfunction of the nerve (recurrent laryngeal) that controls the laryngeal musculature.

Laryngitis: Inflammation of the opening of the windpipe.

Larynx: Cartilaginous and muscular tube connecting the pharynx with the trachea and deeper airways. It contains the vocal cords. The voice box.

Laser acupuncture treatment: In the modern form of acupuncture, a laser beam is focused directly (and painlessly) on the acupuncture point.

Lashing tail: A powerful, swishing tail.

Lasix: A brand name for furosemide, a diuretic prescribed for pulmonary edema, congestive heart failure, and similar conditions. Furosemide acts on the kidney to increase the body's loss of water and assorted minerals and electrolytes.

Lassie: Any of a line of popular collies in movies and a television series. The first Lassie starred in the 1942 movie *Lassie Come Home.*

Lat: Lateral.

Latency: In training, the time between the cue and the response.

Latent: Dormant or inactive form of a disease.

Late-onset disease: A disease that is expressed later in life, usually after a dog has had a chance to reproduce.

Lateral: Toward the side.

Lateral recumbency: Lying on its side.

Laverack setter: English setter ancestor of conformation, as opposed to field examples of English setters.

Laxity: The looseness or extensibility of the skin or a joint.

Layback: (1) Angle at which the shoulder meets the body. **(2)** The receding nose of such breeds as the bulldog and pug.

Lay-on: Angle of the shoulder blade viewed from the front.

Layup: In coon hunting, a coon that has not been on the ground recently and is hiding up in the tree.

LCM: Lure Courser of Merit, a title awarded by the American Sighthound Field Association.

LCM2: Lure Courser of Merit 2, a title awarded by the American Sighthound Field Association. To earn the title, a dog must meet the requirements for LCM twice over. LCM3, LCM4, etc. are also available.

LDDS: Low-dose dexamethasone suppression.

LE: Lupus erythematosus.

Lead: (1) A leash. **(2)** A metal found in many insecticides; it can be poisonous.

Lead dog(s): In sledding, the front dog(s).

Leaky gut syndrome: A condition in which large protein molecules infiltrate the GI tract and initiate an autoimmune response.

Leash: (1) A line to keep the dog attached to the handler. **(2)** A set of three animals, such as hounds.

Leash law: Ordinance requiring animals to be kept contained on their property or on a leash.

Leather: The flap of the ear, especially of long, pendulous ears.

Le Diable: A famous dog that smuggled lace and treasures across the French border under a false skin dyed various colors by its owners to baffle the customs officials.

Ledum palustre: Homeopathic remedy for small puncture wound.

Leg: (1) A qualifying score in obedience or agility. **(2)** In tracking, the part of a track between the start and the first turn or between subsequent turns.

Legg-Calves Perthes disease: Destruction of the head of the femur that causes rear-end lameness. Occurs in young toy dogs. Also called Legg-Perthes disease.

Leggy: Tall; high off the ground.

Leonberger: Large German water dog, known for its life-saving skills.

Lens luxation: Displacement or dislocation of the lens of the eye.

Lenticular sclerosis: A bluish or greenish coloration within the pupil, characteristic of many older dogs. It does not affect vision significantly. Also called nuclear sclerosis.

Leonine: Looking like a lion, in respect to chow chows.

Leptospirosis: Bacterial disease usually affecting the kidney and reproductive tract; caused by various *Leptospira* spirochetes and characterized by jaundice, vomiting, and kidney failure. Symptoms can be severe and include loss of appetite fever, jaundice, and internal bleeding, showing up as blood in the stool. Can cause malfunction or failure in the liver, kidneys, and other internal organs. Infection occurs on contact with the urine of infected dogs. Bacteria enter the host animal through mucous membranes or through breaks in the skin. This disease can be fatal to dogs, and it can spread to humans.

Lesion: Wound, injury.

Lethargy: Listlessness, malaise. Common causes include fever, pain, anemia, obesity, and thyroid deficiency.

Leucopenia: Low white blood cell count.

Leukemia: Cancerous proliferation of certain white blood cells.

Leukeran: Brand name for chlorambucil, a chemotherapy drug.

Leukocyte: White blood cell.

Leukotrienes: Arachidonic acid metabolites produced by granulocytes, which mediate many inflammatory responses.

Level back: A back that makes a straight line from withers to tail, but is not necessarily parallel to the ground.

Level bite: Where the upper and lower incisors meet edge to edge. Also called an even bite or level mouth.

Level gait: Moving without rise or fall of withers or topline when at a standard show ring gait.

Leydig cell tumor: Small, inconsequential tumor of the testicle.

LF: Left fore (veterinary notation).

LGD: Livestock guard dog.

LH: (1) Left hind (veterinary notation). **(2)** Luteinizing hormone.

Lhasa apso: Native to Tibet, a tough, long-haired, long-lived dog between 14 and 18 pounds. The Lhasa is known for its assertive temperament.

LI: Large intestine (veterinary notation).

Liar: In field trials, a dog that calls its bracemate out to a non-existent trail (ghost-trailing).

Liberty: Golden retriever owned by Gerald Ford.

Lice: Parasites found mostly in dogs in bad condition and with matted coats. Signs of an infestation include itching and scratching.

Licensed club: Dog club licensed by the AKC that is approved to hold events at which championship points and titles may be won.

Lichenification: Thickening and hardening of the skin.

Lick granuloma: Common ulcerlike skin condition caused by excessive licking.

Lick sores: See acral pruritus dermatitis.

Licorice (*Glycyrrhiza glabra*): In herbal medicine, prescribed for gastric ulcers.

Lidocaine: Local anesthetic injected intramuscularly. Also an anti-arrhythmic drug, prepared in an injectable form and used intravenously. Often used in heart cases. Also called xylocaine.

Life stage information: On a dog food label, required information about what phase of life the food is intended for: puppies, adults, reproduction, or all life stages.

Life stage nutrition: Adapting the nutrient profile of the food to the specific requirements of the animal.

Lift: In herding events, the time at which the dog reaches the opposite side of the stock and moves them directly toward the handler. Also, the moment between the outrun and start of the fetch.

Ligament: Collection of dense connective tissue crossing the joints and holding them together.

Ligament tear in the stifle: The anterior cruciate ligament may tear, leading to an unstable joint and eventually arthritis.

Ligand: A molecule that bonds to another molecule through a coordinate covalent bond.

Light stock: In herding events, stock that are moved with only slight pressure from the dog and have a flight zone a substantial distance from them.

Limbic system: Brain system controlling the nervous and hormonal systems.

Limer: Old name for a greyhound-harrier dog cross, also possibly a bloodhound.

Lime sulfur/sulfonated lime solution: Antiseptic, antifungal, miticidal, and keratolytic dip used to treat ringworm, scaly skin, and bacterial or fungal infections.

Limited stakes: In AKC field trials, an event in which entry is limited to those dogs that have previously placed in a similar stake.

Limonene: A citrus oil insecticide used for flea control in dogs. May be toxic to cats.

Limping: Common causes include cuts, sprains, overlong toenails, arthritis, Lyme disease, and bone cancer.

Lincomycin: Older antibiotic prescribed for gram-positive bacteria such as streptococcus, staphylococcus, and anaerobic bacteria.

Line: A related group of dogs.

Line breeding: Breeding within in a line.

Line marshal: In hunting tests, the person responsible for making sure the handlers and dogs are at the line when they are called.

Line out: In sledding, a command to the lead dog to pull the team out straight from the sled. Used mostly while hooking or unhooking dogs into the team. "Stay tight!" or "Up front!" may also be used.

Line running: In field events, running in a straight-away manner without quartering or seeking objectives.

Line-steady: A dog that remains quietly at heel or beside the blind until sent to retrieve.

Lining of the ear: Inside of the ear flap.

Liniment: A medicinal preparation designed to be rubbed on the skin.

Linolenic acid: Alpha-linolenic acid.

Linty: A soft-textured coat.

Lion: Tawny color.

Lion clip: Cut in which the coat is clipped from the last rib, leaving the mane of the forequarters.

Lion dog: Pekingese.

Lipase: An enzyme produced by the pancreas, responsible for digesting fats.

Lipemia retinalis: A milky appearance of the veins and arteries of the retina, a result of hyperlipidemia.

Lipfold dermatitis: Lipfold pyoderma.

Lipfold pyoderma: Bacterial infection of the skin around the folds of the lips.

Lipid: Class of nutrients including fats, oils, and cholesterol.

Lipidosis: A lipid storage disease resulting in the accumulation of fat in the tissues.

Lipogenesis: The formation of fat by the body.

Lipogranuloma: A small aggregation of lipid cells. Also called a xanthoma.

Lipolysis: The breaking down of fat to supply glucose to the body.

Lipoma: A benign tumor of fatty cells.

Lippy: Pendulous lips, or lips that don't fit closely together.

List of ingredients: In dog-food labeling, the substances making up the food, usually listed in descending order by weight.

Literal casting: In retrieving work, a cast that, if taken properly, would lead directly to the blind.

Lithe: Graceful.

Litter: A group of puppies of one whelping.

Little griffon Vendéen basset: Petit basset griffon Vendéen.

Little lion dog: Lowchen.

Liver: (1) Large organ that removes toxins and bacteria from the blood, produces immune agents, produces bile, and makes proteins that regulate blood clotting. It has the ability to regenerate to some degree. **(2)** Deep red/brown color produced by recessive alleles. **(3)** In the diet, an excellent source of iron, protein, copper, vitamin D, and several B vitamins. It is excessively high in vitamin A and deficient in calcium.

Liver disease: Most common kinds include chronic, active, or infectious hepatitis, vacuolar hepatopathy, hepatic lipidosis, cirrhosis, cancer, and congenital portacaval shunt. Signs can include inappetance, abdominal upset, weight loss, vomiting and diarrhea or constipation, lethargy, buildup of abdominal fluid, pale stool, orange urine, jaundice, behavior changes, and PU/PD.

LL: Left lower, such as left lower eyelid (veterinary notation).

Llewellin setter: Ancestor of English setter, primarily used as a field dog.

Ln: lymph nodes (veterinary notation).

Loaded: Pertaining to overdevelopment of certain groups of muscles

Loaded shoulders: Lumpy, overmuscled shoulders.

Lobe-shaped ears: Ears like a cocker spaniel.

Lobular ears: Pendulous ears.

Locate: In treeing, finding the tree where the game is. Also the announcement of the tree by the dog.

Lockjaw: Tetanus.

Locus: Location of a gene on a chromosome.

Loin: The area of the body between the last ribcage and the beginning of the pelvis.

Lolling tongue: Overlong, hanging tongue.

Lomotil: Brand name anti-diarrhea medication.

Long back: A back longer than the dog is high at the withers.

Long bones: General term for the bones found in the limbs, namely the femur, tibia, fibula, radius, ulna, and humerus.

Long-coupled: Having a long loin.

Long dog: A sight hound.

Long in hock (high in hock): Hocks farther from the ground than desired.

Loose elbow: Out at elbow.

Loose front: Loose attachment of muscles to the shoulder, producing a gait in which the front is slung all about.

Loosely coupled: A weak, excessively long loin.

Loose mouth: A hound that begins barking as soon as an event begins, without necessarily scenting anything. A babbler.

Loose movement: Erratic, rather uncoordinated movement.

Loose shoulders: Where the attachment of muscles at the shoulders is looser than desirable.

Loose slung: Loose shoulders.

Loose tail: Tail not fitting tightly over the back.

Low at shoulders: Flat withers.

Lowchen: A companion dog standing 12 to 14 inches with a long dense coat in any color. May have been developed in Germany in the fifteenth century or even earlier.

Low-dose dexamethasone suppression (LDDS) test: A test to distinguish between cases of adrenal-dependent and pituitary-dependent HAC.

Lower arm: The region of the radius and ulna.

Lower thigh: Area from stifle to hock, also known as second thigh.

Low passage vaccine: A low passage vaccine contains virus particles that have been weakened, less than those in the average vaccine. Low passage vaccines can generally elicit an immune system response in young animals that have a maternal antibody level that would prevent them from responding to an average vaccine.

Low set: A tail set below the level of the topline.

Low set ears: Ears placed low on the skull, like those of a basset hound or bloodhound.

Low-stationed: Where the ground-to-brisket distance is less that the withers-to-brisket distance.

Lozenge: A marking on the head of a King Charles spaniel and cavalier King Charles spaniel, sometimes called the Blenheim spot.

LP: UKC's Listing Privilege for unpapered purebreds or mixed breeds.

LR: Labrador retriever.

LTF: Learning to fly, dog fell off balcony (veterinary notation).

LU: Left upper (veterinary notation).

Lubricant laxative: A laxative whose primary ingredient is mineral oil, prescribed for constipation and fecal impaction.

Lufenuron: Insect development inhibitor (Program) that prevents the development of flea eggs by interfering with the development of chitin.

Lumbar: Pertaining to the lower back.

Lumbar vertebrae: The vertebrae between thoracic (over ribs) and coccygeal (tail).

Lumbering: Heavy, rough gait.

Lumbosacral arthritis: Arthritis at the junction of the lower back and pelvis.

Lumbosacral instability: Lumbosacral syndrome.

Lumbosacral syndrome: Group of neurological signs resulting from compression of the spinal nerves of the lumbosacral vertebral region. This disease is also known as the cauda equina syndrome.

Lumen: The cavity within a tubular organ such as the intestine.

Lumps: Common lumps can be fatty tumors, infected hair follicles, cysts, warts, or cancer.

Lungroom: A large chest area, roomy enough to permit optimum lung and heart development.

Lungworm: Nematodes that infect the dog's lungs; a rare infection in dogs.

Luo points: Connection points.

Lupod onychopathy (also onychodystrophy): a condition resulting in toenail loss on all four feet. German Shepherd Dogs predisposed. Possibly relating to food allergies. May also have a genetic basis.

Lupus erythematosus: Systemic lupus erythematosus.

Lurcher: A crossbred hound.

Lure coursing: An event where dogs, usually sight-hounds, chase plastic bags pulled by motorized pulleys.

Luteinizing hormone (LH): Hormone that stimulates ovulation in females and testosterone production in males.

Luxating patella: Patellar luxation, dislocation of the "kneecap."

Luxating tarsus: Dislocation of the "ankle."

Luxation: Dislocation of an anatomical structure such as a lens or patella.

LVT: Licensed veterinary technician.

Lyemmer: See limer.

Lyme disease: Tick-borne disease caused by the bacteria (spirochete) Borrelia burgdorferi. Signs include loss of appetite, lethargy, shifting leg lameness, and fever. Treatment is usually by antibiotics.

Lymph: Fluid taken up by the lymphatic system from the tissues. It has both fluid and cellular components and is similar in composition to blood plasma.

Lymphatic system: The body system, which includes the lymph nodes and lymph vessels, responsible for cleansing the tissues and the production of antibodies. It is part of the immune system; it also returns fluids that escape from the blood vessels to the blood stream. Fats digested in the intestine are mostly absorbed into the lymphatic system.

Lymphatic (or lymphocytic) thyroiditis: Condition in which the immune system attacks the thyroid gland, replacing normal tissue with lymphocytes and fibrous material.

Lymphatic vessel: Vessel that originates in tissue spaces and returns excess fluid to the central circulation. Lymphatic channels are the main route of metastasis for various cancers.

Lymphedema: Swelling and pitting of the legs, resulting from an accumulation of lymph fluid, caused by obstructions in the lymph vessels.

Lymph nodes: Part of the immune system of an animal. Small masses of tissue that contain white blood cells called lymphocytes. Blood from the nearby area is filtered through the lymph node, allowing foreign or infectious material to be recognized and destroyed if possible.

Lymphocytes: The class of cells in the body responsible for mounting an immune response. Two main types are B cells and T cells.

Lymphokines: Signaling chemicals produced by T lymphocytes.

Lymphoma: Cancer of the blood cells and tissues of the lymphatic system. Also known as lymphosarcoma. One of the most common cancers in dogs, usually affecting middle-aged and older dogs. Lumps may appear in swollen lymph nodes at the base of the jaw, in the rear legs behind the knee, in the "armpits," in the groin, and in front of the shoulder blades. It responds well to chemotherapy if caught early.

Lymphosarcoma (lymphoma, malignant lymphoma): General term that includes various cancers of the lymphoid system.

Lysosomal storage disease: An inherited brain disorder caused by a deficiency of certain enzymes, resulting in incomplete metabolism and accumulation of some intermediate metabolites.

Lysosome: Small structure within the cell that carries out digestive functions.

M

M: (1) Male. (2) Molar tooth, followed by a number to indicate which (veterinary notation). (3) Abbreviation for meter.

MACH: Master Agility Champion. The title is prefixed to the dog's name.

Macroblepharon: An extremely large eyelid opening, often associated with lower lid entropion.

Macronutrients: Protein, fat, and carbohydrates.

Macrophage: A type of phagocyte (cell in the body that eats damaged cells and foreign substances such as viruses and bacteria).

MAD: Master Agility Dog (USDAA title).

Madam Moose: Dalmatian owned by Martha Washington.

MADC: Master Agility Dog of Canada (AAC title).

Mad dog: A dog with rabies.

Mafia: Poodle owned by Marilyn Monroe. A gift from Frank Sinatra.

Maggie: Bulldog owned by Truman Capote.

Magnesium: Mineral that helps the body utilize phosphorus and calcium in bone and muscle. Found in soy.

Magnesium phosphate: Homeopathic remedy for eclampsia.

Magnesium phosphorica: Homeopathic remedy for muscle spasms.

Magnetic resonance imaging (MRI): A technique in which a powerful magnet is used to produce a three-dimensional picture of a structure in the body.

Magyar vizsla: Vizsla.

Maida: Scottish deerhound owned by Sir Walter Scott.

Maiden: A greyhound that has not won an official race.

Maintenance energy requirement (MER): Amount of energy used by an adult dog at room temperature, expressed as kilocalories per kilogram of body weight.

Major: A win of three, four, or five points in a conformation show. The point schedule is determined by the number of entries and is different for each breed, sex, and region of the country.

Major pointed: A dog that has won at least one major toward an AKC bench or field championship.

Make a stand: Point.

Making a wheel: The circling of the tail over the back, characteristic of the Great Pyrenees when alerted.

Malabsorption syndrome: A condition involving the intestine, in which food may not be properly digested or the nutrients not absorbed.

Malar abscess: An abscess on the root of the carnassial tooth.

Malassezia: Common yeast infection. The organism is most commonly found in the ears, anus, and vulva, usually in low numbers. When numbers rise uncontrollably, the dog has a yeast infection. Yeast infections are often itchy, with red or yellow greasy, smelly scales. Most commonly affected breeds are certain terriers (silky, Australian, Jack Russell, West Highland white), bassets, dachshunds, collies, Shetland sheepdogs, Chihuahuas, German shepherds, cockers, and springer spaniels. Treatment involves medicated shampoos and antifungal drugs.

Malignancy: Cancer.

Malignant: Metastasizing, severe, or life-threatening, usually used in reference to cancer.

Malignant hyperthermia: Sudden onset of high fever and rigid muscles due to drug reaction or abnormally low calcium levels.

Malignant lymphoma (lymphoma): Common internal form of cancer, mainly affecting the lymph nodes.

Malinois: Belgian Malinois.

Malocclusion: A condition in which the upper and lower teeth do not line up properly.

Maltese: Toy dog weighing less than 7 pounds. Has a long, silky, usually pure-white coat hanging nearly to the ground.

Mammary: Pertaining to the breast.

Mammary cyst: Cyst of the mammary gland.

Mammary gland: Modified sweat glands that produce milk. Larger breeds typically have four to six glands on each side of the midline; smaller breeds generally have four.

Mammary tumors and cancers: Growth in the mammary gland. About half of these growths are benign and removed easily. Best prevention is early (before the first heat cycle) spaying.

Manchester terrier: Small black-and-tan terrier used to kill vermin. Comes in standard (less than 22 pounds) and toy (less than 12 pound) types.

Mandible: Lower jaw.

Mane: Long hair around the neck.

Maned wolf (Chrysocyon brachyurus): Wild South American canid.

Manganese: Trace mineral found in egg yolks, nuts, seeds, and whole grain cereals.

Mange: Microscopic parasitic mite that infects the skin and hair follicles and causes intense itching. Most common cause of itching other than allergies. Two most common types are demodectic mange and sarcoptic mange.

manip: Manipulation (veterinary notation).

Mantle: The dark hair on the shoulders, back, and sides.

Manubrium: Frontal area of chest.

Many-tailed bandage: A bandage used to protect the belly. Made by cutting the sides of a rectangular cloth into four or five strips and tying them over the back.

MAOI: Monoamine oxidase inhibitor. Substances that inactivate the enzyme monoamine oxidase, which regulates certain transmitter chemicals between nerves. These compounds include certain types of antidepressants and also insecticides containing amitraz (such as Mitaban and Preventic collars).

Marble eye: Walleye.

Marcel effect: Regular, continuous waves.

Marea: In Greek myth, a dog belonging to Erigone, daughter of Icarus.

Maremma Sheepdog: Ancient breed of sheep-guard dog. Has a white coat.

Mark: (1) In pointing breed events, a dog's watching the flight or fall of a bird. **(2)** In retrieving breeds, the bird or dummy thrown so the dog can watch it descend.

Marked flag: Hanging hair on the tail that forms a flag.

Marked stop: Noticeable stop.

Marked wrinkles: Noticeable wrinkles.

Markings: Usually white areas or feet on a colored coat.

Marshal: In pointing breed events, the person assigned to assist the judges. He also controls the gallery.

Martha: Sheepdog owned by Paul McCartney and featured in the song "Martha, My Dear."

Martingale: One-piece lead that permits some tightening at the neck.

Mask: Dark areas on face.

Massage therapy: A technique in which the practitioner uses the hands to massage soft tissues.

Mast cell tumors (MCT): Also known as mastocytomas. Nodular growths, usually on the skin, liver, or intestines. Vary in appearance from smooth and hard to soft or rough or warty. May appear alone or in clusters, and be either slow- or fast-growing. Treatment may include surgery, radiation therapy, chemotherapy, and cryotherapy.

Master Agility Champion: A dog who has won at least 750 championship points and 20 double qualifying scores obtained from the Excellent B Standard Agility class and the Excellent B Jumpers with Weaves class.

Master Agility Excellent: For a title, dog must earn ten qualifying scores in Excellent B Agility class under at least two different judges. Trial at which AX was earned does not count toward the ten.

Master Agility Jumper: For a title, dog must earn ten qualifying scores in Excellent B Agility class under at least

two different judges. Trial at which AX was earned does not count toward the ten.

Master Courser: Title awarded to hounds that have acquired the Senior Courser title and that have earned an additional twenty-five qualifying scores (with competition) in the Open, Open Veteran, or Specials stake at AKC licensed or member club lure coursing trials.

Master Earthdog: A dog must have a record of having qualified in the Master Earthdog test at four AKC licensed or member club hunting tests under two different Judges.

Master hair: Guard hair.

Master Hunter: For a title, a dog must receive qualifying scores at six licensed or member tests. If the dog has already received an SH, the dog need only qualify five times.

Master of the Hounds: One responsible for a pack of foxhounds.

Master testing level: The highest level in AKC hunting tests.

Masticate: Chew.

Mastiff: A large breed with pendulous lips and drooping ears, used for guarding. In ancient days, the mastiffs were used to hunt wild horses and lions, as well as for sentry duty and protection. Has a short coat, usually fawn, apricot, or brindle.

Mastitis: Mammary gland (milk gland) infection.

Mastocytoma: Mast cell tumor.

Matador: A frequently used sire.

Match: Informal, "practice" dog show. Every AKC Kennel Club holds at least one match a year.

Materia Medica: In homeopathy, a book of provings and properties of remedies.

Maternal antibody: Antibody in a newborn animal that the newborn acquired through the placenta or colostrum (the first milk).

Mathe: Greyhound owned by Richard II.

Mature milk: Nutrient secreted by the mammary gland starting several days after birth.

Mauthe Doog: Legendary dog from Wales and parts of Great Britain. Also known as Gwyllgi, the Dog of Darkness, or Barghest.

Maxilla: Upper jawbone.

Maxillary: Relating to the upper jawbone.

Mayhem: In animal law, the act of illegally and violently depriving an animal of the use of its members so that it cannot defend itself.

MBDCA: Mixed Breed Dog Clubs of America.

MC: Master Courser. Title follows the dog's name.

M/c: Metacarpal (veterinary notation).

MCT: Mast cell tumor.

MCV: Mean corpuscular volume.

MDR: Minimum daily requirement.

Me: Male, unneutered (veterinary notation).

ME: (1) Master Earthdog. Title follows the dog's name. **(2)** Metabolizable energy.

Meal: A food ingredient that has been ground.

Meal-induced thermogenesis: The heat produced following the consumption of a meal.

Meat: In dog-food labeling, meat (beef, lamb, chicken) is the clean flesh derived from slaughtered mammals and is limited to that part of the muscle which is skeletal or that which is found in the tongue, diaphragm, heart, or esophagus; with or without accompanying and overlying fat and the portions of the skin, sinew, nerve, and blood vessels.

Meat and bone meal: In dog-food labeling, the rendered product from mammal tissues, including bone, excluding any added blood, hair, hoof, horn, hide trimmings, manure, and stomach and rumen contents, except in such amounts as may occur unavoidably in good processing practices.

Meat by-products: In dog-food labeling, the non-rendered, clean parts, other than meat, derived from slaughtered mammals. It includes, but is not limited to, lungs, spleen, kidneys, brain, livers, blood, bone, partially defatted low temperature fatty tissues, and stomachs and intestines.

Meat meal: In dog food labeling, the rendered product from mammal tissues, exclusive of any added blood, hair, hoof, horn and hide trimmings, manure, and stomach and rumen contents except in such amounts as may occur unavoidably in good processing practices.

Meat/meat products: In dog-food labeling, ingredients coming only from cattle, hogs, sheep, or goats. Any other animal ingredient must be named specifically.

Meclizine: Antihistamine and anti-emetic drug prescribed for motion sickness.

Meclofenamic acid: NSAID (Arquel) prescribed for arthritis.

Med: Medial (veterinary notation).

Medial: Toward the midline.

Megacolon: A condition in which the colon enlarges and dilates, resulting in feces accumulating in the colon and consequent constipation. This condition is more common in cats than dogs.

Megaesophagus: A condition in which the esophagus is enlarged and unable to push food into the stomach. The affected dog will regurgitate food.

Meiosis: Type of cellular division that produces reproductive cells.

Melanin: Pigments chiefly responsible for coloration of skin and hair.

Melanocytes: Pigment-containing cells.

Melanoma: A malignant, dark-pigmented tumor. It can develop from a pre-existing mole. Some melanomas are very aggressive.

Melatonin: Natural hormone produced in the pineal gland, responsible for wake/sleep cycles.

Melena: Black stools resulting from internal bleeding.

Melissa: An essential oil used in aromatherapy.

Melon pips: Pips.

Memory Bird: In retrieving work, any item in a multiple mark situation, other than the last item, thrown for a dog to retrieve.

Meninges: The membranes covering the brain and spinal cord.

Meningitis: The inflammation of the meninges. Can be caused by bacteria, a virus, fungi, or chemical toxins. Signs include fever and lethargy.

Meniscus: Crescent-shaped cartilage in the stifle joint.

Meridian: In acupuncture, the channel along the skin through which *Chi (qi)*, or energy, passes.

Merle: Dark patches on a lighter background (blue or gray), often with flecks of black. In some breeds called dapple. The merle gene (M or Merling Series) is dominant, and is associated with deafness and blindness.

Merle eye: Flecked eye, brown and blue with black iris.

Merry tail: A constantly wagging tail.

Mesaticephalic: Medium-width head and muzzle, a balanced head.

Mesentery: A membranous sheet attaching various organs to the wall of the body, especially the peritoneal fold that attaches the intestine to the body wall.

Metabolic acidosis: A condition in which the pH of the blood is too acidic because of the production of certain types of acids.

Metabolic enzymes: Natural chemical in the blood and tissues that assist other chemical processes, such as the conversion of food into energy.

Metabolism: Chemical reactions and biochemical processes of the body, especially assimilating food and providing energy.

Metabolizable energy (ME): Energy from food that is available to tissues, after losses in the feces and urine.

Metacarpal pads: The pads on the forefeet.

Metacarpals: A group of five bones within the wrist and toes.

Metacarpus: Front leg between carpus and toes.

Metaldehyde: Poison used in rodent and snail bait. Often combined with arsenic and mixed with bran.

Metamusil: Fiber-containing laxative. Helps diarrhea and constipation. Sprinkle some on your dog's food.

Metaphysis: The wide part at the end of the shaft of a long bone, next to the epiphyseal disk.

Metastatic lung disease: The spread of a malignant tumor into the lungs.

Metastasis: Spread of a tumor from its original location to a remote one, by tumor cells that are carried in the blood.

Metastasize: Spread to other parts of the body. A characteristic of cancer.

Metatarsal pad: The large pad on the hind feet.

Metatarsals: A group of approximately five bones between the tarsal bones and the toes.

Metatarsus: Pastern.

Metestrus: The last stage of the estrous cycle, lasting from two to three months. It may include pregnancy, or if not fertilized, the period during which the uterus repairs itself. False pregnancies may appear during this phase.

Methemoglobin: An altered hemoglobin which does not carry oxygen.

Methemoglobinemia: The presence of excessive methemoglobin in the blood.

Methionine: (1) An essential amino acid. **(2)** Urine acidifier prescribed for cystitis, alkaline urinary stones, and urinary tract infections.

Methocarbamol: Muscle relaxant prescribed for the reduction of muscle spasms.

Methoxyflurane: A gas anesthetic with a fairly long recovery time.

Metoclopramide: Anti-emetic and gastrointestinal stimulant prescribed for nausea and vomiting.

Metritis: Serious bacterial infection or inflammation of the uterus, usually occurring within a week of whelping.

Metro-: Pertaining to the uterus.

Metronidazole: Antiprotozoal, antibiotic, and anti-inflammatory, prescribed for Giardia, colitis, and bacterial intestinal infections. It is especially effective against anaerobic infections.

Mexican hairless: Xoloitzcuintli.

Mg: Magnesium.

Mg/dL: Milligrams per deciliter.

MH: Master Hunter (AKC suffix).

MHR: (1) Master Hunter Retriever (UK). **(2)** Master Hunting Retriever (NAHRA).

Miasm: A homeopathic term for in infective agent that underlies chronic disease.

Mibolerone: Synthetic male sex steroid hormone prescribed for the prevention of estrus and for signs of false pregnancy.

MIC: Minimum inhibitory concentration.

Miconazole: Antifungal prescribed for superficial skin infestations, malassezia infections, and ringworm topical treatment.

Microchipping: An identification technique in which a microchip, a tiny device encoded with an unalterable identification number, is implanted under the skin between the shoulder blades. It is read by a scanner.

Microfilaria: Primarily heartworm larvae, but also any prelarval stage of filarial worm transmitted to the biting insect from the primary host.

Microfilaricide: Compound that kills microfilaria, the immature forms of heartworms that circulate in the blood

Microingredients: Vitamins, minerals, antibiotics, and other substances usually measured in small amounts such as milligrams, micrograms, or parts per million (ppm).

Micronutrients: Vitamins and minerals.

Microphthalmia: Small eyes.

Microsporum canis: A fungus that can cause ringworm in dogs and humans.

Micturition: Urination.

Midwestern Pet Foods: Telephone: (812) 867-7466. Web site: www.propacpetfoods.com.

Milbemycin: An antibiotic compound (Interceptor) used as a once-a-month heartworm treatment. Also controls hookworm, whipworm, lungworm, and mites.

Millie: George and Barbara Bush's English springer spaniel.

Milk fever: See Eclampsia.

Milk teeth: Baby or deciduous teeth.

Milk thistle: In herbal medicine, prescribed for liver disorders, poisoning.

Mimi: Papillon owned by Madame Pompador.

Mincing gait: Short, choppy gait.

Mineralization: The process in which minerals are laid down within tissue in an abnormal pattern, causing a hardening of the tissue.

Mineralocorticoid: A group of adrenal gland hormones that affect sodium and potassium levels.

Minerals: Inorganic substances that

assist in vitamin absorption, digestion, and, in fact, all body systems.

Miniature bull terrier: Bull terrier identical to the standard in every particular but size. Size: 10 to 14 inches.

Miniature pinscher: Developed centuries ago in Germany to kill vermin. Resembles a scaled-down Doberman pincher. Size: 10 to 12 inches.

Miniature schnauzer: Developed in Germany by the fifteenth century. An active, robust dog 12 to 14 inches tall, with a hard, wiry outer coat, usually salt-and-pepper, black-and-silver, or solid black in color.

Minimum daily requirement: The least amount of available nutrients needed in the diet each day to permit normal body metabolism.

Miscellaneous class: Transitional class for breeds attempting to advance to full AKC recognition.

Mismarks: (1) Self colors with white on the back between the withers and tail or sides between the elbows and back of hindquarters. Also black with white markings and no tan present. **(2)** A specimen with highly undesirable coloring or markings for its breed.

Mismating: Accidental mating.

Misoprostol: Anti-ulcer medication, sometimes prescribed for damage to the intestinal tract from NSAIDs.

Miticide: A substance that kills mites.

Mitochondria: Enzyme-containing structures within cells that convert food to energy.

Mitotane: Chemotherapeutic and adrenal function inhibitor, prescribed for Cushing's disease and adrenal tumors.

Mitral valve defect or insufficiency (MVI): A defect in the heart valve that separates the left atrium and the left ventricle. This allows backflow of blood into the left atrium, or mitral regurgitation. Less commonly, a narrowing (stenosis) of the valve can be identified. The leaky valve makes the heart less efficient.

Mittelschnauzer: Standard schnauzer.

Mixed Breed Dog Clubs of America (MBDCA): National registry for mixed breeds, offering titles in obedience, tracking, retrieving, and lure coursing. 13884 State Route 104, Lucasville, OH 45648-8586. Telephone (740) 259-3941. Web site: http://mbdca.tripod.com.

Mixed litter: A litter in which the puppies are the product of more than one male. This phenomenon can occur because eggs can mature and become fertilizable at different times.

mL: Milliliter.

MLV: Modified live virus, usually referring to a vaccine.

mm: (1) Mucous membranes (veterinary notation). **(2)** Millimeter.

Mmb: Mucous membranes (veterinary notation).

Mn: (1) Male, neutered (veterinary notation). **(2)** Chemical symbol for manganese.

MO: Months old, following a number (veterinary notation).

Mobile ears: Ears that can move.

Modeling: See chiseled.

Modified live vaccine: A vaccine made by taking the real, disease-causing virus and altering (attenuating) it in a laboratory to a non-disease-causing virus.

Modular liquid food: A food with greater than 90 percent moisture, containing primarily one nutrient.

Molars: Cheek teeth used by dogs for shearing.

Mold: Fungi that are a common cause of allergies. Dehumidifiers can help lessen the problem.

Mole: (1) Marking on cheeks. **(2)** Gray or blue color.

Molera: The fetal soft spot in the skull that fails to close properly, common in the Chihuahua.

Molossus: Archaic Mastiffs used by the Romans as bodyguards and fighting dogs.

Molting: Shedding (loss of hair and change of coat).

Momma-poppa: See flower pot marks.

Monadic feeding test: A feeding trial that tests the acceptance of a single food.

Money bird: In retrieving work, the last item, in a multiple mark situation, that the dog picks up.

Mongrel: A mixed breed descended from random matings.

Mongolian eyes: Obliquely placed eyes.

Monkey dog: A nickname for the Serra de Aires sheepdog, a breed of Portugal.

Monk's cap: Brown spot on a background of white at the top of the head between the ears, usually spoken of in reference to Saint Bernards.

Mono: Prefix signifying one or single.

Monoamine oxidase inhibitor (MAOI): Substance that inactivates the enzyme monoamine oxidase, which regulates certain transmitter chemicals between nerves. These compounds include certain types of antidepressants and also insecticides containing amitraz (such as Mitaban and Preventic collars).

Monochrome: Hair of one solid color.

Monocyte: Kind of white blood cell.

Monorchid: A male with only one testicle developed. These dogs must be neutered.

Monosaccharide: Sugar composed of a single carbohydrate unit such as glucose.

Monovalent vaccine: A vaccine that is manufactured to stimulate the body to produce protection against only one disease, as in the rabies vaccine.

Moose: Real name of Eddie, the Jack Russell Terrier on *Frasier.*

Mops: Pug.

Morphological: Relating to the morphology or observable physical form of a trait.

Morphology: Form or structure of an organism.

Mother tincture: In homeopathy, undiluted alcoholic preparation obtained from the original source material of a remedy.

Motility: Movement; e.g., intestinal motility is the muscular contractions of the intestines that move the food from the stomach to the anus.

Mottled: Bicolored coat, consisting of dark patches on lighter background.

Mountain Boy: Greyhound belonging to Woodrow Wilson when he was a boy.

Moving close: An incorrect gait in which the fore or hind legs are insufficiently separated from each other during movement.

Moving straight: (1) A balanced gait. **(2)** Dog with little reach and drive in gaiting.

Moving wide behind: The movement of a bow-hocked dog.

Moxibustion: An acupuncture therapy in which the Chinese herb moxa (*Artemisia vulgaris*) is burned and the resulting heat applied directly to the needle or to the skin over the acupuncture point. The heat is thought to enhance the healing effect.

Moxidectin: Heartworm preventative (ProHeart).

MRI: Magnetic resonance imaging.

MT: Mammary tumor (veterinary notation).

M/t: Metatarsal (veterinary notation).

Mucilage: In herbal medicine, gelatinous parts of herbs that act as emollients and demulcents.

Mucolytic: Breaks down mucus.

Mucosa: The lining of an organ; a mucous membrane.

Mucus: Clear, lubricating secretion produced in the mucous membranes.

Mudi: Medium-sized Hungarian sheep-guard dog.

Mute trailing: Remaining silent while hunting.

Multifactorial: In genetics, influenced by many non-genetic factors.

Multigenic disease: Polygenic disease, a disease under the control of more than one gene.

Multivalent vaccine: Vaccine against several diseases administered together.

Multum in parvo: "Much in little." Latin motto of the pug.

Mupirocin: Antibiotic prescribed for skin infections, especially those resistant to older antibiotics.

Murmur: See heart murmur.

Muscle-bound: Excessive development of certain muscle groups.

Muscle tone: Quality of muscular development.

Muscular dystrophy: Progressive degeneration of the skeletal muscles.

Musculation: The arrangement and development of muscles.

Musculoskeletal system: This body system includes all the muscles, joints, and bones.

Mush: See Hike. The only sledders who use "Mush" are the ones in the movies.

Musher: Sled driver.

Music: The sound of baying hounds.

Mustache: Long hair of varying texture around the lip area of some breeds.

Mutation: An unexpected genetic change.

Mute: Running quiet on the trail, not baying.

Muzzle: (1) The foreface. (2) A fabric or leather device to keep the dog from biting but allowing it to breathe comfortably.

Muzzle folliculitis: canine acne, a chronic inflammation of the chin and lip. Affecting young dogs.

MVA: Motor vehicle accident (veterinary notation).

MVI: Mitral valve insufficiency.

MX: Master Agility Excellent (AKC title). The title follows the dog's name.

MXJ: Master Agility Jumper (AKC title). The title follows the dog's name.

Myasthenia gravis: A neuromuscular disease in which there is a failure of the nerves' ability to stimulate and control the actions of certain muscles. Treated using anticholinesterase drugs.

Mycetoma: Fungus-caused granulomatous nodules of the subcutaneous tissues.

Mycobacterium bovis/Bacillus Calmette-Guerin (BCG): Mycobacterial immunosuppressant prescribed for cancer cases. Sometimes used as a tuberculosis vaccine.

Mycosis: A disease caused by a fungus.

Mydriasis: Small pupil size.

Myelin: The fatty layer surrounding and insulating nerve fibers.

Myelogram: Diagnostic procedure to detect diseases of the spinal cord.

Myelosuppression: A suppression of the bone marrow so that it does not produce normal numbers of red blood cells, white blood cells, and platelets.

Myo-: Pertaining to the muscles.

Myocarditis: Inflammation of the myocardium, the muscular tissue of the heart.

Myocardium: Middle layer of heart muscle.

Myoclonus: Involuntary, rapid tremors, often seen in canine distemper.

Myopathy: Usually refers to muscle degeneration but may be applied to any disease of the muscles.

Myositis: Inflammation of muscle.

Myotonia: Muscle spasms.

Myxedema: Thickening of the skin, especially around the head and face. Characterisitc of hypothyroidism.

N

N: Normal (veterinary notation).

Na: Sodium.

NA: Novice Agility (AKC suffix).

NAC, NAC-V, NAC-JH: Novice Standard, Veterans, Junior Handler (NADAC).

NACA: North American Coursing Association.

NACC: NACA Coursing Champion.

NACM: NACA Courser of Merit.

NAD: No abnormality detected (veterinary notation).

NADAC: North American Dog Agility Council.

NAF: No abnormalities found (veterinary notation).

NAFC: (1) National amateur field champion. The title is prefixed to the dog's name and is won in the annual AKC national amateur field trial conducted by each of the several pointing breeds. **(2)** No abnormal findings (veterinary notation).

NAHRA: North American Versatile Hunting Retriever Association.

Nail bed: The point from which the dog's toenail emerges from the skin.

NAJ: Novice agility jumper. The title follows the dog's name.

NAOFA: North American Open Field Association.

Nape: The junction of the base of the skull and the top of the neck.

Narcolepsy: Excessive daytime sleep, in which the dog plunges suddenly into deep slumber.

Narrow front: Where the chest is narrower than desired.

Narrow palpebral fissure: Abnormally small opening between the eyelids.

Nasal: Pertaining to the nose.

Nasal cancer: Most common in long-snouted dogs and dogs exposed to herbicides and pesticides.

Nasal-fold dermatitis: Bacterial infection of the skin folds on the face of brachycephalic breeds.

Nasal mites: Microscopic mites that invade a dog's nose and can migrate to the sinuses.

Nasal septal disease: A condition affecting the nasal septum, resulting in abnormal air movement through the nostrils.

Nasal solar dermatitis: Inflammation of the nose surface owing to exposure to sun. Also known as "collie nose."

Naso-labial line: The groove dividing the right and left upper lip halves.

Nasolacrimal duct: Duct that transmits tears from the medial corner of the eye to the nose.

NATCh: Agility Trial Champion (NADAC).

National: Shorthand term for a national specialty show.

National Amateur Field Champion: AKC title. A dog that has won first place in a stake that has been designated a National Amateur Championship stake.

National Animal Poison Control Center: Telephone: (900) 680-0000, (800) 548-2423, (888) 426-4425.

National Association for Search and Rescue: P.O. Box 3709; Fairfax, VA 22038.

National Center for Homeopathy: 801 North Fairfax Street, Suite 306, Alexandria, VA 22314. Telephone: (703) 548-7790.

National Derby Champion: Erroneous appellation for High Point Derby Dog.

National field champion: AKC title. A dog that has won first place in a stake designated a National Open Championship stake.

National Greyhound Association: Organization made up of greyhound owners, breeders, and trainers; recognized as a registry for racing greyhounds in the United States.

National Gun Dog Champion: A dog that has won first place in a stake that has been designated a National Open Gun Dog Championship stake.

National Obedience Champion: A dog who has won the National Obedience Invitational.

National Shoot-to-Retrieve Field Trial Association: Organization sponsoring field trials open to all pointing breed dogs. The trials are conducted under circumstances closely resembling actual wild bird hunting. Web site: www.nstra.org.

National specialty show: The show sponsored by the national breed club.

Natrum sulphicum: Homeopathic remedy prescribed for liver disease and jaundice, especially when accompanied by diarrhea, vomiting, or tenderness in the abdominal region near the liver.

Natural ears: Uncropped ears.

Natural Life Pet Products: Telephone: (620) 724-8012. Web site: www.nlpp.com.

Natura Pet Products: Telephone: (800) 532-7261.

Nausea: A feeling of sickness with an impulse to vomit.

NAVHDA: North American Versatile Hunting Dog Association, created in 1983 as a not-for-profit organization to preserve the hunting instincts of sporting breeds.

n-Butyl chloride: Dewormer, especially for roundworm and hook worm. No longer widely used.

ND: Doctor of Naturopathy.

N def: nerve deficit (veterinary notation).

NDGA: Nordihydroguaiaretic acid. Causes kidney disease in experimental animals.

Neapolitan mastiff: Ancient Italian breed (150 pounds or more) used as a guard dog and watchdog.

Neckline: In sledding, the line attached to the dog's collar that keeps it close to the gangline.

Neck well set on: Good neckline.

Necropsy: Postmortem examination.

Necrosis: Cell and tissue death.

Needle aspiration biopsy: A sampling of fluid and soft tissue from a lesion, done by inserting a needle.

Negative punishment: In operative conditioning dog training, removing something the animal desires in order to suppress or weaken the unwanted behavior. Turing one's back on a jumping dog is an example of negative punishment.

Negative reinforcement: In operant conditioning dog training, removing something the animal fears or dislikes in order to strengthen or increase the frequency of a behavior. Marginally different from positive punishment, because the negative reinforcer must be present or at least threatened before it can be removed.

Nematodes: Parasitic worms including roundworms, filarial worms, lungworms, kidney worms, and heartworms.

Nemex (Pyrantel pamoate): Dewormer prescribed for hookworms and roundworms.

Neomycin: A topical antibiotic. Part of NeoSporin.

Neonate: A newborn.

Neophobia: Fear of the unknown.

Neoplasia: Progressive abnormal multiplication of cells; may be cancerous.

Neoplasis: Abnormal cell growth.

Neoplasm: A lump; may be cancerous.

NeoSporin: Topical antibiotic combination.

Neoteny: The retention of juvenile characteristics into adulthood.

Nephric: Relating to the kidneys.

Nephritis: Inflammation of the kidneys, either acute or chronic.

Nephro-: Pertaining to the kidneys.

Nephrology: Study of kidney disorders.

Nephropathy: Non-specific kidney disease.

Nephrosclerosis: Sclerosis of the kidney.

Nephrotoxic: Toxic to the kidneys.

Nerve: (1) Fiber conducting nerve transmission.(2) The ability to remain calm in a tough situation.

Nervine: In herbal medicine, a substance that tones and strengthens the nervous system.

Nervous system: Body system that includes the brain, the spinal cord, and all the nerves that communicate between tissues and the brain and spinal cord.

Nestle Purina Pet Care Co.: Telephone: (800) 551-7392. Web site: www.proplan.com.

Net energy: Energy available to the animal for maintenance, growth, work, gestation, and lactation.

Neuritis: Inflammation of a nerve.

Neuro-: Pertaining to the nervous system.

Neurocranium: Braincase.

Neurofibroma: Spindle cell tumors that arise from the connective tissue components of the peripheral nerve.

Neurohypophysis: Posterior lobe of the pituitary gland.

Neurology: The study of the disease and functions of the nervous system.

Neuron: Brain cell.

Neuropathy: Functional disturbance in the peripheral nervous system.

Neurotoxin: A chemical that causes injury to a nerve cell.

Neurotransmitter: Chemical that transmits a signal between two nerve cells.

Neutering: Another name for castration, the surgical removal of the testicles. Employed for purposes of birth control and reducing territoriality and aggression, also sometimes used as medical treatment for disorder directly influenced by testosterone, such as prostate disease, perianal hernias, and some tumors.

Neutrophil: Most common type of white blood cell.

Newfie: Affectionate name for a Newfoundland.

Newfoundland: Canadian breed developed for its lifesaving skills. Size: 26 to 30 inches, 100 to 150 pounds. Known for its sweet disposition.

New Guinea singing dog (*Canis familiaris hallstromi*): Wild dog similar to the Australian dingo, but much smaller. They possess a DNA triplet not found in any other canid.

NFC: National field champion. The title is prefixed to the dog's name. The title is won in the annual AKC national amateur field trial conducted by each of the several pointing breeds.

NGA: National Greyhound Association.

NGC, NGC-V, NCG-JH: Novice Gamblers, Veterans, Junior Handlers (NADAC).

NGDC: National Gun dog champion. The title is prefixed to the name.

Nick: Breeding that produces excellent puppies.

Nictitating membrane: Third eyelid, a pink membrane normally folded out of sight in the inner corner of the dog's eye.

Nidation: In pregnancy, the critical time when the embryos attach to the uterine wall.

NIDDM: Non-insulin dependent diabetes mellitus, a less severe type of diabetes mellitus in which supplemental insulin is not required. Also called Type II diabetes.

Night blindness: Poor vision at night, an early sign of PRA.

Nimrod: Bloodhound owned by Sir Walter Scott.

Nipper: Name of the smooth fox terrier that served as the RCA mascot.

Nite Champion: A dog that has won one hundred AKC points with at least one first place in an AKC-licensed Nite Hunt.

Nite hunt: Competition hunts for coons that are held at night.

Nitrofuran antibacterials: Antibacterial agents prescribed for urinary tract infections and superficial bacterial infections of the skin.

Nitrogen: A chemical element occurring in proteins and amino acids, and is thus present in all living cells.

Nitroglycerin: A vasodilator prescribed for acute heart failure.

Nitrous oxide (laughing gas): An anesthetic often combined with halothane or methoxyflurane in a mix that allows the dog to be kept on a lighter anesthesia level.

NJC, NJC-V, NJC-JH: Novice Jumpers Certificate, Veterans, Junior Handlers (NADAC).

NNTSA: No need to see again (veterinary notation).

NOAD: No other abnormality detected (veterinary notation).

NOAF: No other abnormal findings (veterinary notation).

NOC: National Obedience Champion. The title is prefixed to the name.

Nocardia: A type of bacteria that commonly live in the soil, but which can cause infection in animals.

No C/S/V/D: No coughing, sneezing, vomiting or diarrhea (veterinary notation).

Nocturia: Excessive urination at night.

Nociception: Perception of pain.

Nodular dermatofibrosis: A condition of lumps in the leg that signal cancer in the kidneys or uterus. Primarily affecting German shepherd dogs.

Nodule: Solid bump or lump in the skin that is over one-third of an inch in diameter.

No go: A dog that refuses to leave its handler when ordered to retrieve.

Nonessential amino acids: Amino acids required for protein synthesis but which are made by animals in their bodies. The animals do not need to consume them in their food.

Nonessential nutrients: Nutrients that can be synthesized by the body at levels sufficient to meet its needs.

Nonslip retriever: Dog who walks at heel, marks the fall, and retrieves game on command. It is not expected to find or flush.

Nonspherocytic hemolytic anemia: Mild anemia caused by abnormal red blood cells.

Non-sporting: This diverse group includes the chow chow, bulldog, dalmatian, and poodle. While ancestral functions varied, most today are used as companions.

Nonsteroidal Anti-Inflammatory Drugs (NSAIDs): Painkiller and anti-inflammatory medications including aspirin, acetaminophen, and ibuprofen. This class of drugs prevents pain by blocking production of certain prostaglandins, hormone-like compounds with a wide range of functions in the body, including those that produce inflammation. Those most commonly prescribed for dogs include long-acting carprofen (Rimadyl) and short-acting etodolac (Etogesic).

Nonsuppurative: pertaining to inflammation without the production of pus.

Nonviable: Unable to live.

Norepinephrine: Noradrenaline, a neutrotransmitter and hormone released by the adrenal gland to increase blood pressure.

Norfolk terrier: A small, good-natured, fearless dog. Size: 9 to 10 inches, 10 to 12 pounds. One of the smallest of the working dogs. Has a hard, wiry, straight coat in all shades of red, wheaten, black-and-tan, or grizzle. May have dark points.

Normokalemia: Normal potassium level in the blood.

Norsk elghund: Norwegian elkhound.

North American Dog Agility Council, Inc.: 11522 South Highway 3, Catalso, ID 38310. Web site: www.nandac.com.

North American Flyball Association Inc.: 1400 W. Devon Avenue, #512, Chicago, IL 60660. Web site: www.flyball.org.

North American Hunting Retriever Association: A not-for-profit organization created in 1983 to preserve the hunting instincts of our retrieving breeds.

North American Veterinary Technicians Association: P. O. Box 224; Battle Ground, IN 47920. Telephone: (317) 742-2216.

Norweign elkhound: Used in antiquity by the Vikings to hunt bear and other large game. Size: 19 to 20 inches, 45 to 55 pounds, with a thick weather-resistant coat, usually in various shades of gray with a silver undercoat.

Norwich terrier: Developed in the late nineteenth century. A small, spirited, stock dog. Has a hard, wiry, straight coat in all shades of red, wheaten, black-and-tan, or grizzle. Size: about 10 inches, 12 pounds.

NOS: (1) No other symptoms (veterinary notation). **(2)** Not otherwise specified.

Nosebleed (Epistaxis): Generally indicating an ulceration or injury to the mucous membrane.

Nose rope: The heavy horizontal wrinkle that lies across the nose of the bulldog and similar breeds.

Nosode: Homeopathic remedy prepared from infected tissue or disease organism. Often administered like a vaccine.

Notoedres: A genus of mites.

Nova Scotia duck tolling retriever: Smallest of the retrievers.

Novice: In a conformation show, a class for any dog who has not yet won a championship point or has won fewer than three first-place ribbons in the Novice class.

Novice A/B: Basic level obedience classes. Dogs successfully achieving three qualifying scores ("legs") of at least 170 out of 200 points (including earning at least 50 percent of available points for each separate exercise) are awarded the title Companion Dog and are allowed to add the CD suffix to their registered name.

Novice Agility: For a title, dog must earn three qualifying scores in Novice A and/or B Agility class under at least two different judges.

Novice Agility Jumper: For a title, dog must earn three qualifying scores in Novice A and/or B Jumpers with Weaves class under at least two different judges.

Novice Junior: A handling class for young people between the ages of ten and fourteen who have not yet won three first-place awards in a novice handling class against competition.

Novice Senior: A handling class for young people between the ages of fourteen and eighteen who have not yet won three first-place awards in a novice handling class against competition.

NPD: Non-prescription drug.

NQ'd: Not qualified, due to failure to complete an exercise.

NRC: National Research Council.

N/S: Next step (veterinary notation).

NSAID: Nonsteroidal anti-inflammatory drug.

NSF: No significant finding (veterinary notation).

NSTRA: National Shoot-to-Retrieve Field Trial Association.

Nuchal crest: Top of occiput.

Nuclear sclerosis (lenticular sclerosis): An eye condition of aging dogs in which the lens compacts and hardens, changing its refractive property. Pupils may appear bluish. Eyesight is not affected much.

Nutraceutical: A nontoxic food component that has scientifically proven health benefits.

Nutrient: A food ingredient that will support life. Nutrients are usually considered to be proteins, carbohydrates, fats, minerals, and vitamins.

Nutritional adequacy statement: In dog-food labeling, a statement that informs the consumer about the completeness of the food for growth, maintenance, or lactation.

Nutro Products, Inc: Telephone: (800) 833-5330. Web site: www.nutroproducts.com.

O

O-: Outstanding Performance, prefixed to any NADAC title.

O: Owner.

O₂: Oxygen.

OA: (1) Open Agility (AKC title). Title follows the dog's name. (2) Osteoarthritis.

OAC, OAC-V, OAC-JH: Open Agility Certificate Standard, Veterans, Junior Handlers (NADAC).

OAJ: Open Agility Jumper (AKC title). Title follows the dog's name.

Obedience trial: A competitive AKC performance event in which dogs are tested on their ability to respond to specific instructions. Dogs are scored on their tractability, style, and execution using a scale of 0 to 200 points. Dogs achieving three qualifying scores ("legs") of at least 170 are awarded official AKC/CKC titles as suffixes to their registered name.

Obedience trial champion: A dog that has won one hundred points, plus at least one first-place Open B (with at least six in competition), one first-place Utility (with at least three in competition) and a third-place ribbon in either class. The first places must be awarded by two different judges. The placements must be at all-breed events. One of the required first places may have been won at a Specialty Show.

Nux vomica: A homeopathic remedy for cancer, digestive upset, constipation, gastritis, liver disease, and poisoning.

Nystagmus: Constant involuntary movement of the eye, often from side to side.

Nystatin: Antifungal prescribed for superficial fungal infections due to yeasts (Candida and Malassezia).

NZCh: New Zealand Champion.

Obese: Overweight. Fat.

Oblique fracture: Bone broken at an angle.

Oblique shoulders: Shoulders well laid back.

Obliquely placed eyes: Eyes at an angle so that the outer corner is higher than the inner corner. Required in the Alaskan malamute and bull terrier.

Oblong eyes: Eye formation in which the eyelid aperture appears longer than it is high, with gently rounded corners.

Obsessive-compulsive disorder: A condition in which a dog is psychologically driven to repeat the same behavior, such as licking or snapping at flies.

Obstipation: Complete blockage of the lower bowel, often caused by a piece or splinter of bone.

Obtuse turn: In tracking, an oblique or open turn of more than 90 degrees.

Occipital protuberance: A prominently raised occiput, characteristic of many sporting and hound breeds.

Occiput: Highest point at the back of the skull; the crest or peak.

Occlude: To close off or constrict.

Occult heartworm test: A test for antibodies to heartworms. This is the most accurate heartworm test.

OCD: Osteochondritis dessicans.

OCNE: Off color, not eating (veterinary notation).

OCT: Over-the-counter medication.

Ocular: Pertaining to the eye.

OD: Right eye (veterinary notation).

OED: Old English sheepdog.

OFA: Orthopedic Foundation for Animals.

Offal: Animal organs rejected at slaughter as unfit for human consumption. Often used as by-products in dog food.

Off game: Any unwanted game.

Off label: Term used to describe the use of a medication for a condition for which it was not formally FDA approved. A large number of medications used in veterinary medicine are used off label.

OGC, OGC-V, OCG-JH: Open Gamblers Certificate, Veterans, Junior Handlers (NADAC).

OHE: Ovariohysterectomy; surgical removal of the ovaries.

Ointment: A semi-solid medicinal preparation to be applied to the skin or eyes.

OJC, OJC-V, OJC-JH: Open Jumpers Certificate, Veterans, Junior Handlers (NADAC).

Old dog vestibular syndrome: A condition in geriatric dogs characterized by sudden onset of circling and abnormal eye movements. It generally resolves itself.

Old English sheepdog: Stocky drover's dog with a bobtail, used for herding, guarding, and sledding. Developed in the early nineteenth century although similar dogs were reported much earlier. Its profuse, shaggy coat covers the whole dog, including the face and eyes. Size: 21 to 22 inches, 65 to 70 pounds.

Old Mother Hubbard Dog Food Company: Telephone: (800) 225-0904. Web site: www.old motherhubbard.com.

Olecranon: Bony point of the elbow.

Olfactory: Referring to the sense of smell.

Olfactory abilities: Sense of smell.

Olfactory nerve: One of the twelve cranial nerves of the dog.

Oliguria: An abnormally small amount of urine. Usually due to dehydration or acute kidney failure.

-ology: A suffix meaning "study of."

Omeprazole: Anti-ulcer drug prescribed for ulcers of the gastrointestinal tract.

Omnivorous: Subsisting on both plants and animals.

Oncology: The study of cancer and tumors.

Onion: Vegetable causing hemolytic anemia in dogs.

Ontogeny: Development of an individual from birth to adulthood.

Onychodystrophy: Malformed nails.

Onyx: An award given in flyball competitions based on points earned, named after its first recipient.

Oocyst: Resting stage of a parasite.

op: Operation (veterinary notation).

-opathy: Disease or dysfunction of.

Open: (1) In a conformation dog show, any dog of the breed, at least six months of age. **(2)** In hunting, the announcement by a dog that a track has been located.

Open A/B (Obedience): Mid-level obedience classes (off lead) that earn the title of Companion Dog Excellent (CDX) if a dog earns three qualifying scores of at least 170 out of 200 points (including earning at least 50 percent of available points for each exercise) from three different judges. Obedience classes are divided into two groups (A and B). "A" is for exhibitors who have not yet added this title to a dog's name that they have either handled or trained, and "B" is for more experienced exhibitors who have done so.

Open Agility: For a title, dog must earn three qualifying scores in Open Agility class under at least two different judges.

Open Agility Jumper: For a title, dog must earn three qualifying scores in Open Jumpers with Weaves classes under at least two different judges.

Open bitch: A bitch that can be bred.

Open coat: A sparse coat, usually lacking in undercoat.

Open face with cap: In malamutes, facial markings where the face itself is all white with a widow's peak or cap of dark color.

Open feet: Splay-footed.

Open fontanel (or fontanelle): Incomplete closure of the bones of the skull.

Open Junior: A handling class for young people between the ages of ten and fourteen who have already won three first-place awards in a novice handling class against competition.

Open registry: Health database that allows full access to its information.

Open Senior: A handling class for young people between the ages of fourteen and eighteen who have already won three first-place awards in a novice handling class against competition.

Open stakes: Open field trial stakes open to all handlers, both amateur and professional. These have the highest level of competition.

Open trailing: Vocalizing while hunting.

Open tunnel: In agility, a long, rigid open tube, often sharply bent in competition. Also called a pipe tunnel.

Operant conditioning: A system of training in which the trainer gets a dog to change its response to a specific stimulus by manipulating the consequences to the response.

Ophthalmo-: Pertaining to the eye.

Ophthalmology: Study of the diseases and function of the eye.

Ophthalmoneuritis: Inflammation of the optic nerve.

Ophthalmoplegia: Paralysis of the eye muscles.

Ophthalmoscope: Instrument for examining the interior of the eye.

Opiate: A sedative narcotic containing opium or its derivatives.

Opioid: Narcotic drug that has an activity similar to that of opium.

Opium: (1) A homeopathic remedy for constipation, the dried latex of poppy. **(2)** A narcotic.

Optic nerve colobomas: Holes in the optic disc.

Optic nerve hypoplasia: Incomplete development of the optic nerve in one or both eyes.

Oral: Referring to the mouth.

Oral dosing: Administering a liquid medication by squirting it in the mouth.

Oral melanoma: Cancer most common in dogs with dark-pigmented mouths.

Orb: Eyeball.

Orbit: Eye socket.

Orchitis: Inflammation of the testicles.

Order up a dog: In field events, the judges' command to a handler to remove his dog from the course upon completion of judging or for an infraction that disqualifies the dog.

Organophosphates: Phosphorus-containing organic pesticides.

Organotropy: In homeopathy, the affinity of a substance for a particular organ or organ system.

Organ system: A group of organs that function together.

Ornamentation: Furnishings.

Oro-nasal fistula: Result of an opening between the hard palate and nasal cavity.

Orthomolecular therapy: Provides a combination of vitamins and minerals. Because of the toxicity of some of the minerals, this therapy should be carried out only under the direction of a veterinarian.

Orthopedic Foundation for Animals (OFA): 2300 East Nifong Boulevard, Columbia,

MO 65201-3856. Telephone: (573) 442-0418. A research, diagnostic, and closed registry organization of veterinary orthopedists whose mission is to organize, collate, and disseminate information concerning orthopedic and genetic disease of animals. Founded in 1966. It maintains records on orthopedic diseases, craniomandibular osteopathy, autoimmune thyroiditis, congenital heart disease, copper toxicosis in Bedlington terriers, and DNA registries. Web site: www.offa.org

Orthopedics: The study of the bones and joints.

OS: Left eye (veterinary notation).

-osis: Disease condition.

Osmosis: The tendency of water to pass through a membrane (such as a cell or mucosal membrane) separating two solutions of unequal concentration. The water moves from the less concentrated to the more concentrated solution until the concentrations are equal or the increased osmotic pressure stops further passage of water.

Osmotic pressure: The pressure caused by osmosis. It is equal to the increased pressure in the more concentrated solution.

Os penis: A bone that forms the skeleton of the penis.

Ossicle: The three bones of the middle ear that transmit sound waves.

Ossification: Formation of bone.

Osteoarthritis: Inflammation of joint cells.

Osteoarthrosis: Pathological damage to joint cells.

Osteochondritis dissecans (OCD): A common arthritic-like condition usually occurring in the shoulder, in which the cartilage covering the head of a long bone thickens and grows abnormally; the bone beneath the cartilage is easily traumatized and can develop fractures. The cause is thought to be partly genetic and partly environmental. Signs include mild or moderate lameness, usually appearing in large, rapidly growing dogs between four and twelve months.

Osteochondrosis: Abnormal development of the joint cartilage, usually shoulder, knee, and elbow. Similar to osteochondritis dissecans.

Osteomyelitis: An inflammation and infection of the bone.

Osteosarcoma: Very malignant and common bone cancer that typically strikes large and giant breeds, especially the long bones of the leg. Spreads readily to the lungs. Signs may mimic that of a sprain. Treatment of choice is amputation followed by chemotherapy.

OTC: Over the counter.

OTCH: Obedience Trial Champion. This is a competitive title and is prefixed to the dog's name.

OTD: Open Trial Dog, title awarded to herding dogs by the Australian Shepherd Club of America.

Otic: Relating to the ear.

Otitis externa: Ear canker; infection of the outer ear, including the ear canal.

Otitis interna: Infection of the inner ear. It is usually preceded by middle ear infection.

Otitis media: Infection of the middle ear.

Oto: Pertaining to the ear.

Otoscope: An instrument to examine the dog's ear.

Ototoxic: Destructive to the structures of the ear.

Otter head: Head shape characteristic of the border terrier.

Otterhound: A large, rough-coated hound developed during the Middle Ages. Size: 24 to 27 inches, 80 to 115 pounds, with a long, dense coat of any color.

Otter tail: A round, thick-rooted, tapering tail.

Out at elbow: A condition in which the elbows stick out from the side.

Out at shoulder: Shoulder blades too loosely attached to the body.

Outcrossing: The mating of unrelated individuals of the same breed.

Out of coat: Lacking sufficient coat.

Oval chest: A chest deeper than it is wide.

Oval eye: Egg-shaped eye.

Oval foot: Spoon-shaped foot.

Ovariohysterectomy: Removal of the ovaries and uterus; spaying.

Ovcharka: Large livestock guardian dog from Russia and Central Asia. Also called Caucasian Mountain dog. Used for police, protection, and sheep guarding work.

Overbuilt back: Excessive development over the rump.

Overdone: A dog with extreme angulation.

Over gee: In sledding, move to the right side of the trail.

Overhang: A heavy or pronounced brow.

Over haw: In sledding, move to the left side of the trail.

Overlapping: Crossing over.

Overlay: Mantle of dark color on a lighter background.

Overreaching: A faulty trot in which the rear legs reach beyond and to the outside of the front feet. This is a common fault, caused by more angulation and drive behind than in front.

Overrun: In lure coursing, the failure of the lure operator to maintain a ten- to thirty-yard distance in front of the lead hound, resulting in the lead hound passing or overtaking the lure.

Overshot bite: The upper incisors overlap or extend beyond the lower incisors, leaving a gap.

Oviohysterectomy (OHE): Spaying; the ovaries and uterus are removed. The procedure involves a small incision just below the navel, and usually takes only ten to twenty minutes. Contrary to popular belief, female dogs do not need to have a heat cycle before being spayed.

Ovulation: Release of eggs from the ovary.

Ovum: Egg.

Owner Handler's Association of America: An organization devoted to the education of the owner handler. Web site: www.canineworld.com/oha.

Oxalate: Mineral sediment of stones produced in the bladder.

Oxidation: (1) Metabolism of food by adding oxygen to release energy. **(2)** Any process adding oxygen or removing electrons, such as oxidative damage to cell membranes.

Oxytocin: Hormone that stimulates urine contraction and milk letdown.

P

P: Chemical symbol for phosphorus.

PABA: Para-aminobenzoic acid.

Pace: Moving legs on the same side together, as opposed to a trot, in which diagonal legs move together.

Pack: A group of hounds kept together in one kennel.

Packed cell volume (PCV): The amount of space taken up by cells, when they are permitted to settle, in comparison with the whole blood volume.

Pad: Thick, cushiony skin on the underside of the foot; the sole.

Padding: A gaiting fault in which the front feet flip up and outward to avoid clipping with the rear.

Paddling: A gaiting fault in which the front feet are thrown out sideways. Often cause by an east-west front.

PAF: Platelet-activating factor.

Palatable: Good-tasting.

Palate: Fleshy structure located at the roof of the mouth; it separates the oral cavity from the nasal passage.

Pale gums: May indicate anemia, dehydration, or shock.

Palliative: A substance that relieves some of the signs of the disease without curing it.

Palmar: In reference to the front foot pads.

palp: Palpate or palpation (veterinary notation).

Palpation: Feeling with the hand to make a physical diagnosis.

Palpebrae: Eyelids.

Palpebral fissure: Space between the eye and the eyelid when the eyes are open.

Pan-: Word prefix meaning all.

Panacur: A dewormer (hookworms, roundworms, whipworms, and, to a lesser extent, tapeworms). Also called Fenbendazole.

Pancreat-: Pertianing to the pancreas.

Pancreatic degenerative atrophy: Disease of the pancreas, resulting in the inability to digest and absorb food.

Pancreatic enzymes: Enzymes secreted into the intestine including amylase, endo- and exopeptidases, and lipase.

Pancreatic enzyme test: Test for levels of lipase, amylase, and pancreatic function.

Pancreatic exocrine insufficiency (PEI): Exocrine pancreatic insufficiency, the inability of the exocrine pancreas to produce adequate amounts of digestive enzymes.

Pancreatic insufficiency: See pancreatic exocrine insufficiency.

Pancreatinum: A homeopathic remedy and nosode prepared from pancreatic extract; administered for pancreatitis, and can be used in conjunction with trypsinum.

Pancreatitis: Inflammation of the pancreas. This is a painful condition in which the pancreas over produces digestive enzymes that then start to damage the pancreas itself.

Panmixia: Random breeding; a mating system in which mating is governed entirely by chance.

Pannus (chronic superficial keratitis): Ongoing inflammation of the cornea (the surface of one or both eyes). Progressive and potentially blinding. Most common in German shepherd dogs.

Panolog: Brand name for medication that combines antifungal, antibiotic, and corticosteroid for topical use in cases of superficial bacterial or fungal infections, especially in the ear.

Panosteitis (pano): Inflammation of the bone, particularly the long bones, in rapidly growing puppies. Also known as "growing pains" or shifting-leg lameness, since the limp may shift from one leg to another. Causes pain and limping, but usually resolves without treatment.

Panting: While some panting is normal for dogs (if they couldn't pant they would die from overheating), excessive panting when external heat is not a factor may indicate anxiety, fever, anemia, or thyroid disease.

Pantothenic acid: B vitamin needed for good skin and coat. It also acts with vitamin A to promote growth. Found in organ and muscle meat, eggs, and cereal.

Paper foot: Flat-footed.

Papilloma: A wart, usually noncancerous.

Papillon: A small, playful dog (8 to 11 inches) with large, rounded eyes and a silky coat, white with any other color. The phalene variety has droopy ears.

Papules: Small red bumps, less than one-third of an inch.

Para-aminobenzoic acid: Active ingredient in sunscreen that absorbs ultraviolet rays, preventing them from reaching the skin.

Parainfluenza: Virus that causes respiratory infections. Highly contagious, but not terribly dangerous. Transmitted by sneezing or coughing.

Paralysis: Loss of motor function.

Paraphimosis: Condition in which the penis cannot be withdrawn into its sheath.

Parasite: An organism living in or on another organism.

Parasympathetic: The portion of the nervous system that stimulates the pancreas to produce digestive enzymes. Also stimulates many of the smooth muscles in the body, including those of the stomach and intestine.

Parathyroid: One of the small glands imbedded in the thyroid that control calcium storage in the body.

Parent club: A nationally recognized AKC club that sets the standard for a breed. The AKC recognizes only one parent club for each breed. The national breed club.

Parenteral: Administration of a medication by some means other than by mouth, including intravenous, intramuscular, and subcutaneous.

Parenteral fluids: Fluid given subcutaneously or intravenously rather than orally.

Parenteral nutrition: Administering nutritional support by intravenous or intraperitoneal means.

Paresis: Partial or slight paralysis.

Paronychia: Inflammation of the nail beds.

Parotid duct transposition: Eye surgery to correct KCS (dry eye).

Paroxysm: (1) Sudden onset of a sign that recurs. **(2)** A seizure or spasm.

Parsley: In herbal medicine, administered for arthritis and indigestion.

Parson Russell terrier: Jack Russell Terrier. The AKC, beginning in April 2003, changed the official name from Jack Russell terrier to the Parson Russell terrier. The name Parson Russell Terrier is the correct name of the breed in England and in most kennel clubs around the world. The breed was developed to hunt foxes above and below ground.

Partial dominance: In genetics, a condition in which dominance is shared with other genes.

Parti-colored: Spotted or variegated mix of two or more colors.

Parturition: The birthing process, also called whelping. Consists of three phases: prelabor, true labor, and expulsion.

Parvovirus: Highly contagious and dangerous viral disease spread through contact with infected feces. Symptoms include high fever, depression, vomiting, and bloody diarrhea. In many cases (especially in puppies), it can lead to shock and death.

Pas: Pyrrolizidine alkaloids. Natural chemicals found in ragwort; poisonous to dogs and other animals.

Passing gas: Flatulence.

Passive immunity: Immunity produced by providing an animal with antibodies or immunologic cells from another source, such as colostrum.

Pastern: The metacarpal region; the foot, just above the toes.

Pastore Maremmano-Abruzzese: Maremma sheepdog.

Patchy tongue: Incompletely pigmented tongue.

Patella: The kneecap.

Patellar luxation: A looseness or hyperextension of the joining tendons affecting the knee or stifle joint that allows the kneecap to slip, causing inability to move correctly. The groove in the kneecap may be too shallow. It is thought to be a genetically inheritable tendency, but it can also be caused by injury. Luxated patellae can be surgically corrected. This is a condition affecting mostly smaller breeds, although some larger breeds are prone to a specific type of patellar luxation. Signs include locked leg, or skipping. The dog may walk normally between bouts of lameness.

Patent ductus arteriosus (PDA): A condition in which the normal opening between the aorta and pulmonary artery, which allows blood to bypass the unoxygenated lung in utero, fails to close after birth.

Pathogen: Disease-causing bacteria or other microorganisms.

Pathogenic: Capable of causing disease.

Pathology: The study of damaging changes to tissues.

Patterdale: Old name for a Lakeland terrier.

Pattern: In pointing breed events, the movement of the dog back and forth into the wind as it checks objectives.

Pause box: In agility, a low platform or marked area about four feet square in which the dog must demonstrate control by sitting or lying down until "released" by the handler.

Pause table: In agility, a raised three-foot-square platform in which the dog must demonstrate control by sitting or lying down until "released" by the handler.

PBGV: Petit basset griffon Vendéen.

PBT: Pit bull terrier.

PCR: Polymerase chain reaction.

PCV: Packed cell volume, hematocrit (veterinary notation)

PD: Polydipsia.

PDA: Patent ductus arteriosus.

PE: Physical exam (veterinary notation).

Peak: Occiput.

Peanut hulls: A filler in some dog foods.

Pearled barley: Hulled barley grain.

Pear-shaped head: Head shape characteristic of the Bedlington terrier.

Pearson square: A method of determining the relative proportions of two ingredients required to achieve an intermediate nutrient concentration.

Pedaling: In dog sledding, the driver rides the runners behind the sled and pushes the sled with one foot.

Pedialyte: Solution of salts and dextrose to be given after a bout of diarrhea or vomiting or when your dog is stressed by heat.

Pediculosis: Lice infection, usually seen in young animals kept in an unclean environment.

Pedigree: A dog's family tree, usually showing four or five generations. It is not the same as a registration.

Pekingese: Scaled-down version of an ancient Chinese breed, sometimes called the lion dog or sun dog. A stocky dog weighing less than 14 pounds, with a long, coarse coat of any color.

Peking Palasthund: Pekingese.

Pelger-Huet: Abnormal development of neutrophils.

Pelvic angulation: Lay of the pelvis; pelvic slope.

Pelvic girdle: Two fused bony halves attached to the sides of sacral vertebrae.

Pelvis: Basin-shaped area formed by the hipbones.

Pembroke Welsh corgi: Similar to the Cardigan Welsh corgi, but with a very short tail.

Pemphigus (Pemphigus foliaceous): Autoimmune disease of the skin, producing lesions.

Pemphigus complex: A group of rare viral diseases such as pemphigus foliaceous, pemphigus erythematosus, and pemphigus vegetans, characterized by depression, mouth ulcers, swollen joints, rashes, blisters, and crusty sores. One type, pemphigus vulgaris, is often fatal. Treatment may include prednisone and other immuno-suppressive drugs.

Pemphigus erythematosus: An autoimmune condition that is probably a less aggressive form of pemphigus foliaceous.

Pencilled: Lay of coat on Dandie Dinmont terrier.

Pencilling: Black lines on tan-colored toes.

Penetrance: The probability or frequency of observing a particular phenotype or trait, conditional on having a particular genotype. If penetrance is less than 100 percent, it is called incomplete penetrance.

Penicillin antibiotics: A large group of bacteria-killing drugs.

Penn Hip Improvement Program: A closed registry of hip looseness measurements that relies on a radiograph. Uses a DI (distraction index), a number from 0.0 to 1.00. The lower the number, the better the hip. See OFA for a similar program. Web site: www.pennhip.org

Pepper and salt: Mixture of light and dark hair.

Peppering: Black and white hairs, usually referring to schnauzers.

Peppermint and peppermint tea: In herbal medicine, administered for nausea, coughing, and gastritis. In aromatherapy, used to suppress a cough.

Peptic ulcer: Ulcer in the lower end of the esophagus, stomach, or duodenum caused by the secretion of pepsin, an enzyme produced in the mucous lining of the stomach.

Peracute: Extremely rapid onset.

Performance dog: Physically fit and trained dog that competes in performance events.

Performance events: Events in which dogs are evaluated according to how they perform tasks for which they were bred, such as hunting, herding, and tracking.

Performance food: Usually a dog food with at least 30 percent crude protein and 20 percent fat, with 82 to 86 percent digestibility.

Perianal: The region around the anus.

Perianal adenoma: A generally benign tumor arising from the glands located around the anus.

Perianal fistula: A draining lesion in the area around the anus. Common in German shepherd dogs.

Perianal hernia: Rupture in the abdominal wall near the anal opening.

Periarteritis nodosa: Polyarteritis nodosa.

Pericardium: Sac-like tissue surrounding the heart.

Perineum: Region between the anus and the urethral opening.

Periodontal disease: A tooth and gum infection that is the main cause of bad breath in dogs. It affects as many as 85 percent of all dogs.

Periosteum: Connective tissue covering all the bones of the body.

Peripheral nervous system: Part of the nervous system that include the cranial nerves (except the optic nerve), the spinal nerves, and the autonomic nervous system.

Peristalsis: Wavelike muscular contractions of the gastrointestinal organs that squeeze food along the gut.

Peritoneal: The lining of the abdominal cavity.

Peritoneum: The membrane lining the wall of the abdominal cavity.

Peritonitis: Inflammation of membranes lining the abdominal cavity.

Permethrin: Altered form of the flea-killing preparation pyrethrum; lasts for about ten days.

Persian greyhound: Saluki.

Persistent pupillary membranes: Developmental abnormality in which membranes from the back of the eye attached to the cornea. may obstruct vision. Common in basenjis.

Persistent right aortic arch: Failure of the embryonic right aorta to realign in the puppy, resulting in constriction of the esophagus.

Petit basset griffon Vendéen: A small scent hound developed from similar but larger dogs dating back to at least the sixteenth century. Size: 13 to 15 inches, 20 to 30 pounds, with a long, rough coat in any combination of lemon, orange, black, tricolor, or grizzle markings.

Pet quality: A dog with faults that make it unsuitable to be shown.

Pet Sitters International: Founder Patti Moran; 418 East King Street, King, NC 27021-91630. Telephone: (336) 983-9222.

Pet therapy: See animal therapy.

Peyer's patches: Aggregated lymphoid tissues found in the lining of the small intestine.

pH: A numerical measurement of acidity or alkalinity. A pH of 7 is neutral; lower numbers are acidic, higher are basic or alkaline.

PHA: Professional Handlers' Association.

Phagocytes: Some white blood cells and other cells that eat damaged cells and foreign particles such as viruses and bacteria. A macrophage is a type of phagocyte.

Phalanges: Toes.

Pharaoh hound: A breed used for hunting by the ancient Egyptians. Size: 21 to 25 inches, with a short, glossy coat, usually tan or chestnut with white markings.

Pharyngitis: Inflammation of the pharynx, where the nasal and oral cavities converge.

Pharynx: Back of the throat.

Phenobarbital: A long-acting barbiturate (four to eight hours) and anticonvulsant used primarily to prevent epileptic seizures. It is administered orally.

Phenotype: The physical expression of a genetic characteristic.

Phenoxybenzamine: Smooth muscle relaxant prescribed for urethral spasms and some types of high blood pressure.

Phenylbutazone: NSAID prescribed as a pain reliever and fever reducer.

Phenylpropanolamine: Prescribed to improve urethral sphincter tone in cases of urinary incontinence.

Phenytoin: Antiseizure drug, prescribed for epilepsy and digitalis toxicity. Also called diphenylhydantoin.

Pheromones: Hormone-like substances that affect the behavior of another animal of the same species.

Philtrum: Line separating left and right upper lip and nostril halves.

Phimosis: The inability to extrude (extend out of the prepuce opening) the penis.

Phosphofructokinase deficiency: (1) Deficiency in a red blood cell enzyme, causing anemia. (2) Inherited disorder in glucose metabolism.

Phosphorus: (1) Mineral essential for bones and teeth, along with energy. Found in milk, eggs, meats, and cereals. (2) Homeopathic remedy for pneumonia.

Photodynamic therapy (PDT): Laser therapy for cancer, in which the patient is injected with a light-sensitive agent that precisely marks the tumor before the application of the laser. It is cheaper and less destructive than radiation therapy and is often effective as a one-time treatment.

Photophobia: Sensitivity to light.

Photosensitivity: A condition in which the skin reacts abnormally to light, especially ultraviolet light or sunlight.

Phylogeny: The evolutionary history of a group of organisms.

Phytochemicals: Substances in plants that affect a body system and may promote health and decrease the risk of a disease such as cancer.

Pica: Condition in which the dog devours non-food material such as carpets and rocks.

Picardy sheepdog: Rather large dog with harsh coat, erect ears, and long tail.

Piccolo levrievo Italiano: Italian greyhound.

Pi-dog: Crossbred dog, usually of eastern origin.

Piebald: Large, uneven black patches on white coat color. The piebald gene is found in many white or near white breeds. The whiter the coat, the more influential the piebald gene. The piebald gene is recessive and is associated with deafness, especially in dogs with blue eyes.

Pied: See piebald.

Pig: Colloquial term for a slowly moving, uninterested retriever in the field.

PIG: Pulled in group (making the cut).

Pigeon chest: A chest with a short protruding breastbone.

Pigeon toed: Feet (front or rear) pointing inward, toward each other

Pig-eye: A small, hard eye. Eyes set too close.

Pig-jaw: Overshot jaw.

Pigmentary keratitis: Deposit of pigment on the cornea, usually secondary to chronic irritation.

Pigmentation: (1) Natural color of the skin and other tissues. **(2)** The color of the lip line and eyes.

Pig mouth: Overshot jaw.

Pile: Soft, dense undercoat.

Pill curing: A Chinese patent medicine prescribed for gastritis.

Pill gun: An instrument used to administer pills.

Piloerection: Reflex that causes the hairs on the dog's back to stand up.

Pily coat: Dense, harsh outer coat coupled with a soft, fur-like inner coat.

Pin: In retriever work, when a dog runs directly to the fall and picks up the item without a hunt.

Pin bones: Upper bony protuberance of the pelvis.

Pincer bite: Even bite.

Pinched front: Narrow front.

Pinched muzzle: See snipelike muzzle.

Pinched nostrils: Narrow, closed nostrils, a fault in any breed.

Pincher bite: Level bite.

Pink nose: Lightly pigmented nose.

Pinna: Ear flap.

Pinscher: German breed, smaller than the Doberman.

Piperazine: Dewormer prescribed for roundworms.

Pipestopper tail: A short, upright tail.

Pipette: (1) A piece of equipment used to insert a rectal suppository. **(2)** A dropper for drawing fluid.

Pips: Spots above the eyes in black-and-tan breeds. Often called "eyebrows."

Piroxicam: NSAID prescribed for pain and fever. Also an antitumor agent.

Pitted teeth: Teeth disfigured by distemper.

Pituitary adenoma: Benign tumor on the pituitary gland, often leading to Cushing's disease.

Pituitary dwarfism: A rare disorder in which the function of the pituitary gland, located at the base of the brain, is reduced. All parts of the body are reduced proportionally in size.

Pituitary gland: An endocrine gland at the base of the brain.

It regulates growth and controls the functioning of many other glands and processes.

PK: Pyruvate kinase.

Placebo: An inert medicine given to humor or reassure a patient, or as a control in a medical test.

Placed: Awarded first, second, third, or fourth place in a competition.

Placenta: Tissue forming the lining of the uterus to supply nourishment to and remove waste products from the fetus.

Plaiting: See crossover.

Planes: Referring to the head, the flat area of the muzzle, and the flat area of the top skull.

Planing: Comparison of the angles of the two planes of the head.

Plantar: In reference to the back foot pads.

Planter: Person who places birds at a field trial, hunting test, or working certificate test.

Plaque: Sticky film of decaying matter that clings to the teeth.

-plasia: Suffix indicating abnormal growth.

Plasma: The clear part of blood that remains after the separation of the cells and before clot formation. If the blood is first allowed to clot and then separated, the fluid is called serum.

Plastic dish dermatitis: Skin irritation and depigmentation caused by contact with plastic food dishes.

Platelet-activating factor: Substance that causes platelets to clump together.

Platelets: Cell fragments that float in the bloodstream and help stop bleeding.

PLE: Protein-losing enteropathy.

Pleiotropism: In genetics, the connection between the expression of a certain trait, such as hair color, and a seemingly unrelated physical abnormality, such as deafness.

Pleomorphic: Existing in two or more distinct forms during the life cycle.

Plot: In tracking, to lay out a track and/or make a map. Also called "chart."

plt: Platelet.

Pluck: To remove hairs from the coat.

Plum Pudding Dog: Nickname for the Dalmatian.

Plume: Profusely feathered tail carried over the back, as in a Pomeranian or Pekingese.

PM: (1) Premolar tooth, followed by a number to indicate which one (veterinary notation). **(2)** Post-mortem. **(3)** Pairs Master (USDAA title).

PMI Nutrition: Telephone: (800) 332-4738. Web site: www.pminutrition.com.

Pneumo-: Pertaining to the lungs.

Pneumonia: Inflammation of the lung tissues, sometimes occurring after a viral upper respiratory infection.

Pneumonitis: Inflammation of lung tissue.

Pneumothorax: The presence of air or gas in the pleural cavity, usually the result of a penetrating wound.

PO (per os): Medication administered orally.

Pocket beagle: Beagles of the sixteenth century, small enough to fit in a pocket.

Podenco: Type of sight hound.

Podenco Ibicenco: Ibizan hound.

Podengo Portugues: A small-game hunter.

Point: Stance taken by a hunting dog to indicate the presence of game, usually by standing immobile and directing its muzzle toward it.

Point dead: When a dog continues to point at a dead bird instead of going to pick it up.

Point dogs: In sledding, the dogs directly behind the lead dogs.

Pointed: A dog that has least one point toward an AKC bench or field championship.

Pointer: Sporting dog bred for field work. Size: 23 to 28 inches, 45 to 75 pounds. Comes in many colors, including liver, black, and orange, either solid or combined with white. Developed to hold a point while hunters loaded and got into position with their old muzzle-loading guns.

Pointillage: To massage with the tips of the fingers.

Pointing breeds: Breeds eligible to enter AKC hunting tests. They include Brittany, pointer, German shorthaired pointer, German wirehaired pointer, English setter, Gordon setter, Irish setter, vizsla, weimaraner, and wirehaired pointing griffon.

Pointing intensity: Pointing with exceptional concentration, power, or force.

Pointing lab (PL): A lab that points at birds during an upland hunt instead of flushing them as regular labs (RL) do.

Pointing style: The degree of intensity, loftiness, or elegance a dog shows while pointing.

Pointing wirehaired griffon: Wirehaired pointing griffon.

Points: (1) Matching color on face, ears, legs, and tail that contrasts with coat color. (2) Credits toward a show or field championship.

Poison bird: A mark the dog must ignore to successfully complete the assigned task, usually a blind.

Poisonous house plants: Amaryllis, asparagus fern, crown of thorns, many ivy plants, chrysanthemum, and others.

Poisonous outdoor plants: Daffodils, azalea, yew, and others.

Poke: To carry the head forward in a low, ungainly way.

Polish lowland sheepdog: Long-haired sheep-guard dog reportedly brought to Poland by the Phoenicians.

Poltalloch terrier: West Highland white terrier.

Poly-: Prefix meaning several or too many.

Polyarteritis nodosa: An inflammatory disease of the smaller arteries.

Polyarthritis: Arthritis involving two or more joints.

Polyarthropathy: Inflammation in multiple joints.

Polycrest: In homeopathy, a deep-acting, consistently applicable remedy that has a wide action on several body systems.

Polycystic kidney: Kidney with a number of fluid-filled sacs. Usually does not cause clinical illness.

Polydactyl: Extra toes.

Polydipsia: Excessive thirst.

Polygenic disease: A disease under the control of more than one gene. Also called multigenic disease.

Polygenic traits: Characteristics controlled by an unknown number of genes.

Polymerase chain reaction (PCR): Analytical or diagnostic tool that detects minute amounts of a particular protein in a mixture.

Polymorphism: The variation between a particular gene and its mate on a pair of homologous chromosomes. Literally, having many forms.

Polymyositis: Inflammation of several muscles at once.

Polyneuropathy: Weakness of the limbs due to problems in peripheral nerves.

Polyp: A small growth from mucous membranes such as those lining the nasal cavity and intestinal tract.

Polyphagia: Excessive appetite.

Polysaccharide: Complex carbohydrate consisting of many simple monosaccharides linked together. Includes starch, glycogen, cellulose, and hemicellulose.

Polysulfated glycosaminoglycan (PSGAG): Anti-degenerative arthritic agent (Adequan).

Polyuria: Excessive urination.

Pomeranian: 3- to 7-pound spitz-type dog descended from Icelandic sled dogs. Long, straight outer coat, often a rich tan but may be any color.

Pompom (Pompon): The tuft of hair left at the end of the tail after a dog is clipped, as in poodles.

Pont-Audemer spaniel: Small spaniel developed in southern France for hunting in swamps. Colors include solid liver and liver-and-white with or without ticking in the white.

Poodle: Long-coated dog that comes in three sizes: standard (more than 15 inches), miniature (less than 15 inches), and toy (no more than 10 inches). The coat is any solid color.

Poodle eye: Condition in which tears stain the face; characteristic of poodles and some other breeds.

Poodle sheepdog (schafpudel): Medium-sized shaggy dog with long, pendant ears and a long tail. Usually pure white. Used as a sheepdog in Germany.

Pop: (1) When a dog stops to look to its handler for guidance in the hunting field. Considered a fault. **(2)** Popliteal (lymph node); veterinary notation.

Popper: Blank shotgun shell.

Popping hock: Gaiting fault describing an accentuated lift of the hock portion just after full extension of the rear.

Portacaval (also portocaval) shunt: See portosystemic shunt.

Portosystemic shunt (PSS): Congenital blood vessel abnormalities that result in venous blood from the intestine bypassing the liver. This blood vessel is operative in the embryo, but should disappear in the puppy. (Blood should flow from the digestive tract to the liver via the portal system, into the blood vessels of the liver, and then to the caudal vena cava, the large blood vessel carrying blood back to

the heart.) Also called portocaval or portacaval shunt.

Portuguese water dog: Web-footed dog that can be traced back 2,000 years or more. Size: 17 to 23 inches, 35 to 60 pounds. Comes in curly- and wavy-coated varieties of black, white, and various shades of brown.

Positive punishment: A method of training in which the trainer adds a consequence the animal will work to avoid in order to suppress or lessen the frequency of a behavior. For example, spraying water on a dog that barks.

Positive reinforcement: A method of training in which the trainer adds a reward in order to strengthen or increase the frequency of a behavior. Food treats and praise are both positive reinforcers.

Possessive aggression or possession aggression: The term used to describe threatening behavior such as staring, standing over, growling, snarling, snapping, or biting (these are increasing aggressive behaviors) to protect food, toys, or other items.

Post: Posterior (veterinary notation).

Posterior: In veterinary medicine, structures of the head (especially the eye) closer to the optic nerve or back part of the head.

Postictus: The period following an epileptic seizure. During this period, the dog may be confused, disoriented, restless, or unresponsive, or may wander or suffer from temporary blindness.

Posting: Leaning backward when stacked.

Postoperative: After surgery.

Postpartum: Period of time after giving birth.

Postprandial: Period of time immediately after eating.

Post sternum: The breastbone; located on the forechest, midway between the points of shoulders. A prominent post sternum is desirable in most sporting, working, and herding breeds and is believed to indicate a chest cavity large enough to accommodate lungs and heart expansion.

Potassium: Mineral necessary for kidney function, nerve transmission, and muscle contraction. Found in green vegetables.

Potassium bromide: Anti-seizure medication.

Pot-casse: A bark with a bell-like tone, used for the Old English sheepdog.

Potency: In homeopathy, the power of a remedy that increases with successive dilutions and succussion.

Potentization: In homeopathy, the process of increasing the potency of a remedy by diluting and shaking it.

Pot hook tail: A tail held over the back in an arc, as in the shih tzu.

Pottering: In hound field trials, dwelling too long on a scent without making progress.

Pouch: Fold of loose skin around the hock, as in the basset hound.

Poultry: In dog-food labeling, the clean flesh and skin with or without bone, exclusive of feathers, heads, feet, or entrails.

Poultry by-product: The non-rendered, clean parts of carcasses of slaughtered poultry, including heads, feet, and viscera, free from fecal content and foreign matter.

Poultry by-product meal: In dog-food labeling, the ground, rendered, clean parts of the carcass of slaughtered poultry, including necks, feet, undeveloped eggs, and intestines, exclusive of feathers.

Poultry fat (feed grade): Fat obtained from the tissue of poultry during the process of rendering or extracting.

Poultry meal (including chicken meal if the only poultry used is chicken): The dry, rendered, clean parts of the carcasses of slaughtered poultry such as necks, feet, undeveloped eggs, and intestines, exclusive of feathers except in such amounts as might occur unavoidably in good processing practices.

Pounding: When the front feet hit the ground hard; a gaiting fault resulting from a front stride shorter than the rear.

Powdered cellulose: Purified, mechanically disintegrated cellulose. Sawdust.

Powder puff: The hairy version of the Chinese crested.

PPB: Parts per billion.

PPM (ppm): (1) Persistent papillary membrane. **(2)** Parts per million.

PPP: Pretty poor prognosis (veterinary notation).

PRA: Progressive retinal atrophy.

Praziquantel: Dewormer (Droncit) prescribed for tapeworm and lung fluke.

Pre-anesthetic: Drug given before general anesthesia, usually a sedative or tranquilizer.

Preceptor: In animal law, a veterinarian serving as an instructor for a veterinary student or assistant.

Pred: Prednisolone or prednisone (veterinary notation).

Predatory expression: Bird of prey eyes.

Prednisone: Intermediate-acting (12 to 36 hours) corticosteroid. Prescribed for relief of itching and inflammation.

Prelabor: Early birthing stage in which the bitch may show nesting behavior, anxiety, lack of appetite, vomiting, or shivering. Lasts two to thirty-six hours.

Premature closure of distal radius: A condition in which one side of the radius stops growing before the other.

Premium foods: Usually considered to be a food using a fixed formula with at least 21 percent crude protein and 10 percent crude fat with 82 to 86 percent digestibility.

Premium list: Advance notice of a dog show or field trial, giving details of the event and an entry form.

Premolars: Small teeth located just behind the canine teeth and in front of the molars.

Prepotency: Very strong ability to pass on qualities to offspring.

Prepuce: The tissue that covers the penis; the sheath.

Preservative: A substance added to protect food against decay, discoloration, or spoilage.

Pressure tree dog: A dog that will stay treed until the hunter arrives and will not leave the tree for any reason. Will stand the pressure of other dogs barking nearby.

Pre-Trial Tested: Dog that has been certified by two different judges to have qualified by passing two licensed or member club Pre-Trial tests. Dog may qualify twice in one day at the same event, provided that it is judged by different judges.

Prey drive: The instinct to chase and grab.

Prick ears: Upright, usually pointed, ears.

Primary ciliary dyskinesia: Abnormal functioning of small, hairlike projections in the respiratory system.

Primary epilepsy: Chronic nervous disorder characterized by convulsions.

Primary track: In tracking, the main track the dog is supposed to follow.

prn: As needed (veterinary notation). From Latin *pro re nata*.

Prob: Problem or probably (veterinary notation).

Prodrome: (1) In epilepsy, the period that may precede the actual seizure by hours or days. It is characterized by a change in mood or behavior. **(2)** Sign indicating an oncoming disease.

Produce: The offspring of a brood bitch.

Proestrus: During this "pre-heat" period, the ovaries produce more estrogen. There may be some bleeding and gradual swelling of the vulva. This period may last from one to two weeks. Normally, females cannot be mated during this time.

Progesterone: Sex hormone produced in the ovaries after the eggs are released.

Progestins: Steroid hormones produced in the ovary and placenta, prescribed for estrus suppression.

Proglottid: Segment of a tapeworm.

Prognathism: A condition in which the upper jaw is shorter than the lower.

Prognosis: Prediction of the probable course of a disease.

Progressive posterior paresis: Paralysis of one or both hind limbs.

Progressive retinal atrophy (PRA): A family of inherited diseases characterized by slow deterioration of the retina, leading to blindness. Generally starts with difficulty seeing in the dark, then in daylight. Also called progressive retinal degeneration.

Prolapse: Structure that protrudes (usually abnormally) into another space, such as a rectal prolapse.

Prolapsed gland of the third eyelid: Cherry eye. Hypertrophy of the gland of the third eyelid. It is thought to be associated with a looseness of a small ligament that holds the gland in a normal position.

Prolapsed rectum: The inner part of the rectum pushed out so that it is visible as a pink mass protruding from the anus, usually due to injury or irritation.

Prolapse of nictitans gland: See prolapsed gland of the third eyelid.

Promace: Brand name for acepromazine.

Prong collar: Device of interlocking metal links with blunt prongs that can be worn facing either inward or outward. Used for large, hard-to-handle dogs.

Propeller ears: Ears that stick out sideways.

Propionibacterium acnes: Immunostimulant bacterial medication prescribed to treat chronic pyoderma. It activates macrophages and stimulates resistance to bacterial infection.

Proprioception: The awareness of position provided by sensory nerve terminals.

Proptosis: Displacement of the eyeball from its socket.

Prostacyclin: A protoglandin synthesized by endothelial cells lining the cardiovascular system. A potent vasodilator.

Prostaglandins: Any of a group of components derived from unsaturated 20-carbon fatty acids, primarily arachidonic acid; as medication, used to induce abortion and to treat pyometra. Prostaglandins resemble hormones.

Prostate problems: Indicated by bloody urine, or swollen penis and testicles.

Prostatitis: Condition in which the prostate gland is enlarged, causing constipation or urinary problems.

Protease: Pancreatic enzyme responsible for digesting protein.

Protein: Made from strings of amino acids. Forms the structural part of muscles and organ tissues. Nearly all enzymes and many hormones are proteins.

Protein-calorie malnutrition: A clinical syndrome produced by severe protein and calorie deficiency.

Proteinuria: Presence of excess protein in the urine.

Protein-wasting disease: Wasting disease caused by loss of protein through the kidneys or the failure to absorb protein by the intestines.

Prothrombin time: A measure of time from injury to blood clot formation.

Protamine zinc insulin: Insulin combined with large quantities of a protein called protamine, which slows the absorption of insulin from a subcutaneous injection site.

Protozoa: A single-celled animal such as an ameba.

Proving: In homeopathy, the administration of a remedy to a healthy animal sufficient to cause the symptoms noted in the *Materia Medica.*

Proximal: Toward the center of the body.

Pruritis: Itching.

Pseudocyesis: False pregnancy.

Pseudo hyperkalemia: High level of potassium in red blood that causes a falsely high reading on clotted blood samples.

Pseudopregnancy: False pregnancy.

PSGAG: Polysulfated glycosaminoglycan.

PSS: Portosystemic shunt.

Psychogenic water consumption: Drinking water without thirst, usually from stress or boredom.

Psychoneuroimmunology: A field of medicine that studies the interactions between the psyche, the nervous system, and the immune system.

Psyllium: Bulk laxative made from the seeds of certain plants such as *Plantago pysyllium;* Metamucil.

PT: (1) Pretrial Tested. **(2)** Prothrombin time.

PTH: Parathyroid hormone.

Ptosis: Drooping of the upper eyelid.

PTS: "Put to sleep;" euthanize (veterinary notation).

PU/PD: Polyuria/polydipsia (veterinary notation).

Puerperal tetany: Eclampsia.

Pug: (1) A small Chinese breed dating to at least 400 B.C. Size: 14 to 18 pounds, with a short glossy coat in silver, apricot-fawn, or black. **(2)** A pug owned by George Eliot.

Puli: Hungarian sheep-guarding dog; the name means "leader." Size: 16 to 17 inches, with a dense, weather-resistant, corded coat in various solid colors.

Pulled in group: A dog that "made the cut" in the group ring.

Pulmo: Pertaining to the lungs.

Pulmonary edema: Accumulation of fluid in the lungs.

Pulmonary embolism: Blood clot that travels to the blood vessel in the lung and obstructs them.

Pulmonic stenosis: A partial obstruction of normal blood flow of the pulmonary artery, usually due to a congenital malformation of the pulmonic valve. The effect is to force the heart to work harder to pump blood to the lungs.

Pulpitis: Inflammation of the pulp of the tooth.

Pulsatilla: A homeopathic remedy for irregular heat cycles.

Pulse: The normal pulse is 60 to 160 heart beats per minute for most adult dogs, and up to 180 beats per minute in toy breeds; it is as much as 220 beats per minute in puppies.

Pulse oximeter: An instrument that measures the oxygen saturation of a dog's red blood cells during surgery. It also measures heart rate, pulse character, and respiration.

Pumi: Curly-haired Hungarian cattle herder and guard dog.

Pump handle: Long tail carried low with an upward curve at the end.

Punch bird: In retrieving work, a term used to identify the placement of a longer mark in relation to the other marks in the field.

Punishing mouth: Powerful jaws.

PUO: Pyrexia of unknown original (veterinary notation).

Puppy: Dog less than twelve months old. In conformation dog shows, an animal between six and twelve months old, who is not yet a champion.

Puppy breath: The characteristic breath odor of all puppies, no matter what breed. The source is a certain population of bacteria that makes its home in teething gums (which bleed slightly). The bacteria produce the sweet-sour-garlicky scent. As teeth come in, the bacteria disappear, along with the puppy breath.

Puppy classes: In large dog shows there are usually two classes for puppies: Puppy Dog (or Bitch) 6 to 9 months, and Puppy Dog (or Bitch) 9 to 12 months.

Puppy clip: A coat style used for show poodles between nine and twelve months of age. Only the hair on face, feet, and tail root are clipped.

Puppy dermatitis: A term covering both impetigo and acne.

Puppyish: Immature in overall conformation.

Puppy kindergarten classes: Socialization classes held for two- to-five-month-old dogs; the classes also focus on elementary training.

Puppy mill: Commercial mass-producer of puppies, usually dealing with many breeds, often in unhealthy conditions.

Puppy stakes: Field trial stakes with age limits.

Pup trainer: Older dog that is hunted with the pup so the pup can learn by doing.

Purebred: A dog whose parents belong to the same breed and who themselves are purebred.

Purling: See crossover.

Purple-and-gold ribbon: Awarded to the dog judged "Best of Breed" in each breed competition.

Purple-and-white ribbon: Awarded to the Reserve Winners; that is, the runners-up to the winner of the Winners Dog and Winners Bitch classes in a dog show.

Purple ribbon: Awarded to the winners of the Winners Dog and Winners Bitch classes in a dog show.

Purple-ribbon bred: United Kennel Club classification of a dog that has at least three generations of registered ancestors.

Purpura: Red or purple spots on the skin resembling bruises, usually the result of blood vessel inflammation.

Purulent: Containing pus.

Pus: Yellow or greenish, foul-smelling discharge resulting from an infected wound. Contains white blood cells that accumulate in the infected tissue.

Pustule: Pimple-like, pus-filled lesion.

Put down: (1) Euthanize. (2) Get ready to be presented in a show ring.

Putty nose: See Dudley nose.

Put up: Awarded first place.

PWC: Pembroke Welsh corgi.

PWD: Portuguese water dog.

Px: (1) Physical examination or physical examination findings (veterinary notation). (2) Prognosis.

Pyelogram or pyelography: See intravenous pyelogram.

Pyloric stenosis: A narrowing of the muscular outlet of the stomach, causing frequent vomiting.

Pylorus: The distal opening of the stomach into the small intestine. Also the distal region of the stomach.

Pyo-: Pus-containing.

Pyoderma: Any purulent skin disease.

Pyometra: Accumulation of pus within the uterus, usually occurring one to two months after a bitch has been in heat. Possibly caused by hormone imbalance. Signs include excessive thirst and urination, depression, and a high temperature. There may be a brown discharge from the vulva. Associated with cystic endometrial hyperplasia. Requires emergency surgery.

Pyrantel pamoate: Active ingredient in the dewormers Nemex, Pyratabs, and Strongid T.

Pyrenean mountain dog: Great Pyrenees.

Pyrethrin: Natural flea-killing chemical, derived from chrysanthemums. Frequent application needed.

Pyrexia: Fever.

Pyridoxine: Vitamin B-6.

Pyrrolizidine alkolids: A group of poisonous plant chemicals.

Pyruvate kinase (PK) deficiency: Enzyme deficiency causing premature red blood cell destruction. Occurs in beagles and basenjis.

Pyuria: White blood cells (pus) in the urine.

PZI: Protamine zinc insulin.

Q

Q: Every (veterinary notation). Usually used with a unit of time such as hours or days.

Q2h: Every two hours.

Q4h: Every four hours.

Qi: Chi.

QID: Four times daily (veterinary notation).

Qiqirn: In Inuit myth, a spirit of a large, bald dog who both frightens people and is frightened by them.

QOD: Every other day.

Quad: In retrieving tests, four marks thrown in one series.

Qualifying Stakes: In the AKC, a competition for dogs over six months and who have never won first, second, third, or fourth place or a Judges Award of Merit (JAM) in an Open All-Age, Limited All-Age, or won first, second, third, or fourth place in an Amateur All-Age stake or two first places in Qualifying stakes. This stake is the only intermediate stake between the Derby and the Amateur or Open stakes.

Quality: Refinement, fitness. Degree of excellence.

Quarry: Prey.

Quartering: In field events, to traverse (back and forth) an area of ground while advancing forward.

Queen Anne front: Forelegs out at elbows, pasterns close, feet turned out.

Queensland Heeler: Australian Cattle Dog.

Quick: Endpoint of the blood supply in the nail; the vein in the nail.

Quicksilver: (1) Able to make abrupt turns, used for herding dogs. **(2)** Old name for mercury.

Quinidine: Anti-arrhythmic prescribed for abnormal heart rhythms.

Quinolone antibiotics: Prescribed primarily for infections of the urinary tract, prostate, lungs, GI tract, and liver.

R

R: (1) Right (veterinary notation). **(2)** Roentgen.

RA: (1) Rheumatoid arthritis **(2)** Rally Advanced, a title given in Rally.

Rabid: Having rabies.

Rabies: Fatal viral infection affecting nearly all mammals, although it is not common among rodents. It primarily attacks the nervous system. It can be spread by saliva.

Raccoon dog (*Nyctereutes procyonoides*): Canid resembling a raccoon, native to Eastern Asia.

Racy: Slight, long-legged build.

Radiation therapy: Treatment for cancer in which a series of directed bursts of radiation are focused on cancer cells to neutralize them; it kills cells by damaging their DNA. Highly effective for controlling localized tumors. A typical course is twelve treatments over four weeks. It is also sometimes done before surgery to shrink a tumor. The disadvantage of radiation therapy is that it destroys healthy as well as cancerous cells.

Radical surgery: Surgery aimed at removing all traces of a disease or growth.

Radiograph: Image created by an X-ray.

Radius: Smaller of the two bones of the foreleg.

RAE: Rally Advanced Excellent. Highest title awarded in Rally.

Rage syndrome: Sudden episode of unprovoked and unexplained aggression, possibly a form of epilepsy. Most common in English springer spaniels and cocker spaniels.

Ragged: A condition in which the muscling appears rough and ragged, instead of smooth.

Rally or Rally-O (obedience): A canine obedience sport in which the dog performs obedience exercises while moving from one instructional sign to another. (The handler reads the signs.) Unlike classic obedience, owners are permitted to encourage their dogs.

Ram's head: Convex profile, as in the bull terrier and Bedlington terrier.

Ram's nose: A nose that is straight and aquiline in profile, as in the Scottish deerhound.

Range: In field events, the distance at which a dog works from its handler.

Rangy: Disproportionately tall, long, and of a lighter build than is desired.

Ranula: Blocking of the salivary

glands beneath the tongue, producing a fluid-filled swelling.

Rapid breathing: Can indicate pain, stress, fever, overheating, or overexertion.

RAST: Radioallergosorbent.

Ration type: Canned dog food ground and blended into a uniform semi-solid substance.

Rat tail: A tapered tail that is thick at the root and devoid of most hair, such as that of the Irish water spaniel.

RBC (rbc): Red blood cells.

RBKC: Rare Breed Kennel Club.

RC: Recheck (veterinary notation). For example, RC 1Wk indicates "recheck in one week."

RCM: Restrictive cardiomyopathy.

R. C. Steele Pet Supply Company: 1989 Transit Way, Box 905, Brockport, NY 14420-0905. Telephone: (800) 872-3733. Web Site: www.rcsteele.com.

RD (Ranch Dog): Title awarded to herding dogs by the Australian Shepherd Club of America. Dog is evaluated by a judge while doing its routine farm tasks and certified to be a useful working dog.

RDA: Recommended daily allowance.

RE: Rally Excellent; a Rally Obedience title, higher than Rally Advanced.

Reach: Length of forward stride taken by the forelegs.

Reachy: With a long neck.

Rear angulation: Angles formed between the pelvis, femur, and second thigh.

Recessive gene: A gene whose characteristics are overridden by the dominant gene in a pairing.

Recessive trait: A trait that requires a copy of the gene from both parents to exhibit the trait.

Recombination: The breakage and reuniting of DNA strands that results in genetic variation.

Rectal prolapse: Protrusion of a portion of the anal canal lining through the rectum, usually due to straining.

Rectum: The terminal portion of the large intestine.

Recumbency: Lying down.

Red-and-white ribbon: Awarded to the Best of Opposite Sex in a dog show.

Red blood cell: Small cell containing hemoglobin that carries oxygen from the lungs to the tissues.

Red clover (*Trifolium pratense*): In herbal medicine, administered for dermatitis.

Red factored: Black pup carrying a red gene.

Red raspberry (*Rubus idaeus*): In herbal medicine, prescribed for strengthening and toning the uterus during pregnancy.

Red ribbon: Awarded for second place in any regular class in a dog show.

Red setter: Irish setter. However, the name now is used almost exclusively for hunting dogs registered with the FDSB, which differ considerably from their AKC counterpoints (both show and field varieties).

Red-white-and-blue ribbon: Given to the Best in Show at a dog show.

Red wolf (*Canis rufus*): Rare wolf of South America.

Reduction: Chemical or metabolic process that is the opposite of oxidation.

Reedwater terrier: Old name for the Border terrier.

Refined: Elegant.

Refinement: Describing the amount of raciness.

Regional: A grouping of states with similar numbers of entries, used for the purposes of calculating a major.

Register: List of pedigreed dogs.

Registration: Official certificate of ownership.

Regular lab: (RL) A lab that flushes birds during an upland game hunting event instead of pointing at them as pointing labs (PL) do.

Regurgitation: Throwing up undigested food from the esophagus (vomiting is from the stomach).

Reh pinscher: Miniature pinscher. Reh refers to a kind of roe deer.

Relaxin: Reproductive hormone that helps prepare the uterus to give birth.

Release: An obedience command telling the dog it is free from obeying the previous command.

Release trap: A training device that holds a bird and then releases it.

Relocate: When a dog follows and continues to point at moving birds.

Renal: Relating to the kidneys.

Renal cortical hypoplasia: Abnormally small kidneys that fail to function normally.

Renal disease: Unspecified kidney disease.

Renal dysplasia: Renal cortical hypoplasia.

Renal threshold: The point at which the kidneys can no longer process glucose, allowing it spill into the urine.

Rendering: In dog-food manufacturing, cooking animal tissues at high temperatures to separate the fat from the protein.

Repertory: A homeopathic term referring to a dictionary of symptoms with indicated remedies. See Rubric.

Replication: Duplication or copy.

Resco: Adjustable, non-choking, one-piece lead.

Rescue Remedy: A Bach flower essence consisting of five of the original essences. To be used in cases of accident and trauma: one drop every five minutes for one hour.

Reserve Winner: The dog declared the winner if for some reason the original winner is declared ineligible.

Residual: Remaining for a certain period of time.

Residual scent: In search and rescue work, a human scent from a person no longer in the area.

Resorption: (1) Biochemical dissolution of tissue. **(2)** In pregnancy, a condition in which the fetus dies, and instead of being aborted, the fetal tissue dissolves within the uterus and is absorbed by the mother.

Respiration: (1) Absorption of oxygen into the tissues and the release of carbon dioxide. **(2)** The act of breathing. The normal respiration rate is ten to thirty breaths per minute.

Respiratory: Relating to breathing.

Respiratory depression: Decrease in the rate or depth of breathing.

Respiratory quotient: The ratio of the volume of carbon dioxide given off by the tissues to the volume of oxygen absorbed by them.

Respiratory system: This body system includes the mouth, nose, trachea, lungs, and smaller airways. It is responsible for taking in oxygen and eliminating waste gases. It also plays an important role in regulation of temperature.

Resting energy expenditure: Resting energy requirement.

Resting metabolic rate (RMR): The amount of energy expended while resting quietly, several hours after a meal.

Restricted: A gaiting fault caused by under-angulation, in which either the front or the rear appears painfully constricted.

Restrictive cardiomyopathy: Heart disease resulting in reduced filling of the ventricles.

Retained testicle: Testicle that has failed to descend into the scrotum. It should be removed, since it has a high likelihood of becoming cancerous.

Retina: The light-sensitive inner layer of the eye.

Retinal detachment: Detachment of the retina from the back of the eye, causing partial blindness. Can be due to trauma, cysts, tumor, or eye inflammation.

Retinal dysplasia: Abnormal development of the retina, possibly leading to blindness.

Retinal folds: Folds in the retinal layer, often caused by differences in growth rate of different layers of the eye.

Retrieve: When a dog runs forward, picks up the object, and returns it to the handler.

Retriever: A hunting dog that can be trained to pick up and bring back shot game.

Retrieving Gun Dog Stake Champion: A dog that has won first place in a stake that has been designated a Retrieving Gun Dog Championship Stake.

Return: Set-back of the upper arm under the dog's body.

Reverse scissors bite: A lower jaw longer than the upper jaw, causing the lower incisors to be placed slightly in front of the upper ones.

Reverse sneeze: A peculiar snort, probably caused by a spasm of the throat muscles, sometimes due to mucus, food, or a foreign body. It is not dangerous.

Rex: (1) Reexamine (veterinary notation). **(2)** Cavalier King Charles spaniel owned by former President Ronald Reagan.

RF: Right fore (veterinary notation).

RGDSC: Retrieving Gun Dog Stake Champion. The title is prefixed to the name.

RH: Right hind (veterinary notation).

Rhinitis: Inflammation of the nasal passages.

Rhodesian ridgeback: A hound originating from South Africa. Best known for the line of hairs making a ridge along the back in the shape of a dagger. A strong, muscular dog. Size: 24 to 27 inches, 70 to 85 pounds, with a short wheaten coat. Also known as an African Lion Hound.

Rhus toxicodendron: A homeopathic remedy commonly administered for arthritis. Often called just Rhus tox.

Ribbed up: Ribs carried well back, along rib cage.

Ribbon: In dog-food manufacturing, a semi-moist food created by alternating strips of red and white material to look like meat marbled with fat.

Rib spring: Arch of the ribcage.

Rice field disease: An old name for leptospirosis.

Rickettsia: Genus of small bacteria causing a variety of mostly tick-borne diseases in animals and humans.

Ridge: Narrow strip formed by hair growing in the opposite direction to that of the surrounding hair.

Ridgeback: Rhodesian ridgeback or Thai ridgeback.

Riesenschnauzer: Giant schnauzer.

Rig: In sledding, a three- or four-wheeled cart used when no snow is present.

Rimadyl: A brand name of carporfen, an NSAID used in the treatment of arthritis and similar complaints. On rare occasions, it can cause digestive upset or liver problems.

Rin Tin Tin: German shepherd movie star. "Rinty" starred in nineteen movies before his death in 1932.

Ring: The roped-off enclosure in which dogs are judged.

Ringed eyes: An abnormal amount of clearly visible sclera surrounding the eye.

Ringer: One dog substituted for another which closely resembles it.

Ringtail: An almost completely circular tail that is carried high.

Ringworm: (*dermatophytosis*): A fungal skin infection caused by *Microsporum canis* (which lives in skin and hair), *Microsporum gypseum* (which lives in soil), or *Trichophyton metnagrophytes* (found on rodents). The first is most common. More rarely, dogs can catch ringworm from people, and vice versa. Symptoms include a circular hair loss patch, crusting, and scaling. However, the classic circle is not always present, and the condition is easy to confuse with other skin conditions. Usually ringworm does not produce itchiness. It is usually treated with medicated shampoos and antifungal drugs for several weeks.

Rintal (febantel): A dewormer.

Riot: When a hound goes off to hunt something other than the designated prey.

RL: Right lower (veterinary notation).

RMSF: Rocky Mountain spotted fever.

RN: Rally Novice, an obedience title given in Rally.

RNA: Ribonucleic acid.

R/O: Rule out (veterinary notation).

Roach back: Arched, convex back.

Roading a bird: Repeated pointing and relocating demonstrated by a dog while following the ground scent trail of a bird.

Roadwork: To exercise a dog by walking or jogging. Usually used in reference to preparing for a show.

Roan: A fine mixture of white and colored hairs, such as orange roan and lemon roan.

Rob Roy: Collie belonging to Grace Coolidge, wife of Calvin Coolidge.

Rocker-fashion tail: Tail that curves like the runners of a rocking chair.

Rocking horse: Front and back legs extended away from the body like a rocking horse.

Rocky Mountain spotted fever: Tick-borne rickettsial disease. Signs include lethargy, loss of appetite, vomiting, diarrhea, mucus discharge, fever, depression, and joint pain. Some dogs never become ill, but remain carriers.

Roentgen: Old unit of X-ray exposure, now superseded by coulomb/kg.

ROF: Retrieve on the flat.

ROH: Retrieve over the high jump.

Rolled: In dog-food manufactur-

ing, flattening the food particles to change their appearance.

Rolled ears: Long, pendant folding ears with lower tip and edge curled inwards.

Rolling gait: An ambling motion.

ROM: Register of Merit, awarded by parent clubs of specific breeds.

Roman finish: Slightly sharper downward inclination at the end of downface. More exaggerated than a Roman nose.

Roman Lady's Dog: An old name for the Maltese.

Roman nose: A nose with a convex bridge. Characteristic of the borzoi and bull terrier.

Rompum: Brand name of Xylazine hydrochloride, a drug used as a muscle relaxant, sedative, and calming agent; it also provides some analgesia.

Ropy tail: A normally feathered tail now devoid of hair.

Rose ears: Small drop ears folded back, exposing part of the ear canal when the animal is resting, as in greyhounds.

Rosette: (1) Small tan patch on either side of the chest above the front legs. **(2)** Two patches of hair on the loin of a poodle. **(3)** A rose-shaped ribbon awarded at AKC events.

Roseval Golden Eagle: Pembroke Welsh Corgi owned by Queen Elizabeth II.

Rosie: Ulysses S. Grant's dog.

rost: Rostral (veterinary notation).

Rostral: Toward the nose (used to describe structures on the head).

Rotary motion: Strong, purposeful gait.

Rotenone: Botanical insecticide used for control of fleas and lice.

Rothbury terrier: Bedlington terrier.

Rottweiler: Originally a cattle drover, later a police dog. A sturdy dog with a short coat with black and tan markings. Size: 22 to 27 inches.

Rough coat: Medium to long coarse outer coat.

Round foot: Cat foot.

Rounding: Cutting or trimming the edges of the ears.

Roundworms: Thick-bodied, spaghetti-like whitish nematode parasites (ascarids) living in the dog's digestive tract. They can be one to seven inches long, and may show up in the stool. Also known as spool worms. Most puppies are infested with roundworms.

Royal Canin USA Dog Food: Telephone: (800) 592-6687. Web site: www.royalcanin.com.

Royal collar: A well-developed, symmetrical full white collar of hair.

rpt: Repeat (veterinary notation).

RR: In genetics, a genetically normal animal.

rr: In genetics, an affected animal.

Rr: In genetics, represents a carrier animal.

RS: Remove sutures (veterinary notation).

RSPCA: Royal Society for the Prevention of Cruelty to Animals.

RU: Right upper (veterinary notation).

Rubber hocks: A gaiting fault in which the hocks flex and twist both ways to bear the weight of the rear.

Rubric: In homeopathy, a text that catalogs symptoms and remedies for diseases. Also called a repertory.

Ruby: Rich red color, referring to a Cavalier King Charles spaniel.

Ruby eye: Whole eye tinged with red.

Rudder: Tail.

Ruff: Long, thick hair on the neck. Collar.

Rufus gene: The unique gene responsible for the deep red or mahogany of the Irish setter.

Runner: One who acts as an assistant at the judging ring and aids the stewards in getting entered dogs into the ring.

Runners: In sledding, the two bottom pieces of the sled, which slide across the snow.

Running order: A listing of the bracing and running order of dogs entered in all stakes in a field trial.

Runny nose: Watery discharge from the nose usually indicates excitement, not a cold.

Runt: Weak, undersized puppy in a litter.

Ruptured cervical disk: Herniated disk in neck region of the spine.

Ruptured disk: Herniated disk.

Rural Rube Award: In greyhound racing, an award to the nation's top sprint ($\frac{5}{16}$-mile) greyhound by the National Greyhound Association; named for an outstanding sprinter of the late 1930s.

Russet gold: Reddish brown.

Russian sheepdog: A category including three different breeds: the South Russian, the Central Asian, and the Caucasian.

Russian wolfhound: Borzoi.

Rv: Recheck (veterinary notation).

RVT: Registered veterinary technician.

RWB: Reserve Winner's Bitch.

RWD: Reserve Winner's Dog.

Rx: (1) Prescription (veterinary notation). **(2)** Recheck (veterinary notation).

S

S-: Superior performance, prefixed to any NADAC title.

SA: Sebaceous adenitis.

Saarloos wolfhound: A new breed from the Netherlands. Resembles a wolf in appearance. Size: 23 to 29 inches, 70 to 80 pounds.

Saber tail: Slight curved tail, carried low.

Sable: Black-tipped hairs over a lighter, often silver or gold, undercoat.

Sacral vertebrae: The three vertebrae in croup area.

Sacrum: The part of the vertebral column between the hip bones that consists of three fused vertebrae.

Saddle: Large, dark patch over back.

Saddle back: Overlong back with a dip behind the withers.

S-adenosylmethionine: A nutritional supplement synthesized by cells throughout the body, especially the liver. Often used to treat a variety of liver diseases.

Sailor Boy: Chesapeake Bay retriever owned by Theodore Roosevelt.

Saint Bernard: A large rescue dog developed in the eighteenth century. Size: 25 to 27 inches; the males can weigh up to 200 pounds. White with various shades of red or yellow-brown.

Saint Bernardshund: Saint Bernard.

Saint Hubert's hound: Bloodhound.

Salivary cysts: Cysts occurring when salivary ducts become blocked with secretions or foreign bodies.

Salivary duct stone: Formation of a stone in the salivary duct, causing a lump behind the jawbone.

Salmonellosis: Contagious bacterial infection caused by a variety of *Salmonella* species. Causes severe diarrhea. Can also affect humans.

Salmon Poisoning Disease: Highly fatal rickettsial disease affecting canids. It requires several intermediate hosts, including snails, flukes, fish, and mammals. It is seen in dogs that eat certain types of raw fish, notably salmon and other fish that swim upstream to breed. These fish can be infected with a parasite called *Nanophyetus salmincola*. While the parasite is relatively harmless, it can be infected with a rickettsial organism called *Neorickettsia helminthoeca*. It is this microorganism that causes salmon poisoning.

Salt-and-pepper: See Peppering.

Saluki: An ancient Egyptian sight hound. Size: 23 to 28 inches, 29 to 66 pounds, although the females may be considerably smaller. Has a smooth, soft coat in a variety of colors.

Sam: Beagle owned by James Herriot.

Samoyed: Sled dog developed in antiquity by Nordic people in Siberia. Size: 19 to 23 inches, with a luxurious silvery-white coat.

Samoyedskaya: Samoyed.

Samoyed smile: Special expression created by the upward tilt of the lips at the corners of the mouth.

Sanctioned A match: Less common than Sanction B matches, these are offered only by new clubs who have already held a number of sanctioned B matches and are working up to AKC permission to host a full-scale dog show. The show is run just like a regular dog show, with the same classes and mail-in entries. Judged by anyone in good standing with the AKC.

Sanctioned B match: Similar to a fun match, but conducted under AKC rules. Most have classes for puppies younger than at a regular show for practice. Judged by anyone in good standing with the AKC.

Sanctioned Club: Club that has been approved to hold sanctioned B or A events, but not AKC-licensed events at which titles may be won.

Sanctioned Matches and Events A: Events held in order to establish eligibility to hold licensed events. More formal than Sanctioned B Matches.

Sanctioned Matches and Events B: Informal AKC-approved events at which no championship titles or points are earned.

SAR: Search and rescue dog.

Sarcoma: Malignant tumor arising in the underlying connective tissue.

Sarcoptic mange: Also called scabies. Skin disease caused by the *Sarcoptes scabei* var. *canis* mite. Often misdiagnosed as an allergy, sarcoptic mange is intensely itchy and is easily transmitted to other pets in the house, as well as to owners. In people it is manifested as small, itchy, red bumps. In dogs the mites cause skin lesions most often on the face, chest, abdomen, and legs. The ends of the ears are often crusty. Sarcoptic mange can be detected by your vet with a deep skin scraping.

SARDS: Sudden acquired retinal degeneration syndrome.

Sarplaninac: Sheep-herding dog.

SAS: Subaortal arterial stenosis.

Saur (Suening): A dog declared "king" of Norway for three years in the eleventh century. The Norwegian king, furious with his subjects for once deposing him, put Saur on the throne and demanded that he be treated royally.

Savoy sheepdog: Medium-sized, long-bodied dog with drop ear, thick coat, and fairly long tail.

Sawhorse stance: Position in which the longitudinal axes of the forearms or rear pasterns are not vertical to the ground.

S/b: Submandibular.

SBISweeps: Best in Specialty Sweepstakes

SBT: Staffordhshire bull terrier.

SC: (1) Senior Courser (AKC title placed after the dog's name). **(2)** Subcutaneous (veterinary notation).

Scabies: See Sarcoptic mange.

Scale: Flakes due to excess keratin in the skin. Can lead to itching.

Scapula: Shoulder blade.

Scent article: In search-and-rescue and tracking, an object that was in contact with the search subject and contains his or her body odor.

Scent cone: A pattern that scent molecules take as they disperse downwind.

Scent discrimination: The ability of a dog to distinguish one individual from all others by its unique body odor.

Scent drag: a drag made of cloth or canvas with scent on it, dragged across the ground to lay a scent trail for training or competitive events.

Scent hound: A hunting dog that tracks by nose. This group of hounds emerged later than the sight hounds, and originated in Europe. Examples include the beagle and basset.

Scent Hurdle Dog Champion: CKC certificate awarded to a dog that competes successfully in Scent Hurdle Dog Racing.

Scent marking: The method by which a dog marks his territory, using urine or special glands in the face and paws.

SCFA: Short-chain fatty acid.

SCH I, II, III: Schutzhund titles comprising three phases: tracking, obedience, and protection. A dog must pass all three phases to earn title.

Schapendoes: Also called the Dutch sheepdog, a sheep guardian and herder.

Schiff-Sherrington posture: A condition, caused by a lesion in the spinal cord, in which the front legs are held rigid and the rear legs are weak or paralyzed. Sometimes the neck is hyper-extended, with the head held up and over the back.

Schipperke: Small, black Belgian dog with a long black coat. Originally used for hunting small game and guarding barges. Now mostly a companion dog. Size: 10 to 13 inches, 7 to 20 pounds. Also spelled Schipperkee.

Schnauzer comedo syndrome: Skin disease characterized by blackheads. Also called follicular dermatitis.

Schutzhund: Literally, "protection dog." Training program for protective work that includes tracking, obedience, and attack training.

Scimitar: A tail much like the saber tail, but with a more exaggerated curve.

Scissors bite: The upper teeth come down next to the under teeth.

Sclera: White membrane surrounding the cornea of the eye.

Sclerosis: A hardening of tissue, usually the result of chronic inflammation.

Scolex: Headlike portion of the tapeworm that attaches to the intestinal lining.

Scooting: Scraping the rear end on the ground. It may indicate blocked anal sacs, worms, or other irritation.

Scottish collie: Collie.

Scottish deerhound: Tall, shaggy hound dating to the sixteenth century or earlier. Size: 28 to 32 inches, 85 to 110 pounds, with a long, shaggy coat, usually dark gray-blue but a variety of other colors as well.

Scottish terrier: A small but spirited dog, loyal to its family, but may be aggressive to other dogs. Size: 10 inches, 19 to 22 pounds, with a long, hard, wiry outer coat that may be black, wheaten, or brindle in color.

Scotty cramp: Periodic leg cramps caused by overexcitement, confined mostly to Scottish terriers. Associated with metabolism of a neurotransmitter.

Scout: In a pointing breed field event, a person, generally mounted, dispatched by a handler, with the approval of a judge, to seek out and report the presence and behavior of a dog.

Scrambled mouth: Misplaced or jumbled incisor teeth.

Scratching: May indicate fleas, mites, or allergies.

Scratching a dog: Withdrawing from competition.

Screw tail: Naturally short, twisted tail.

Scrotal dermatitis: Dermatitis of the scrotum, characterized by red, scaly, itchy skin.

Scrotum: Pouch containing the testicles.

Scuffing: In tracking, the dragging of a tracklayer's feet to leave a concentrated scent.

Scutellaria: A homeopathic remedy for nervousness, apprehension, and excitability.

Se: Chemical symbol for selenium.

SE: Senior Earthdog (AKC suffix).

Sealyham terrier: Terrier developed in Wales during the nineteenth century. Used for hunting badger and fox. Size: 10 inches, 23 to 24 pounds. Hard, wiry outer coat, mostly white in color.

Seaman: Newfoundland owned by Lewis and Clark.

Season: A bitch's heat period.

Sebaceous adenitis (SA): Inflammation of the sebaceous glands in the skin; the condition can lead to baldness.

Sebaceous cyst: Cyst arising from blocked sebaceous glands.

Sebaceous glands: Oil glands in the skin associated with hair follicles.

Seborrhea: Skin condition (probably hereditary) in which dead cells accumulate too quickly, producing a waxy, flaky coat; the combination of dead cells and skin oils (sebum) that can lead to bacterial infection, so that dogs with seborrhea are also prone to skin infections. Vulnerable breeds include cocker spaniels, English springer spaniels and West Highland white terriers.

Sebum: Oily material produced by the sebaceous glands in the skin; it functions to lubricate the skin and coat.

Second thigh: Area of the hind quarters between the hock and the stifle. Also called lower thigh.

Secondary selection: In retrieving work, when the handler decides which bird will be picked up next.

Sectorial tooth: Carnassial tooth.

Sedation points: In acupuncture, points used to decrease energy levels in a specific meridian.

Sedative: A medication that produces deep calm.

Sedge: Red-gold.

Seeing Eye Dog: A dog trained as a guide for the blind.

Seesaw: In agility, a teeter-totter. Consists of a twelve-foot plank attached to a fulcrum.

Seizures: Convulsions. May indicate epilepsy, low blood sugar, low calcium level, or poisoning.

Selamectin: A medication to control heartworm, fleas, ticks, roundworms, and mites. Contained in the heartworm preventative Revolution.

Selective breeding: Planned matings to improve the breed.

Selective cobalamin malabsorption: Erratic absorption of vitamin B12.

Selective serotonin reuptake inhibitor (SSRI): Medication that slows the ability of nerve cells to absorb serotonin, a neurotransmitter (chemical that serves as a messenger between nerves). Prozac is an example.

Selegiline: An MAOI prescribed for Cushing's disease and canine cognitive dysfunction, also called Anipryl or L-deprenyl.

Selenium: Essential trace mineral and antioxidant. It is highly toxic in amounts not much greater than those needed for good health.

Self: A solid color, except for lighter shadings.

Self-colored nose: A nose the same color as the coat.

Self-hunt: Bolt.

Self-marked: A solid-colored dog with white or pale markings.

Self-relocation: In pointing breed events, the alternating self-release and re-pointing behavior

by a dog on a moving bird. The self-relocation should end with the bird being pinned on point. Same as relocate.

Semihare foot: Between oval and hare foot.

Seminoma: A tumor of the testicle. Some can be malignant.

Senescence: The process of growing old.

Senior Courser: (1) Must be eligible to enter the open stake. That requires the dog to have obtained at least one of the following: AKC Junior Courser title, American Sighthound Field Association Field Champion title, Canadian Kennel Club Field Champion title, or American Kennel Club Field Champion title. **(2)** The hound must run with at least one other hound. **(3)** Must receive qualifying scores at four AKC-licensed or member trials, under two different judges or judging panels.

Senior Earthdog: A dog must have a record of having qualified in the Senior Earthdog tests at three AKC-licensed or member club tests under two different judges.

Senior Grand Champion: A dog that has been designated a Grand Bench Show Champion plus thee champion classes with competition.

Senior Grand Field Champion: A dog that has won three First Lines or First Trees in three Final Lines at three different trials with competition. At least one of the three wins must include both Final Line and Final Tree in the same trial on the same date with competition.

Senior Grand Nite Champion: A dog that has won three first-place wins as a Grand Champion in AKC-licensed Nite Hunts. The top four dogs competing in the AKC World Hunt are awarded the title, if they have not already been so recognized.

Senior Grand Water Race Champion: A dog that has won three First Lines or First Trees in three Final Lines or Final Trees at three different Water Races with competition. At least one of the three wins must include both Final Line and Final Tree in the same event on the same date with competition. If a hound wins both First Line and First Tree in the Final Line and Final Tree at the same race, this counts as only one win toward a Senior Grand Race Champion title.

Senior Hunter: For a title, a dog must receive qualifying scores at five licensed or member tests. If the dog has already received a JH, the dog need only qualify four times.

Senior Testing Level: The intermediate testing level at AKC hunting tests.

Separation anxiety: A behavioral condition in which the pet becomes excessively anxious when separated from the owner.

Sepsis: The presence of toxins in the blood or other tissues; the toxins are produced by bacteria or other pathogens.

Septal defect: Structural defect involving the heart wall.

Septic: A condition caused by an infection.

Septicemia: Pathogens and their toxins in the blood; blood poisoning.

Septum: (1) The groove between the nostrils. **(2)** Partition of a body space or cavity.

Seroma: Mature hematoma, filled with serum and shrinking mass of red blood cells.

Serotonin: A neurotransmitter.

Serotype: A subdivision of a species of microorganism based on its reaction with antibodies, e.g., a bacteria, based upon its particular antigens.

Serous: Thin and watery.

Serra de Aires sheepdog: Portuguese dog with small ears and a long tail. Known as a monkey dog in its native land. Size: 16 to 18 inches, 25 to 35 pounds.

Sertoli cell tumor: Estrogen-secreting tumor of the testicle.

Serum: The clear part of blood that remains after removal of the blood cells by clotting.

Service: The act of mating.

Service dog: A dog trained to assist a physically disabled person. Also known as a mobility dog.

Sesamoid bones: Bones embedded in the tendons of freely mobile joints, especially in the foot.

Set on: The placement of the ears and tail.

Setter: A long-haired hunting dog breed that freezes in a characteristic stance, with the hind end low.

Set up: Stack or show pose.

SGC (SGCH): Senior Grand Champion. The title is prefixed to the dog's name.

SGFC: Senior Grand Field Champion. The title is prefixed to the dog's name.

SGOT: Serum glutamic-oxaloacetic transaminase. Also called AST. Liver enzyme normally present at low levels in the blood; often elevated in an animal with liver disease.

SGPT: Serum glutamic-pyruvic transaminase. Also called ALT. Liver enzyme normally present at low levels in the blood; often elevated in an animal with liver disease.

SGWCH: Senior Grand Water Race Champion. The title is prefixed to the dog's name.

SH: Senior Hunter. AKC title. The title follows the dog's name.

Shaker dog: White dog shaker syndrome.

Shanks: Thighs.

Shark mouth: A condition in which the jaw is level but the teeth are not set properly and protrude.

Shar-pei: See Chinese shar-pei.

Sharpey's fibers: The fibers making up the annulus or outer portion of the intervertebral disks.

Sharpness: A natural tendency to respond to a situation with aggression.

Shawl: Long hair on top and sides of the neck.

SHDCH: Scent Hurdle Dog Champion.

Sheath: Covering of the penis.

Shed: To drop hair.

Shedding: In sheepdog trials, separating two animals from the flock.

Shelly: Narrow, shallow chest and body.

Sheltie: Nickname for the Shetland sheepdog.

Shepherd's crook tail: A kink or U shape at the end of the tail.

Shepherd spitz: Medium-sized dog with an abundant white coat and a bushy tail.

Shetland sheepdog: A smaller version of the collie. Size: 13 to 16 inches, 14 to 16 pounds.

Shiatsu: Acupressure.

Shiba inu: Ancient breed indigenous to Japan. Size: 13 to 16 inches, 17 to 23 pounds, with a short, double coat in various colors.

Shifting-leg lameness: See panosteitis.

Shih tzu: A toy breed native to Tibet and China, with a luxuriant, long coat. Size: 9 to 10 inches, 9 to 16 pounds.

Shikoku: Ancient medium-sized breed native to Japan. Originally used for hunting boar.

Shivering: Involuntary, high-frequency contraction and relaxation of muscles.

SGNCH: Senior Grand Nite Champion, awarded to coonhounds. A dog must earn three first-place wins as a Grand Champion in AKC-licensed Nite Hunts. The top four dogs competing in the AKC World Hunt are awarded the title of Senior Grand Nite Champion, if the dog is not already recognized as a SGNC. The title is prefixed to the dog's name.

Shock: A serious condition in which there is inadequate blood flow to meet the body's needs, bringing on circulatory collapse. It follows trauma or emotional catastrophe.

Shock dog: An old name for the Maltese.

Shock-headed: Coarse, tangled hair.

Shooting Dog Stake: FDSB field trial for dogs of all ages, but generally requiring a lower level of skill than stakes designated all-age.

Short bones: Bones of the carpus and tarsus.

Short-chain fatty acid: Acid formed from the bacterial fermentation of fiber in the large intestine. "Short" indicates fewer carbon atoms.

Short-coupled: Short loin area.

Shorts: (1) Fine particles of bran, germ, or flour. (2) Offal from the tail of the mill in commercial milling.

Shot proof: Opposite of gun shy.

Shoulder angulation: Angle formed between the scapula and the humerus.

Shoulder luxation: Dislocation of the shoulder joint.

Show quality: A puppy with potential to succeed in conformation shows.

SI: Small intestine (veterinary notation).

Siberian husky: Sled-pulling dog of the Arctic. Size: 20 to 23 inches, 35 to 60 pounds. Medium-length, heavy coat in a variety of colors.

SIBO: Small intestinal bacterial growth.

Sick sinus syndrome: A disturbance of the normal heart rhythm.

Sickle hocked: Over-angulated hocks (when viewed from the side.)

Sickle tail: Tail carried up and out in a semicircle.

Sid: Once a day (veterinary notation).

Sidegait: The movement of a dog as viewed from the side.

Sidewinding: See crabbing.

Sig: Signalment (veterinary notation). The signs of the disease.

Sight hound: A hound that hunts primarily by eyesight rather than scent. This is one of the earliest groups to emerge, and it originated in Asia. Examples include the Afghan and saluki. Also called long dogs, or gaze hounds.

Signs: The visible clues to what is ailing a dog, such as vomiting, diarrhea, reddened ears, and so forth. Although we often use the word symptom to refer to these things, sign is the correct term. A symptom is a subjective thing, something you feel inside. Since we can never know what a dog feels inside, we refer to these clues as signs. When noting signs of your dog's problems, you should consider what other signs are occurring at the same time, and whether the sign is acute or chronic, local or general, and continuous or intermittent. Common dangerous signs may include breathing difficulties, bleeding, swollen abdomen, bloody vomit or diarrhea, and pale gums.

Silent: A dog who trails game without barking.

Silent retinal syndrome: Suddenly acquired retinal degeneration syndrome.

Silky terrier: Developed in Australia around 1900. Size: 9 to 10 inches, 9 to 11 pounds, with a straight, glossy, silky blue-and-tan coat.

Silver eye: See walleye.

Silver sulfadiazine: Antimicrobial prescribed for wounds and burns.

Silymarin: Milk thistle.

Simillimum: In homeopathy, a remedy that is most similar to the case, and the most correct remedy.

Single: In retrieving tests, one marked retrieve or blind.

Single coat: Dog with no undercoat.

Single tracking: When all footprints fall in a single line of travel. This is the normal canine gait.

Singling: In herding, when a dog comes in too close and allows the sheep to separate.

Sire: Male parent.

Sit: A command telling a dog to repose on his haunches.

SIT: Self-inflicted trauma (veterinary notation).

Skatole: An amine with a strong odor, found in feces.

Skin cancer: Most common in dogs exposed to strong ultraviolet light, especially common in short-haired, light-skinned breeds. Signs include lumps, bumps, and lesions. See a vet—noncancerous skin lesions are indistinguishable from cancerous ones by visual examination. Types of skin cancer can include melanoma, lymphoma, and squamous cell carcinoma. Also see skin tumors.

Skin fold dermatitis: Skin infection caused by moisture and bacteria in the deep folds of the skin.

Skin fragility: Tissue disease causing fragile, easily torn skin. Also called Ehlers-Danlos syndrome.

Skin scrapings: Removal of thin layers of skin to evaluate for disease.

Skin tumors: About one-third of all canine tumors are skin tumors. About 80 percent are benign and do not spread. Common types of tumors include histiocytoma (button tumor), lipoma (fatty tumor), and mast cell tumor, which is the most serious.

Skirting: In a hound field trial, when a hound cuts ahead of its bracemate and continually intercepts.

Skull: In a broad sense, the fused bones of the skull, inner ear bones, and mandible. In a narrow sense the fused bones of the skull and inner ear bones, without the mandible.

Skully: A dog that is thick and coarse in the skull area.

Skunk odor: Remove by applying tomato juice to the skin and then bathing. Douche powder or liquid works even better.

Skye terrier: Double-coated terrier in shades of black, gray, fawn, or cream. Origin: Scotland, perhaps as early as the sixteenth century. Size: about 10 inches, 25 pounds.

Slab-sided: Flat ribbed.

Slack back: Sway back.

Slats: In sledding, thin strips of wood that comprise the bottom of a wooden sled basket.

SLE: Systemic lupus erythematosus.

Sled bag: In sledding, a bag to carry gear.

Sleeve dog: Pekingese, so named because it was carried about in the sleeves of ancient Chinese nobility.

Slew feet: Feet turned out.

Slicker brush: A brush with bent-wire teeth of the slicker brush set close together to help remove mats and dead hair. Slicker brushes will take out large amounts of coat and are useful during periods of shedding.

Slick tree: Referring to when a dog trees at a game-less tree.

Slipper feet: Long, oval feet.

Sloping shoulder: An oblique shoulder, set at an angle.

SM: Snooker Master (USDAA agility title).

SMA-20: Biochemical profile.

Small intestine bacterial overgrowth (SIBO): An intestinal condition in which a pure culture of bacteria increases and displaces other beneficial bacteria.

Sm an: Small animals (cats, dogs).

Smegma: Normal discharge from the sheath of the penis.

Smith, Owen Patrick: Invented the mechanical lure (1912) used in greyhound racing.

Smooth coat: Short, flat hair.

Smooth muscle: The type of muscle found in the internal organs such as stomach and intestines.

Smudge nose: Snow nose.

Sn: (1) Sneezing (veterinary notation). **(2)** Chemical abbreviation for tin.

Snap and release: Form of correction in which the handler gives a quick, upward pull on the leash so that the choke collar momentarily constricts the dog's neck.

Snap-dog: Old name for a whippet, derived from the animal's habit of snapping at game.

Snap tail: A tail carried over the back with the tip making contact.

Snatching hocks: A gaiting fault that causes a rocking in the hindquarters.

Snipey (snipy, snippy): Sharp, pointed muzzle.

Snooker: An agility course patterned after the British billiards game of snooker. The obstacles are labeled as to their color and point value, which ranges from one to seven, with red jumps having a value of one. The dog must successfully complete a red jump prior to attempting an obstacle of any other color.

Snoring: May stem from obesity, obstructed nasal passage, normal aging, or elongated soft palate.

Snow hook: In sledding, a kind of emergency brake that anchors in the snow.

Snow nose: Inflammation of the skin near the nose, primarily a cosmetic problem occurring in white-coated breeds. Occurs in the winter.

Snubline: In sledding, a rope that attaches to a tree while the dog is resting.

SO: Sutures or staples out (veterinary notation).

Social facilitation: The phenomenon of dogs eating more in the presence of other dogs or people.

Socialization: Process of familiarization between animals in a group or between animals and human beings.

Socialization period: Occurs between three and twelve weeks; the period during which it is important for a puppy to get acquainted with others dogs and with human beings, including children.

Socks: Hair of a different color than the main coat (usually white) on the feet to pasterns.

Sodium: Mineral necessary for muscle function, nerve impulse transmission, and electrolyte balance.

Sodium fluoracetamide (1081): Chemical used as a rat poison; highly fatal to dogs.

Sodium fluoroacetate (1080): Chemical used as a rat poison, and highly fatal to dogs.

Soft back: Saddle back.

Soft-coated wheaten terrier: Medium-sized terrier with an unusually soft coat. Size: 17 to 19 inches, 30 to 40 pounds. Color may be any shade of wheaten.

Soft feet: Down in pastern.

Soft mouthed: A dog that retrieves birds without damaging them.

Soft on point: A dog that lacks intensity on point.

Somatotropin: Growth hormone; stimulates body growth and increases milk production.

Somber expression: A facial expression resulting when the mask covers most of the skull area and blends into the surrounding head color.

Somnolence: Sleepiness, a condition of semi-consciousness approaching coma

Somogyi overswing or somogyi effect: A diabetic condition, associated with unusually high doses of insulin and continued clinical signs of polyuria and polydipsia, particularly in the evenings when blood glucose has been increased by the release of protective hormones.

Sooty: Black hairs intermingling with tan.

Soporific: Sleep-inducing.

Soter: One of fifty watchdogs of ancient Greece. Soter alone survived an attack by invaders and ran to the gates of Corinth to warn the citizens.

Source points: In acupuncture, points along the carpal or tarsal area used in the treatment of organ disease or dysfunction.

Soybean meal: The substance obtained by grinding the soybean flakes remaining after removal (by extraction with a solvent) of most of the oil from the hulled soybeans.

Sp/spp: Species (sing./plural).

S & P: Scale and polish (veterinary dentistry notation).

Spaniel: Any of numerous dog breeds of medium or small size, most with rather short legs, luxuriant coats, and feathering. The word refers to Spain, the origin of many of the breeds.

Spaniel Gentle: An old name for the Maltese.

Spanish mastiff: Originally developed as a fighting and military dog.

Spanish pointer: Extinct breed that was the foundation of many of the pointing and retrieving breeds.

Spanning: Method of measuring a terrier's (especially a Parson Russell terrier's) chest using the hands.

Sparring: Allowing two terriers to charge at each other (cautiously) in a show ring.

Spay: To neuter a female dog.

SPAY/USA: (800) 248-7729.

Speak: To bark.

Special: A champion dog that continues to show in Best of Breed Competition.

Specialing: Showing a champion dog with the intention of having that dog become one of the top dogs in that breed.

Specialty: Specialty show.

Specialty pet food: A premium food available in limited distribution.

Specialty show: A show for dogs of a specific breed or for varieties of one breed, usually offering extra classes and prizes.

Speckling: Flecking or ticking.

Spectacles: Dark markings around the eyes.

Speculum: An instrument used to hold open a body orifice.

Sphincter: A ring-like band of muscle that constricts a passage or closes an opening.

Spiculosis: Abnormal bristle-like hairs interspersed among normal hairs.

Spike tail: Short tail that tapers rapidly along its length.

Spina bifida: A defective fusion of spinal vertebrae, causing paralysis.

Spinal column: The backbone; the column of vertebrae along the back of an animal.

Spinal cord: Nerve tissue within the spinal column that relays sensory information to the brain and motor commands from the brain.

Spinal disk disease: Intervertebral disk disease.

Spinal myelinopathy: Disease of the myelin, the covering of the spinal cord.

Spinal tap: Procedure used to obtain cerebrospinal fluid for analysis.

Spinone Italiano: An all-purpose hunting dog, working mostly as a pointer but resembling a sight hound. Size: 20 to 26 inches, about 56 pounds, with a short, rough, wiry coat. The dog is usually white, possibly with yellow or light brown patches.

Spirally twisted tail: A low-carried tail with a spiral twist at the end.

Spirochete: A type of long, slender, spiral-shaped bacteria. *Leptospira* species and the bacteria that cause Lyme disease (*Borrelia burgdorferi*) are spirochetes.

Spitz: A northern dog with wedge-shaped head, pointy ears, a thick double coat, and a powerful build.

Spitz breeds: A group of thick-coated northern breeds resembling wolves.

Splashed: Irregularly patched.

Splashes: Pied brindle spots on a white ground, used in reference to Boston terriers.

Splay footed: Open toes.

Spleen: Large, tongue-shaped organ near the stomach that filters blood and stores blood cells. It is part of the immune system but can also manufacture new blood cells if the animal's bone marrow is damaged. It may be removed if diseased.

Spondylitis: Joint inflammation of the vertebrae.

Spondylosis: Abnormal fusing (ankylosis) of the vertebrae.

Spongia tosta: Homeopathic remedy often administered for heart problems, especially angina or hypertrophy of the heart.

Spoon ear: Bat ear.

Spoon-shaped foot: Oval foot.

Sporozoa: Type of small protozoan parasite.

Sporting dogs: An AKC groups that consists of dogs bred to hunt game birds both on land and in the water, notably pointers, retrievers, setters, and spaniels.

Spotted Dick: Nickname for the Dalmatian.

Spotted nose: Butterfly nose.

Sprain: Stretching or tearing of the tendon or ligament fibers.

Spread: The distance between the front legs.

Spring: Refers to the amount of roundness to the rib cage.

SQ: Subcutaneous (veterinary notation).

Squamous cell carcinoma: Common cancer arising in the epithelium of the skin, oral cavity, or other organ.

Square bodied: A dog whose height at the withers equals the length from point of sternum of point of croup.

Squinting: Squeezing the eyes shut. May indicate something in the eye, corneal injury or ulcer, conjunctivitis, glaucoma, anterior uveitis, or iris atrophy.

Squirrel tail: A curved tail that is carried up and forward.

S/R: Suture removal (veterinary notation).

SR: Started retriever (NAHRA).

SS: Skin scrape (veterinary notation).

SSRI: Selective serotonin reuptake inhibitors: Medications that slow down the ability of nerve cells to absorb serotonin, a neurotransmitter.

Stacking: Posing a dog, usually for a conformation class.

Stafford bull terrier: The smallest of the bull-and-terrier breeds. Size: 14 to 16 inches, 24 to 38 pounds. Of English origin, probably in the sixteenth century. Originally used for bull and bear baiting.

Stake: A separate competitive category in a field trial.

Standard: The official description of the perfect dog.

Standard course time (SCT): In agility, the number of seconds judged to be the maximum time contestants should use over the course without penalty.

Standard schnauzer: Strong, heavy-set dog about 17 to 20 inches high. Has a thick, wiry coat, usually black or salt-and-pepper in color.

Stand game: Point.

Standoff coat: A heavy, somewhat long coat that stands out from the body, rather than lying flat.

Stanozolol: Anabolic steroid prescribed for appetite stimulation and chronic anemia.

Staphylococcal bacterins: Immunosuppressant medication to treat chronic pyoderma.

Staphylococcus: A bacteria of the family Micrococcaceae.

Star: White mark on the forehead.

Staring coat: A harsh, sparse, dry coat; out of condition.

Started hound: Usually refers to a young hound (up to $1^1/_2$ years old) that has only recently started to bark on a hot rabbit scent.

Stasis: In the gastrointestinal tract, a condition in which the food does not move through normally, but remains in one section.

Station: Comparative height from the ground.

Status epilepticus: A severe seizure occurring as one continuous event lasting thirty minutes or more, or a series of multiple seizures in a short time with no periods of normal consciousness.

Staunch: Referring to a bird dog that remains in place after pointing until the handler arrives and flushes the bird.

Stay: A command to the dog to remain in place.

STD: Started Trial Dog, a title awarded by the Australian Shepherd Club of America.

Steady: (1) In retrieving trials, a dog that waits to be sent after the mark, and does not break. **(2)** In pointing dog trials, a dog that remains in place through the flush and shot.

Steady on: In sheepdog trials, a command to go easy or to take some time.

Steady-to-shot: In pointing breed

field events, staying on point during the flight of, and the shot(s) for, a flushed bird.

Steady-to-wing: In pointing breed field events, maintaining a point during the flight of a flushed bird.

Stealingkira point: A dog making continued movement into the area where the game is present after observing another dog on point, rather than honoring. See stolen point.

Steel blue: A dark grayish blue, but not silver, coat.

Steep: Incorrect angles.

Steep croup: A croup that makes a dramatic slope from the hip bones to the root of the tail.

Stem cells: (1) Cells in the bone marrow that give rise to the red blood cells, the platelets, and the cells of the immune system. (2) Any cell that can give rise to multiple types of cells, such as cells in the embryo that develop into all the different types of cells in the body.

Stenosis: A narrowing or constriction of a body opening, such as a duct or canal.

Stenotic nares: An abnormal narrowing of the nasal passages, sometimes interfering with breathing. Generally occurs in brachycephalic breeds, such as pugs.

Steptracking: In tracking, scenting from one footprint to another. Useful technique in distinguishing primary tracks from cross-tracks and working older tracks.

Stern: The tail of a sporting dog or hound.

Sternal recumbency: Lying on its chest.

Sternum: Breastbone.

Steroids (corticosteroids): Drugs related to the adrenal hormone cortisone. Used primarily to treat dermatitis, joint inflammation, and shock. Can be prescribed as pills, creams, or injections.

Stertor: Snoring or other low-pitched sound that arises from air passing over loose tissue projecting into the airway.

Steward: In dog shows, the person who gives out armbands, calls dogs into the ring, and arranges for the correct distribution of ribbons.

Sticky: (1) A dog that is reluctant to let go of a bird. Not necessarily the same as hard-mouthed. (2) A sheepdog that is giving too much eye to the sheep.

Stifle: Upper joint of rear leg, corresponding to the human knee.

Stilted: Stiff, jerking gait.

Stippled: Pattern of dots rather than lines, used in reference to the Harlequin Great Dane.

STO: Speak to owner (veterinary notation).

Stocking: Hair (usually white) on the legs that is a different color from the main coat. Covers most of the leg.

Stolen point: The refusal of a dog to honor the dog on point, moving up and pointing the same bird.

Stomatitis: Inflammation of the mouth, including the gums and tongue.

Stool sample: The collection of feces to be examined microscopically for parasites.

Stop: Junction where the muzzle meets the back skull. Some breeds, such as the boxer, are supposed to have a pronounced stop.

Stopper pad: The fleshy cushion on the front legs at the back of the wrist.

Stop-to-flush: When a dog stops after observing the flush of a bird. This allows the handler to shoot the bird.

Storage disease: Any of several diseases in which cells of the body accumulate a substance that causes the cells to malfunction.

Strabismus: Abnormal positioning, or squint, of the eye, often indicative of a neurological defect.

Straight front: Too little angulation in the front

Straight-hocked: Lacking appreciable angulation of the hock joint.

Straight in the pastern: Not enough give in the pastern area when in a natural stance.

Strain: Damage to muscle tissue.

Straining to urinate: Difficulty in urination. May stem from urinary tract infection, prostate problem, or bladder stones.

Stranguria: Straining to urinate. Also called strangury.

Streptococcus: A spherical bacteria responsible for many pus-forming infections.

Stricture: Narrowing, stenosis.

Stridor: High-pitched sound, usually heard on inhalation, resulting from air passing over more rigidly anchored tissue than is characteristic of stertor.

Strike: When the dog barks or opens when it smells a track.

Stripper: A tool designed to pluck hair.

Stripping: Hand-plucking the dead hairs of the undercoat (usually in terriers) without loss of the harsh outercoat.

Strobila: The whole body (all of the segments) of the tapeworm.

Stroke: A neurological disorder that occurs when a blood clot lodges in a blood vessel in the brain.

Strongid T (*pyrantel pamoate*): A deworming medication used for roundworms and hookworms.

Strung up: Showing a dog on a very tight lead.

Struvite: A urinary calculus composed of magnesium ammonium phosphate.

Strychnine: Highly toxic rodent and mole poison.

Stud: Male dog used for breeding.

Stud dog class: A class in which a male dog is judged by the merits of one or more of its offspring.

Stuffy neck: Short, stocky neck.

Stumpy tail: Short tail.

Stuttgart disease: Leptospirosis.

Subacute: Of intermediate duration, about one week. Between acute and chronic.

Subaortic stenosis: Aortic stenosis.

Subclinical: Applied to a disease whose signs are not apparent.

Subcut: Subcutaneous.

Subcutaneous (SQ): Beneath the skin; usually referring to a method of giving medication.

Subluxation: An incomplete or partial dislocation.

Submandibular: Beneath the mandible (jaw).

Sub Q: Subcutaneously (veterinary notation).

Substance: Having a lot of bone and good musculature.

Subvalvular aoritic stenosis: A heart disease condition, in which there is an abnormally narrow constriction between the left ventricle and the aorta.

Succussing: Shaking a homeopathic preparation vigorously to potentize it. Homeopathic remedies are created by alternately succussing and diluting them.

Succussion: In homeopathy, the violent agitation applied at each step in dilution during the potentization process.

Sucralfate: Anti-ulcer medication composed of aluminum hydroxide and sulfated sucrose.

Sudden acquired retinal degeneration syndrome (SARDS): Acute, sudden blindness often preceded by several weeks of increased eating or drinking. The patient may have symptoms suggestive of Cushing's as well. No cure is available, and the disease is as yet poorly understood. It is most common in older, female dogs.

Sugar diabetes: Diabetes mellitus.

Sulfadimethoxine: Antibiotic and antiprotozoal drug prescribed for a variety of bacteria and coccidia.

Sulfasalazine: Antibiotic (sulfa drug), NSAID, and immunosuppressant, prescribed for inflammatory bowel disease, colitis, irritable bowel syndrome, and some kinds of arthritis.

Sulfonamides: A class of antibiotics that contain sulfur. They are bacteriostatic; they stop the growth (reproduction) of bacteria, but do not kill them.

Sulfur or sulphur: Homeopathic remedy for pneumonia or skin conditions.

Sulky: In carting, a cart designed for a passenger rather than freight.

Sun dog: Pekingese.

Sunken eyes: Eyes that are well recessed into their sockets.

Sunken pastern: Down in the pastern.

Sunscreen: Helpful for preventing sunburn on hairless dogs. Sunscreen containing PABA may be harmful to dogs if they lick it off.

Suomenpystykorva: Finnish spitz.

Sup: Superior (veterinary notation).

Superfecundation: Having a litter with more than one father (or breeding).

Superintendent: In dog shows, the person in charge of mailing out the premium lists, accepting entries, mailing confirmations, printing catalogs, arranging for accommodations, and managing the show in general.

Supernumerary teeth: Extra teeth in the mouth.

Super-premium: Dog food with more than 23 percent crude protein and at least 14 percent crude fat.

Supported entry: Show in which trophies are offered by a breed club. More prestigious than a regular show.

Suppuration: The formation of pus.

Supraventricular tachycardia: A condition in which the heart beats very rapidly because of signals coming from the atria (chambers of the heart that receive the blood) or near the junction of the atria with the ventricles (the chambers of the heart that pump the blood to the body or lungs).

Suspended (or suspension) trot: Flying trot.

Suspension: A preparation of solid particles dispersed, but not dissolved, in a liquid.

Sussex spaniel: A slow-moving bird dog developed in Sussex, England in the eighteenth century or earlier. Good for working in heavy cover, less so for light open country. Size: 13 to 15 inches, 35 to 45 pounds, with a thick coat, usually of a rich golden liver color.

Swampy back: Saddle back.

Swan neck: Goose neck.

Swayback: Sunken, concave topline.

Swedish Vallhund: Native herding breed of Sweden. They are said to be the ancestors of the corgi and bear a resemblance to that breed.

Sweepstakes: Held in conjunction with a regular show, a sweepstakes offers additional classes, especially for younger dogs. Monetary prizes are awarded.

Swimmer: A puppy of three weeks or older that cannot stand.

Swing dogs: In sledding, the dogs following the point dogs.

Swirl: Slight upward tilt of the tail end. Hook tail.

Switch: In retrieving trials, when a dog hunts the area of one mark, then leaves before recovering it, and finds another instead.

Sword tail: A tail that hangs straight down.

Sx: Surgery (veterinary notation).

Sydney silky: Silky terrier.

Sympathetic system: Part of the involuntary nervous system involved primarily with body functions that support "fight or flight."

Sympathomimetic: Producing effects similar to the "fight or flight" response.

Synapse: (1) The space between two nerves. **(2)** In genetics, the joining of homologous chromosomes just before recombination.

Syndrome: Collection of symptoms.

Synovia: Synovial fluid.

Synovial fluid: Joint fluid.

Synovial membrane (syn-ovial cells): The flexible inside lining of the joint capsule; it is only one or two cells thick. This connective-tissue membrane secretes synovial fluid.

Synovitis : Inflammation of the soft membrane lining the joint.

Systemic lupus erythematosus (SLE): An autoimmune disease in which the immune system targets its own body as foreign matter. SLE is commonly characterized by polyarthritis, hemolytic anemia, and skin disease, among many other symptoms.

T

T: Thoracic vertebrae, followed by a number to indicate which (veterinary notation).

T3: Triiodothyronine.

T4: Thyroxine.

Tachy-: Word prefix meaning fast or rapid.

Tachycardia: Faster-than-normal heart rate.

Tack: Equipment.

T.A.F.: Transfer applied for. Transfer of ownership applied for with the Kennel Club (UK).

Tail fold dermatitis: Infection of the skin around the tail due to excessive moisture collecting in the skin folds.

Tail head: Where tail attaches to croup.

Tail line: In a pedigree, the tail line refers to the line on the very top (sire-grandsire-great grandsire) or the very bottom (dam-grand-dam-great granddam).

Tail set: Position of the tail on the croup.

Tally-ho: In hound sports, a cry uttered when a fox or rabbit is spotted.

Talus: The uppermost, protruding tarsal bone of the hock.

Tankage: In dog-food manufacturing, residue from animal tissues, including bones, but excluding hair, hoofs, and horns.

Tapering muzzle: Wedge-shaped, pointed muzzle.

Tapering tail: A shorthaired tail that is long and narrowing at the tip.

Tapetum lucidum: A reflective layer in the choroid (part of the eye); this is the anatomical feature that makes some eyes glow in the dark.

Tapeworm: Segmented flatworm, belonging to a group of organisms called Cestoda. They live in the small intestine and are usually spread by infected fleas. Tapeworm segments can be observed in the feces.

Targus: Knob at the base of the external ear.

Tarsal bones: A group of seven bones arranged in two rows between the lower rear leg bones (tibia and fibula) and the foot bones (metatarsal). Corresponds to the human ankle.

Tarsus: The hock.

Tartar: Hardened (mineralized) plaque that forms a hard shell on the tooth surface.

Tassel: Feathering on the ears, used in reference to the Bedlington terrier.

Taurine: Amino acid and nutritional

supplement for dilated cardiomyopathy and retinal degeneration.

Taut coat: Sleek, stretched skin without folds or wrinkles.

Tavist: Clemastine; an antihistamine used in the treatment of allergic disorders.

Tawny: Light fawn color.

Taxonomy: Classification of organisms into groups such as mammals or dogs.

Tazi: Afghan hound.

TC: Triple Champion. The title is prefixed to the dog's name.

T cell: Also called T lymphocyte. The type of lymphocyte responsible for cell-mediated immunity.

TCM: Traditional Chinese medicine.

TD: Tracking Dog. Title follows the dog's name.

TDI: Therapy Dog title.

TDN: Total digestible nutrients.

TDX: Tracking Dog Excellent. Title follows the dog's name.

Teacup: An unusually small dog, usually a runt, often sold by unscrupulous breeders as something special. A "teacup poodle" is not an accepted AKC designation.

Team: (1) In dog shows, four matched dogs. **(2)** Three or more dogs.

Team dogs: In sledding, the dogs between the swing dogs and the wheel dogs on a big team.

Teapot curve tail: See pothook tail.

Tear stain: Dark brown stain running from the inner corner of the eye.

Teckel: Dachshund.

Telek: Scottish terrier owned by Dwight Eisenhower.

Telogen phase hair: Dead hair.

Temperature: A healthy dog's temperature is 99.5 to 102.5 degrees F. Always use a rectal thermometer made for dogs. Shake it down to 99 degrees and lubricate with petroleum jelly.

Temporomandibular joint: The joint between the lower jaw (mandible) and the temporal bone (part of the skull).

Tender knot: Painful sore at the site of a vaccination.

Tendon: Inelastic tissue that attaches muscle to bone.

Tenerife dog: Bichon frise.

Tenesmus: Straining to defecate.

Tenosynovitis: Inflammation of a tendon and its sheath.

Terbutaline: Bronchodilator medication used to treat asthma, collapsing trachea, and similar conditions.

Terhune, Alfred Payson (1872-1942): Writer of fiction about collies and founder of Sunnybank Kennels.

Terrier: Class of small to medium (usually wirehaired) dogs used primarily for hunting vermin. One subclass resulted from crossing with bulldogs to produce a fighting dog.

Terrier front: Narrow, straight front.

Tervuren: Belgian Tervuren.

Tesem: A dog of ancient times, thought to be an ultimate ancestor of all the sight hounds.

Testicular tumor: Tumor of the testicles.

Testis: Testicle.

Testosterone: Male sex hormone.

Tetanus: Disease resulting from toxins produced by infections with the clostridium family of bacteria. Causes muscle rigidity and spasms. Also called lockjaw.

Tether line: In sledding, a long chain with shorter pieces of chain extending from it. Used to stake out a team when stakes are not available.

Tetracycline: Class of antibiotics prescribed for a variety of conditions, including Rocky Mountain spotted fever, salmon poisoning, ehrlichiosis, Lyme disease, and others.

Tetralogy of Fallot: A fairly uncommon but serious complex of congenital heart defects (pulmonic stenosis plus a defect in the ventricular septum) resulting from abnormal development in the embryo.

Theobromine: A methylxanthine alkaloid (similar to caffeine) found in chocolate, can be toxic to dogs.

Theophylline: Bronchodilator prescribed for bronchial asthma and chronic obstructive pulmonary disease.

Therapeutic: Designed to cure or treat a disease.

Therapy Dogs, Inc: Therapy dog association. P. O. Box 5868, Cheyenne, WY 82003. Telephone: (877) 843-7364, (307) 432-0272. Web site: www.therapydogs.com.

Therapy Dogs International: Dog therapy organization. 88 Bartley Road, Flanders, NJ 07836. Telephone: (973) 252-9800.Web site: www.tdi-dog.org.

Thermic effect of food (TEF): The amount of energy used when digesting and absorbing food.

Thermogenesis: The production of heat by physiological processes.

Thermoneutral zone: The comfort zone, the temperature at which metabolic heat production is minimal.

Thiacetarsamide: Anti-heartworm drug used to kill adult heartworms.

Thiamin: Vitamin B1. As thiamin hydrochloride, it is often used as a nutritional supplement.

Thiaminase: An enzyme that destroys thiamin. It is found in certain types of raw fish, such as carp and herring.

Thiazide diuretics: Prescribed for congestive heart failure and other diseases.

Thighbone: Femur.

Third eyelid: Nictitating membrane.

Thoracic: Pertaining to the chest cavity.

Thoracic vertebrae: The thirteen vertebrae in the chest region.

Thorax: Chest cavity.

Threadworm: (1) Strongyloides stercoralis infestation, usually limited to tropical climates. They are small, round worms that live in the intestine. They can infect humans as well as dogs. **(2)** Any nematode infestation.

Threshold: The point at which a stimulus elicits a response.

Throaty neck: Neck with loose skin, especially where none should exist.

Thrombocytopenia (CPT): Low platelet count, leading to excessive bleeding.

Thromboembolism: Occlusion by an embolus that has broken away from a thrombus.

Thrombopathia: Disorder of the small blood cells, called platelets or thrombocytes, necessary for clotting. In this disease, platelets do not respond normally to the activation signals that occur following injury to a blood vessel, and do not aggregate. Dogs with this condition are therefore more susceptible to bruising and hemorrhage. Primarily affects basset hounds.

Thromboxane: A potent inducer of platelet aggregation.

Thrombus: A clot or obstruction in a blood vessel.

Throwing the bird: Tossing a bird in field trials for the dog to find.

Thumb marks: Black spots on or near the pastern, used to describe the Manchester terrier.

Thunderphobia: A great fear of thunder or other loud noises, such as fireworks or gunshots. An approaching storm may trigger a response in a sensitive dog.

Thymus: Organ located in the neck of young animals. It is part of the immune system.

Thyroid: (1) Small gland in the throat that regulates metabolism. **(2)** Homeopathic remedy for hypothyroidism, and inappropriate urination.

Thyroid deficiency: See hypothyroidism.

Thyroid-stimulating hormone (TSH): Pituitary hormone that stimulates the thyroid to produce thyroxine and tri-iodothyronine (T3 and T4). Also called thyrotropin.

Thyrotropin-releasing hormone: Hormone produced by the hypothalamus. It stimulates the pituitary gland to produce TSH.

Thyroxine: T4. Thyroid hormone that helps regulate metabolism; prescribed for hypothyroidism.

Tibetan mastiff: Ancient livestock guard dog of Tibet.

Tibetan spaniel: An old Oriental breed. Size: about 10 inches, 9 to 15 pounds, with a double silky coat of any color.

Tibetan terrier: An ancient, medium-sized Tibetan breed that has always been used as a companion. Has a profuse outer coat in any color, which may be either wavy or straight.

Tibia: The lower thigh or lower leg bone, the smaller of the two bones in the hock area.

Tick: Parasite that buries its head in the dog's body to suck blood.

Ticking: Color flecks on a white background.

Tick paralysis: Disease caused by a neurotoxin in the saliva of the female wood tick. The disease will usually abate when the tick is removed.

Tid: Three times daily (veterinary notation).

Tied at elbows: Elbows set too close under the body. See paddling.

Tight hunt: In retrieving work, when the dog runs directly to the area of the fall and, after a short hunt in a small area directly around the fall, finds the item.

Tight-mouthed: A dog that does not open much on track.

Timber: Bones, especially a leg bone.

Timolol: Beta-adrenergic blocker; an eye drop, prescribed for glaucoma.

Tincture: An herbal preparation

made by soaking an herb in liquid solvent to draw out the medicinal elements.

Tipped ears: Ears carried erect, with only the tips falling over.

Tire jump: In agility, a raised, circular structure through which a dog must jump. Also called a hoop.

Tissue: A group of specialized cells that together perform a particular function such as muscle tissue, nerve tissue, and bone.

Titer: The quantity of substance required to elicit a reaction with a given volume of another substance. Sometimes used to measure an animal's immunity to an antigen.

T-L: Thoraco-lumbar.

TLI: Trypsin-like immunoreactivity.

TMJ: Temporomandibular joint.

TN: Temperature normal (veterinary notation).

TNT: Toenail trim (veterinary and grooming notation).

Tocopherol: Any of a group of related compounds referred to as vitamin E.

Toed-in front: Pigeon-toed (feet pointing toward each other).

Toed-out front: Feet pointed away from each other. See east-west front.

Toeing-in: Feet are rotated toward each other when the dog moves. Pigeon-toed.

Toeing-out: Feet are rotated away from each other when the dog moves.

Tolling dog: Dog used to attract game.

Tomato juice: Remedy for skunk spraying; may help reduce odor.

Tongue: Barking or baying in pursuit of game.

Tonification: Gentle stimulation of an acupuncture point.

Tonification points: In acupuncture, points used to stimulate energy flow on the corresponding meridians.

Tonsillitis: Inflammation of the tonsils.

Tonsils: Lymphoid tissues located in the back of the oral cavity near the esophagus.

Topical: Refers to a substance, such as a drug, placed on the skin or a mucous membrane.

Topknot: Tuft of hair on the top of the head.

Topline: The spinal section of a dog from withers (top of shoulder blades) to the end of the croup.

Top producer: A dam that has produced at least three, or a stud that has produced at least five, champions in a calendar year.

Torsion: (1) Twisting of the stomach following bloat. **(2)** The twisting of any organ.

Tosa or Tosa Ken: Known as the Japanese mastiff; this short-haired guardian dog is most noted for the sumo costume specially designed for it.

Tosa-Ken Global Spread Association: P. O. Box 52855, Knoxville, TN 37950. Telephone: (865) 693-6453. Web site: www.tosa-inu.com.

Total protein levels: A test to measure albumin and globulins in the blood; used to indicate malnourishment or chronic infectious disease.

Tow line: In dog sledding, the gang line, the main rope that runs from the sled.

Toxascariasis: Infection with roundworms of the genus *Toxascaris.*

Toxascaris leonina: Species of roundworm living in the small intestine of dogs and cats.

Toxemia: (1) Presence of bacterial toxins in the blood. **(2)** Presence of toxins arising from altered metabolism.

Toxic: Poisonous.

Toxin: A poison.

Toxo: Toxoplasmosis (veterinary notation).

Toxocara canis: Species of roundworm living in the small intestine. Most frequently infects pregnant and nursing bitches and their puppies.

Toxocariasis: Infection with roundworms of the genus Toxocara.

Toxoplasma gondii: A small sporozoan parasite, primarily in cats, which uses dogs and people as an intermediary host.

Toxoplasmosis: Contagious infection caused by the sporozoan parasite *Toxoplasma gondii* and resulting in general illness, weight loss, fever, and coughing. More rarely it can cause pneumonia and central nervous system disease. All animals are vulnerable to this disease.

Toy dog: A member of a small-sized breed.

Toy group: An AKC group consisting of small dogs bred mostly as companions.

Toy poodle: Smallest of the poodles. Colors include white, cream, black, blue, silver, silver-beige, brown, café au lait, red, and apricot. Country of origin: Germany. Size: Less than 10 inches; 5 to 14 pounds.

TPLO: Acronym for Tibial Plateau Leveling Osteotomy, a type of surgery for rupture of the cranial cruciate ligament.

TPR: Temperature, pulse, respiration (veterinary notation).

TPRn: Temperature, pulse, respiration all normal (veterinary notation).

Trace: The dark stripe down the back of the fawn-colored pug.

Trachea: Breathing passage, or windpipe, conducting air from the pharynx to the lungs.

Tracheal collapse: Collapsed trachea, in which the tracheal rings are weakened, making the trachea collapse easily in response to pressure. Most common in toy breeds.

Tracheal hypoplasia: A condition in which a dog is born with an underdeveloped trachea, causing insufficient airflow.

Tracheobronchitis: Inflammation occurring within the trachea and bronchi of the respiratory tree.

Tracheoscopy: Examination of the trachea using a special instrument designed for the purpose.

Tracheotomy: An artificial opening made in the windpipe or trachea; usually an emergency procedure.

Track: Scent trail left by a game animal or an article such as a glove used in a tracking test.

Track drifter: A dog that works the track by taking shortcuts and not following the entire trail.

Track straddler: A dog that follows the trail by smelling every step made by the game.

Tracking collar: A collar that has a transmitter and emits a signal, which is tracked by a receiver. Used for locating lost dogs after the hunt as well as locating treed dogs. Also called a telemetry collar.

Tracking Dog: Dog that has been certified by two judges to have passed a licensed or member club TD test, a combined TD/TDX test, a combined TD/VST test, or a TD/TDX/VST test. For the test, a dog follows a track 440 to 500 yards long with three to five changes of direction, laid by a human track layer. The track is "aged" thirty minutes to two hours before the dog begins. The owner follows the dog on a long leash.

Tracking Dog Excellent: Dog that has been certified by two judges to have passed a licensed or member club TDX test, a combined TDX/VST test, a combined TD/TDX test, or a combined TD/TDX/VST test. For the test, the dog follows a track three to five hours old between 800 and 1,000 yards long with five to seven directional changes plus the additional challenge of human cross tracks.

Tragi: (1) Hairs on the external ear. (2) Plural of tragus.

Tragic face: Expression frequently seen in hypothyroid dogs, resulting from myxedema.

Trail: In sledding, a call to yield the right of way.

Trailing: (1) Following a ground scent to its source. (2) When a hunting dog follows its bracemate rather than hunting independently.

Trailing tail: Used for sled dogs, a tail carried straight behind that is apt to become tangled in a sled harness.

Training scent: Scent of game used to lay a trail, used in training and competition events.

Transport host: An animal or insect that carries an immature parasite from one mammalian host to another.

Transudate: Fluid passed through a membrane or extruded from tissue.

Trauma: A physical injury.

Travois: In carting or drafting, poles that drag on the ground with a load-bearing material stretched between them.

Treed: When the dog is at the tree with game in barking. Also called tree bark.

Treeing feist: A hunting breed.

Treeing Walker coonhounds: A hunting breed.

Trematode: Any parasitic organism belonging to the class Trematoda, including flukes.

Tresaderm: Patent topical corticosteroid, antibiotic, antifungal, miticide combination used for superficial bacterial or fungal infections.

Triangular ear: Ear that forms an equilateral triangle, as in the Siberian husky.

Triangular eye: Three-cornered eye as in the Afghan.

TRI-CH: Triple champion.

Trichiasis: Ingrown facial hair causing irritation to the cornea. Pekingese are especially vulnerable.

Trichomoniasis: Protozoan infection caused by various specious of the protozoan *Trichomonas*, resulting in a mucoid and sometimes bloody diarrhea in puppies.

Trichuris vulpis: The dog whipworm; a slender parasite that can attain a length of four inches.

Tricolor: Black, tan, and white.

Tricuspid valve dysplasia: Malformation (dysplasia) of the right atrioventricular (tricuspid) valve in the heart, causing backflow of blood into the right atrium, or tricuspid regurgitation. There may also be narrowing (stenosis) of the valve.

Trigeminal neuritis: Inflammation of the trigeminal nerve, which supplies the facial muscles.

Trigger points: Acupuncture points apparent only when a localized pathologic process occurs.

Triglyceride: A unit of fat containing three fatty acid molecules linked to a glycerol molecule.

Triiodothyronine (T3): An iodine-containing thyroid hormone involved in regulating the metabolism.

Trim: To clip and groom the coat.

Trimmings: Furnishings.

Triple: In retriever tests, three or more marks or blinds.

Triple Champion: A dog who has won the title of Dual Champion (DC) and the title of Obedience Trial Champion (OTCH) or Tracking Champion (CT) or Agility Champion (MACH).

Triple-X syndrome: A condition in which a bitch has three X chromosomes rather than the normal two, preventing normal cycling.

Trochlea: Smooth articular surface of bone on which tendons or another bone glide.

Trot: Moving diagonal legs in unison.

Trousers: Longish hair at the back of the thighs of some breeds.

True front: Straight front.

True ribs: First nine pairs of ribs; those attached directly to the sternum.

Trypsinum: A homeopathic remedy used to treat pancreatitis.

TSH: Thyroid-stimulating hormone.

Tschckt: In sledding, a command to keep moving forward (spelling varies).

T-Touch Massage: Therapy developed by behaviorist Linda Tellington-Jones and derived from the human therapy work of Moshe Feldenkrais. A system of gentle, repeated, circular massage movements. Given three times a day for one week for acute problems, and for four weeks for chronic problems.

TT/TC: Temperament tested/Temperament certified.

Tuberculosis: Disease caused by the tubercle bacillus *Mycobacterium tuberculosis*. The disease usually affects the lungs but may spread to other parts of the body.

Tuck up: Narrower, thinner area around the loins.

Tufted tail: A tail with a plume at the end.

Tugline: In sledding, the line that attaches each sled dog to the gangline.

Tularemia: An uncommon disease caused by the bacteria *Francisella tularensis*. The disease is spread by ticks and most commonly affects rodents.

Tulip ear: A wide ear carried erect and forward, with the edges turning slightly in.

Tumbler: Old name for a rabbit dog.

Tumor: Abnormal growth of tissue. May be benign or malignant.

Turgid: Swollen and congested.

Turn up: An uplifted face.

Tusks: Canine teeth.

TWBC: Total white blood cells (veterinary notation).

twds: Toward (veterinary notation).

Tweedmouth, Lord: An early British breeder largely responsible for producing the first yellow or "golden" retrievers.

Twenty-Nail disease: A rare but interesting disease in which all twenty nails fall out. No one knows the cause, but it may stem from an autoimmune problem.

Twist: The tail of a pug.

Twisted hocks: Rubbery hocks.

Two-Down-the-Shore: In retriever work, a water double thrown in such a way that, after picking up the go bird, the dog must swim by the go bird fall area and pick up the memory bird.

Two-fer: In clicker training or operant conditioning, a situation in which the dog must perform two correct behaviors in order to earn one reward.

Tx: Treatment (veterinary notation).

Tympanic membrane: Eardrum.

Type: Sum total of characteristic physical qualities that distinguish one breed or lineage from another.

Typey: Displaying essential qualities of the breed.

U

U: Unit (veterinary notation).

UA: Urinary analysis (veterinary notation).

U-ACH: Agility Champion (UKC title).

U-ACHX: Agility Champion Excellent (UKC title).

U-AGI: Agility I (UKC title).

U-AGII: Agility II (UKC title).

UAP: Ununited anconeal process.

Ubiquinone: Also called coenzyme Q10, a vitamin-like substance essential for energy production at the cellular level. It makes the enzyme the cell used to create ATP.

U-CD: Companion Dog (prefix) (UKC).

U-CDX: Companion Dog Excellent (prefix) (UKC).

UD: Utility Dog (AKC, CKC). Title follows the dog's name.

UDT: Utility Dog title with a Tracking Dog title (AKC).

UDTX: Utility Dog title with a Tracking Dog Excellent title (AKC).

UDVST: Utility Dog Variable Surface Tracking (AKC). Title follows dog's name.

UDX: Utility Dog Excellent (AKC). Title follows the dog's name.

UGA: Under general anesthetic (veterinary notation).

UH: Upland Hunter (UKC).

UKC: United Kennel Club.

ULA: Under local anesthetic (veterinary notation).

Ulcer: A lesion in which the tissue surface is eroded.

Ulcerated cornea: Damaged cornea, appearing as a white area with a depression in the middle.

Ulna: One of the two bones of the forearm; the other is the radius.

Ultrasound: An imaging technique in which sound waves are passed through body tissues in order to view the size, shape, and location of internal structures.

Umbilical hernia: An "outie" belly button, appearing as a result of a weakness in the abdominal lining at the umbilical site; may be surgically repaired.

Umbilicus: Belly button.

Umbrella: Similar to the veil, but shorter.

Undercoat: A soft, dense coat beneath the more visible outer coat.

Underline: Combined contour of the brisket and abdominal floor.

Undershot: Where the front teeth of the upper jaw are behind the front teeth of the lower jaw when the mouth is closed.

Undescended testicles: Retained testicles.

Undulating: Rising and falling regularly.

United Kennel Club: Second oldest and second largest all-breed registry, founded in 1898 by Chauncey Z. Bennet. It sponsors conformation shows, obedience trials, agility trials, coonhound field trials, water races, nite hunts, bench show, hunting tests for retrieving breeds, and Cur and Feist Squirrel and Coon events. 100 East Kilgore Road, Kalamazoo, MI 49001. Telephone: (616) 343-9020. Web site: www.ukcdogs.com.

United States Dog Agility Association Inc: P.O. Box 850955, Richardson, TX 75085. Telephone: (972) 487-2200. Web site: www.usdaa.com.

United States Pharmacopeia: Agency that sets purity standards for drugs.

Univalent vaccine: Vaccine against only one kind of disease.

Unsound: A dog with one or more severe conformational or health faults that would render it incapable of working.

Ununited anconeal process: Where the anconeal process fails to articulate properly with the ulna, resulting in a fracture of the growth plate. Mainly a condition of young large-breed dogs.

Up on leg: High stationed.

Upwind: In tracking, a wind blowing into the dog's face.

Urajiro: Cream to white ventral color, used in reference to the Shiba inu.

Urate: A chemical compound made from uric acid that can form crystals and stones in the urinary bladder.

Urea: A nitrogen-containing by-product of protein metabolism.

Uremia: Abnormally high concentration of urea, creatinine, and other products of metabolism in the blood. Result of kidney failure.

Ureter: A small, tubular structure leading from the kidney to the bladder. There are two ureters, one from each kidney.

Urethra: Small, tubular structure leading from the bladder to the outside for the discharge of urine.

Urethral prolapse: Protrusion of part of the mucosal lining of the urethra through the external urethral opening.

Urethritis: Inflammation of the urethra, usually due to an infection.

Urethrogram: A radiograph that evaluates the size and contour of the urethra.

Uric acid: Product of DNA metabolism. Excess amounts in the blood indicate inadequate liver function.

Uric acid calculi: Bladder stones resulting from excessive excretion of uric acid.

Urien: Wolfhound owned by Anne Boleyn.

Urinalysis or urinanalysis: A test of kidney function by the evaluation of the composition of urine chemicals.

Urinary system: Includes the kidneys, ureters, bladder, and urethra. The urinary system is responsible for removing waste products from the blood and eliminating them as urine.

Urinary tract infection: Can occur anywhere along the urinary system, including the kidneys, ureters, bladder, urethra, or, in males, the prostate gland. Signs may include painful urination, blood in the urine, excessive urination, and urinary incontinence.

Urine: Liquid waste produced by the kidneys.

Urogenital system: This body system includes the kidneys, ureters, urinary bladder, urethra, and the genital organs involved in reproduction.

Urohydropropulsion: A technique used to dislodge uroliths obstructing the ureters.

Urolith: Crystalline stone, usually in the bladder.

Urolithiasis: Condition of having urinary stones.

Urolitis: Stones in the bladder.

Ursodeoxycholate: A natural bile acid and liver-protecting agent.

URT: Upper respiratory tract (veterinary notation).

URTI: Upper respiratory tract infection (veterinary notation).

Urticaria: A blood vessel reaction in the skin that results in raised areas; hives.

US: (1) Urine sample (veterinary notation). **(2)** Ultrasound (veterinary notation).

USDA: United States Department of Agriculture. The USDA regulates the development and approval of vaccines, serums, antitoxins, and other products.

USDAA: United States Dog Agility Association, established in 1985 and incorporated in 1986 to promote agility trials.

USP: United States Pharmacopeia.

Uterine prolapse: A condition that occurs when a dog's uterus everts and is passed through the vagina.

Uteroverdin: Pale green substance produced in the placenta of some pregnant bitches.

UTI: Urinary tract infection (veterinary notation).

Utility A/B: Highest level of obedience classes to earn the title Utility Dog (UD). Dogs must earn three qualifying scores of at least 170 out of 200 points (including earning at least 50 percent of available points for each separate exercise) from three different judges. Obedience classes are divided into two groups: Utility A for exhibitors who have not yet added this title to a dog's name that they have either handled or trained, and Utility B for more experienced exhibitors who have done so.

Utility Dog: Certified by three obedience trial judges as having received qualifying Utility scores at three licensed or member obedience trials.

Utility Dog Excellent: To earn a Utility Dog Excellent title, the dog must have received qualifying scores in both Open B and Utility B at ten separate licensed or member obedience trials.

Utility Dog Variable Surface Tracking: Dog that has completed its UD and VST titles.

U-UD: Utility Dog (prefix) (UKC).

Uvea: The vascular layer of the eye, composed of the iris, ciliary body, and choroids.

Uveitis: Inflammation of the uvea, the colored iris of the eye. The cause is usually indeterminable.

Uvula: The caudal portion of the palate (roof of the mouth).

V

V: Vomiting. V-: vomiting lessened. V+ Vomiting increased; V++ vomiting severe. (veterinary notation).

V or VA: In a pedigree, highly rated German dogs.

VAAD: Veteran Advanced Agility Dog (USDAA).

vacc: Vaccinate (veterinary notation).

Vaccination: Immunization against communicable diseases.

Vaccine: Material derived from a disease-causing virus or bacteria used to prime the body's immune system and prevent catching the actual disease.

Vaccine titer: A measure of the level of disease-fighting antibodies present in the blood.

Vacuolar hepatopathy: Degenerative changes in the liver, secondary to some underlying cause.

VAD: Veteran Agility Dog (USDAA).

Vaginal culture or swab: A collection of material from the vagina for evaluation.

Vaginal hyperplasia: Overly enlarged vaginal tissue, especially with estrogen stimulation. Usually most visible during the heat cycle.

Vaginitis: Inflammation of the vagina.

Vagus: The tenth cranial nerve, with widespread distribution to the head, neck, thorax, and abdomen.

Valium (Diazepam): A mild sedative.

Vallee owczarek nizinny: Polish Lowland sheepdog. Also called a vallee Sheepdog.

Vaporizer: A precision veterinary instrument used to deliver the anesthetic gas and oxygen to the patient.

Variable formula: In dog-food manufacturing, a food in which ingredients change in response to market prices.

Variable ratio: In operant conditioning, a schedule of reinforcement in which the trainer reinforces the first correct response after varying numbers of correct responses.

Variable Surface Tracker: Dog that has been certified by both judges to have passed a licensed or member club Variable Surface Tracking test, combined TD/VST test, a combined TDX/VST test, or a combined TD/TDX/VST test. For the test, a dog must follow a three- to five-hour-old urban track that may take him down a street, through a building, up stairs, and in other areas devoid of vegetation.

Variety: A subtype of a breed that can be shown separately, but which can be interbred with other varieties of the same breed.

Varminty: A bright, piercing expression.

Vascular: Relating to the blood vessels.

Vascular ring anomaly: One of several disorders that occur due to abnormal development of the blood vessels that arise from the aortic arch in the fetus. The most common type is a persistent right aortic arch that develops instead of the left aortic arch, which normally becomes the permanent aorta, the main blood vessel leading from the heart.

Vascular shunt: Portosystemic shunt.

Vasculitis: Inflammation of the blood vessels. Causes include food allergies, drug reactions (ivermectin and itraconazole), lymphosarcoma, and vaccination.

Vasoconstriction: A decrease in the diameter of blood vessels.

Vasodilator: Agent that dilates, or increases the diameter of, blood vessels

Vasopressin: Antidiuretic hormone (ADH) that raises the blood pressure and increases water retention.

VBMA: Veterinary Botanical Society.

VCCH: Versatile Companion Champion. The title is prefixed to the dog's name.

VCD1: Versatile Companion Dog 1. Title follows dog's name.

VCD2: Versatile Companion Dog 2. Title follows dog's name.

VCD3: Versatile Companion Dog 3. Title follows dog's name.

VCD4: Versatile Companion Dog 4. Title follows dog's name.

V-D: Vomiting/diarrhea (veterinary notation).

Vector: Carriers of a disease, such as ticks.

Veil: The portion of the dog's forelock that hangs straight down over the eyes, often partially covering them.

Veiled coat: Fine, wispy, long-haired coat.

Veins: Blood vessels that carry blood toward the heart.

Venous: Referring to the veins.

Vent: (1) The anal opening. **(2)** Any opening or outlet, such as the opening of an abscess.

Ventilator: A device used to control breathing.

Ventral: Toward the belly.

Ventricle: Either of the two chambers that make up the bottom part of the heart.

Ventricular septal defect: A congenital defect leaving a hole in the muscular wall of the heart (the septum) that separates the right and left ventricles.

Vermifuge: Any substance that kills or expels intestinal parasites.

Versatile Companion Champion: A dog who has completed an OTCH, MACH, and CT.

Versatile Companion Dog 1: Must complete CD, NA, NAJ, and TD.

Versatile Companion Dog 2: Must complete CDX, OA, OAJ, and TD.

Versatile Companion Dog 3: Must complete UD, AX, AXJ, and TDX

Versatile Companion Dog 4: Must complete UDX, MX, MXJ, and VST.

Versatile hunting: Dog skilled not only in pointing and retrieving, but also in retrieving waterfowl, tracking furry animals, or even trailing ducks across water.

Vertebra: Bone of the spine. Plural: vertebrae.

Vesicle: Small, elevated area on the skin filled with a clear fluid.

Vestibular organ: Structure in the inner ear essential for maintaining balance.

Vestibular system: Portions of the inner ear, nerves, and brain that help the body maintain balance.

Veteran: Older dog (usually over seven years old).

Veterinarian: A licensed, trained animal doctor.

Veterinary Botanical Society: Group of veterinarians and herbalists dedicated to developing responsible herbal practices by encouraging research and education, strengthening industry relations, keeping herbal tradition alive as a valid information source, and increasing professional acceptance of herbal medicine for animals. Web site: www.vbma.org/.

Veterinary Cancer Society: The Web site for this organization lists specialists by location and provides link to information on cancer and university-run clinical trials. Web site: www.vetcancersociety.org.

Veterinary Institute for Therapeutic Alternatives: 15 Sunset Terrace, Sherman, CT 06784. Telephone: (860) 354-2287.

Veterinary Medical Database/Canine Eye Registration Foundation (VMD/CERF): 1248 Lynn Hall, Purdue University, West Lafayette, IN 47906. Telephone: (765) 494-8179. Web site: www.yshenvet.purdue.edu.

VG: Veterans Gambler (an agility title).

Vibrissa: Whisker on the muzzle. Plural: vibrissae.

Villi: Threadlike projections that cover the mucosal surface of the small intestine.

Vine leaf ears: Ears that resemble vine leaves.

Viremia: Presence of virus particles in the blood.

Viscera: All the organs in the abdominal and thoracic cavities.

Viscerocutaneous: Pertaining to the internal organs and skin.

Viscous (viscid): (1) Sticky. **(2)** A thick fluid.

Vitamin: Originally, "vital amine." Substances, other than minerals, essential in trace amounts for growth and health.

Vitamin A: Fat-soluble vitamin that helps vision (especially night vision) and aids the immune system, skin, bone growth, and kidney function. Found in green vegetables, liver, milk, and fat.

Vitamin B complex: All the B vitamins. They are essential to the health of the nervous system.

Vitamin B-1 (thiamin): Water-soluble vitamin that helps release energy from carbohydrates. Found in dairy products, cereals, and organ meat.

Vitamin B-6 (pyridoxine): Water-soluble vitamin needed for protein and fat metabolism and for blood renewal. Found in fish, liver, soy, milk, wheat germ, and yeast.

Vitamin B-12: Must be present for protein metabolism and red blood cell formation.

Found in animal products.

Vitamin C: Ascorbic acid, an unstable vitamin whose potency is lost when exposed to light, or air. This powerful antioxidant supports the immune system and is essential for healthy bones and joints. Dogs produce some vitamin C.

Vitamin D: Fat-soluble vitamin that helps calcium and phosphorus absorption and bone growth. Found in animal products, egg yolk, and cod liver oil. Most importantly, dogs can manufacture this vitamin in their skin when exposed to sunlight.

Vitamin E: Fat-soluble antioxidant made up of compounds called tocopherols. Helps in reproduction. Found in green vegetables, vegetable oils, and dairy products.

Vitamin K: Fat-soluble vitamin that helps the blood clot. Found in green vegetables and liver. Dogs can also manufacture their own.

Vitiligo: Skin condition characterized by smooth areas of pigment loss, usually around the nose, lips, and muzzle.

Vitreous: The glassy humor of the eye.

Vizsla: Short-haired Hungarian breed of a golden rust color used to hunt hares and water birds. Size: 21 to 24 inches, 50 to 60 pounds.

Vizsla Club of America: 16 Deer Run Road, Collinsville, CT 06022. Telephone: (860) 693-9403. Web site: http://clubs.akc.org/visla/index.html.

VJ: Veterans Jumper (an agility title).

VKH: Vogt-Koyanagi-Harada-like syndrome.

VLM: Visceral larval migrans.

VMAD: Veteran Master Agility Dog (USDAA).

VMB: Very much better (veterinary notation).

VMI: Very much improved (veterinary notation).

VN: Virus neutralization (veterinary notation).

VO2 max: Maximal oxygen consumption.

VO2: Oxygen consumption.

Vogt-Koyanagi-Harada-like syndrome (VKH): Autoimmune disorder leading to progressive destruction of melanin-containing tissues. Affected dogs have inflamed eyes and loss of skin pigment. Also called uveodermatologic syndrome.

Void: To cast out as urine or feces.

Volhard collar: A variation of the choke collar.

Voluntary muscular activity: Intended movement, such as walking.

Volvulus: Twisting of the stomach or intestine.

Vomiting: Expulsion of food from the stomach through the mouth.

Vomiting blood: Usually indicates a break in the mucous lining somewhere between the mouth and upper small intestine.

Vomitus: The material that is vomited.

Von Willebrand's disease: Blood-clotting defect involving platelet and coagulation function (factor VIII antigen). A blood test is available to determine if the condition is present.

Vorstehund: German wire-haired pointer.

VPD: Veteran Performance Dog (an agility title).

VS: Veterans Snooker (an agility title).

V-shaped ears: Long, triangular ears, usually dropped, as in the vizsla.

VST: Variable Surface Tracker (AKC title). Title follows dog's name.

Vulnerary: In herbal medicine, a substance that is applied externally to wounds to heal them.

Vulva: External female genitalia.

vWD Negative: Tested negative for von Willebrand's disease.

vWD: Von Willebrand's disease.

W

Wagon: In carting, a vehicle (usually four-wheeled) designed to carry freight.

Walking dandruff: See Cheyletiella.

Walk up: (1) In sheepdog trials, a command to walk up to the stock. **(2)** In retriever work, a mark or marks that occur while the dog is in motion, progressing with the handler.

Walleye: An eye with pale bluish iris. Also called glass eye or fish eye.

Waltham Pet Care and Nutrition: Telephone: (800) 528-1838. Web site: www.waltham.com.

Warfarin (Decon, Pindone): Rat and mouse poison causing extensive internal bleeding.

Warrigal: Dingo. Also warragal.

Wasting disease: Cachexia.

Water blind: A bird hidden in a location where a dog is directed to it mostly by water, as opposed to a land blind.

Water fever: An old name for leptospirosis.

Water Race Champion: A dog that has won one First Line and one First Tree in Finals at least once on the same date and in the same Water Race with competition, and has a total of 200 Championship points.

Waterside terrier: Airedale terrier.

Water-soluble vitamins: Vitamins C and the B complex.

Way to me: In herding events, a command to move the dog counter-clockwise around the livestock; to circle to the right.

WB: Western blot (veterinary notation).

Wbc or WBC: White blood cell (veterinary notation).

WC: Working Certificate.

WCH: Water Race Champion. The title is prefixed to the dog's name.

WCX: Working Certificate Excellent.

WD: Winners dog.

Weaning: The change in a puppy's diet from milk to solid food.

Wearing: (1) In herding events, when the dog holds the flock up against the handler by running back and forth on the opposite side. The dog will bring the sheep after the handler wherever the handler walks without additional commands. **(2)** Also in herding events, holding back animals that have been separated from the main flock.

Weaving: See crossover.

Webbed feet: Toes with a membrane of skin between them, characteristic of many water-retrieving breeds.

Weedy: Insufficient amount of bone.

Weil's disease: An old name for leptospirosis.

Weimaraner: Native to Weimar, Germany. A short-haired gray gun-dog developed in the nineteenth century. Size: 23 to 27 inches.

Weimaraner vorstehund: Weimaraner.

Well-laid back: Well angulated shoulders.

Well let down: Short hocks.

Well sprung: Nicely rounded ribbing.

Welsh corgi Cardigan: See Cardigan Welsh corgi.

Welsh corgi Pembroke: See Pembroke Welsh corgi.

Welsh springer spaniel: Red-and-white spaniel that is slightly smaller, more lightly built, and with shorter ears than the English springer spaniel. They are excellent water dogs. Size: 17 to 19 inches.

Welsh terrier: Black-and-tan terrier similar in structure and markings to the Airedale, but smaller. Size: 15 inches, 20 to 21 pounds.

West Highland white terrier: Developed in Scotland during the eighteenth or early nineteenth century. Size: 10 to 11 inches, with a hard, white, straight coat.

Westminster: Prestigious New York dog show (and social event) held by the Westminster Kennel Club, inaugurated in 1877. It is held in February. The WKC show is the second-oldest sporting event in the United States; only the Kentucky Derby is older.

Wet neck: Throaty.

Wetterhoun: Very old breed used to hunt otters in Holland.

WH: (1) Wolf hybrid. **(2)** In schutzhund, a watchdog title.

Wheaten: Pale yellow or fawn color.

Wheel back: A noticeable arch of the thoracic and lumbar vertebrae. A roached back.

Wheel dogs: In sledding, the dogs closest to the sled. The name comes from the horse world, as obviously sleds don't have wheels.

Wheezing: A forceful whistling noise caused by narrowing or spasm in the windpipe.

Whelp: To give birth to a litter of puppies.

Whelps: Unweaned puppies.

Whelpwise: A patented medical device, originally designed for humans, that monitors contractions and fetal heartbeats in the whelping bitch.

Whippet: A small, fast dog resembling a miniature greyhound. Size: 18 to 21 inches, with a short, smooth coat of any color.

Whip tail: A stiff tapered tail that is carried straight out.

Whipworms (*Trichuris vulpis*): Long, whip-shaped parasites attaching to the wall in the colon, causing irritation and bright red bleeding on the surface of the stools. Adults are two to three inches long.

Whiskers: Long hair on the muzzle and jaw.

Whistle refusal: The refusal of a dog to obey a whistle command.

White blood cells: Large disease-fighting cells circulating in the blood. Part of the immune system.

White cavalier: Affectionate name for the bull terrier.

White coat: A term used to identify those people who participate in Field Trial events.

White dog shaker syndrome: Episodic diffuse muscular tremors and incoordination, mostly seen in certain white dogs such as Malteses and West Highland white terriers.

Whitelies: White body and red or dark markings, often used when referring to certain Pembroke Welsh corgis.

White ribbon: Awarded for fourth place in each regular class in a dog show.

Whoa: Basic stop command used with field dogs. A command to a running dog to stop and stand still.

Wicket: A measuring implement that measures the dog's height at the withers. Used in dog events to determine height qualifications.

Wide hunter: A dog that hunts a long distance from the hunter.

Widow's peak: Triangular marking on forehead hair.

Wild boar: A mix of black, brown, and gray coloration.

Wild hunt: Pack of spectral hounds, featured in German folklore.

Wind splitter: Colloquial term for hound that will only carry a line for a short distance before over running and going to look for another line.

Winging: A gaiting fault in which one or both front limbs twist outward.

Winter nose: A normally black nose that takes on a pinkish hue in the winter.

Wire-haired: A harsh, crisp coat.

Wirehaired pointing griffon: A good water dog and retriever developed in Holland and France in the nineteenth century. Size: 20 to 24 inches, with a medium-length wiry coat, usually steel gray with brown markings, but brown or orange with white are also common.

Witch hazel: Plant extract used to cool insect stings, sunburn, and hot spots.

Withers: Top of the shoulder blades; point of shoulder.

WKC: Westminster Kennel Club.

WLD: Working Lead Dog.

WNL: Within normal limits (veterinary notation).

WO: Weeks old, following a number (veterinary notation).

Wobblers (wobblers syndrome): Abnormality of the neck vertebrae causing rear leg incoordination or paralysis. Also called cervical vertebral instability.

Woden's hunt: Pack of spectral hounds in Scandinavian folklore.

Wolf claw: A dewclaw on the hind leg.

Wolf-dog hybrid: The result of a cross between a wolf and a domestic dog, usually a German shepherd dog, Alaskan malamute, or Siberian husky.

Wolf heat: Characteristic of some "primitive" breeds such as huskies and basenjis. In this pattern, a bitch may not come into heat directly from proestrus. The estrous cycle may seem to stop for a couple of weeks, then pick up again in estrus.

Wolf spitz: Keeshond.

Wool hairs: The innermost layer of hair covering most of the skin surface.

Working a line: In hound field trials, following a scent well.

Working certificate test: Any of many field-performance testing programs sponsored by various national breed clubs.

Working Group: An AKC category that includes dogs that were bred to pull carts, guard property, and perform search and rescue services. Among the breeds in this group are the Akita, boxer, Doberman pinscher, and Saint Bernard.

Working Lead Dog: Title awarded by the Alaskan Malamute Club of America in recognition of a dog's ability to work as a single lead dog on a team.

Working Pack Dog: Title awarded by the Alaskan Malamute Club of America in recognition of a dog's ability to work as a pack dog.

Working Team Dog: Title awarded by the Alaskan Malamute Club of America in recognition of a dog's ability to work on a dog team.

Working Weight Pull Dog: A title awarded by the Alaskan Malamute Club of America in recognition of a dog's ability to successfully compete in weight pull competitions.

World Canine Freestyle Organization Inc.: P. O. Box 350122, Brooklyn, NY 11235. Telephone: (718) 332-8336. Web site: www.worldcanine-freestyle.org.

WPD: Working Pack Dog.

WR: Working Retriever. A NAHRA title.

Wrinkle: The loose, folded skin of the skull, as seen in the bulldog, bloodhound, or pug.

wt: Weight (veterinary notation).

WTCH: Working Trial Champion (prefix), a title awarded by the Australian Shepherd Club of America. To earn the title, a dog must earn an ATD on all three types of stock: duck, sheep, and cattle.

WTD: Working Team Dog.

WWPD: Working Weight Pull Dog.

Wysong Corporation: Manufacturers of dog food. 1880 North Eastman Road, Midland, MI 48642-8896. Telephone: (517) 631-0009. Web site: www.wysong.net.

X

Xanthoma: A tumor of lipid foam cells. May indicate defective lipid metabolism.

Xanthosis: yellowish discoloration.

X-back harness: Traditional sledding harness.

X chromosome: The chromosome responsible for the development of female characteristics.

Xenophobia: Fear of strangers.

Xoloitzcuintli: Ancient, primitive hairless Aztec breed, also called the Mexican hairless.

Xolotl: In Aztec myth, a lightning god who is depicted with the head of a dog.

X-pen (ex-pen): An exercise pen.

X-ray: A radiograph picture of the bones or other hard material to search for abnormalities.

Xylazine: Rompum.

Xylocaine: Lidocaine

Y ────────

Yard breaking: For field dogs, a synonym for basic obedience training.

Yard work: In field dog, a term used to describe any number of drills that can be done in and around the kennel area. Similar to yard breaking.

Y chromosome: The chromosome responsible for the development of male characteristics.

Yeast infection: Malassezia, a condition occurring in moist area such as the ears.

Yellow retriever: Golden retriever.

Yellow ribbon: Awarded for third place in each regular class in a dog show.

yo: Years old, following a number (veterinary notation).

Yogurt: Made from curdled or fermented milk. Add yogurt to your dog's food to promote healthy intestinal bacteria, especially after an attack of diarrhea or course of treatment with antibiotics.

Yorkie: Affectionate name for Yorkshire terrier.

Yorkshire terrier: Small terrier, originally used for ratting, now solely as a companion and watchdog. Size: less than seven pounds, with a glossy medium-long blue or tan coat.

Yukon Quest: A famous long-distance (1,000 miles or more) sled race across part of Alaska and Canada.

Z ────────

Zeel: A homeopathic remedy prescribed for arthritis.

Zinc phosphide: A substance found in rat poison. Rarely used today.

Zinc-responsive dermatosis: Skin condition caused by a zinc deficiency that produces crusty skin and cracked feet. Found mostly in Arctic breeds. It responds to dietary changes or zinc supplements.

Zinc: Mineral necessary for skin and coat. Found in meat.

Zollinger-Ellison syndrome: Collection of conditions including gastrointestinal ulceration, secretion of excess stomach acid, and pancreatic islet tumors.

Zoonotic disease: Any disease that can be secondarily transmitted to human beings. Some of the best known are rabies, ringworm, fleas, and roundworm.

Zweigpinscher: Miniature pinscher.

Zweigschnauzer: Miniature schnauzer.

Zweigteckel: Miniature dachshund.

Zygomatic arch: A bony ridge extending from beneath the eye orbits.

Zygote: Fertilized ovum.

Symbols and Numbers

#: Fracture (veterinary notation).

1080: Sodium fluoroaceate (rat poison).

1081: Sodium fluoroactamide (rat poison).

.22 rimfire crimp or acorn shell: The smallest blank round legal for use in Hunting Tests.

Diane Morgan teaches philosophy and literature at Wilson College in Chambersbug, Pennsylvania. She has written on subjects as diverse as beagles and Buddhism, magic and gardening, Tarot and horses. She also writes poetry, plays, and has been nominated for five Maxwell Awards. She is a founding member of Basset Rescue of Old Dominion and lives with four dogs, two cats, some goldfish-and John Warner, her coauthor.

John Warner is a biochemist and technical editor. John is well known for his superior cooking, great patience, and awesome Monopoly playing. He and Diane live in Williamsport, Maryland, near Washington, D.C.

They have retained a strong interest in the alphabet and its eternal mysteries.

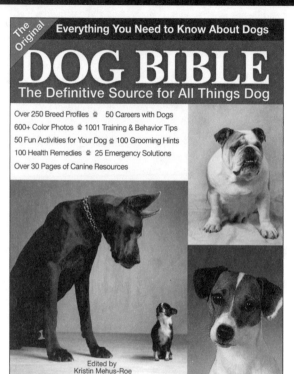